# First Equation

**Aroha Paora**

An Arodyce Book

**First Equation**

Written by Aroha Paora in the course of her lifetime 15 June 1939 – 25 February 2023

Agent and publisher - Dave Fletcher, Arodyce Publishing, Dargaville, New Zealand

Second Edition, January 2025. Includes autobiographical material.

ISBN 978-0-473-73672-9 Paperback POD
ISBN 978-0-473-73673-6 Hardback POD
ISBN 978-0-473-73681-1 ePub
ISBN 978-0-473-73674-3 Kindle
ISBN 978-0-473-73675-0 Digital Audiobook

Book and cover design by Catherine Morgan and Dave Fletcher.

**Contents**

# Introduction

This is a book that the world does not expect, written by a woman the world does not expect to be its author.

That a woman is the bringer of all the truth it contains, contravenes the teachings and expectations of thousands of years of religious hypocrisy. The advent of this book brings the truth of God, the universe, the evolution of life and the planets from first beginning to present day and beyond. The woman Messiah is named as Love and represents, in her own state of extreme suffering, the truth of love, abandoned, neglected, broken and unwanted.

Christ was called to teach, briefly, and to suffer briefly and die for love, for God, for the truth of eternal life and conscience of the soul within the heart of mankind. The Messiah is a woman, called as the suffered representation of Love itself, to bring the truth and call for the Earth to be saved. Christ's Calling was not burdened with such a grave responsibility over a lifetime of suffering.

It has fallen to me to publish this book. I do so in humility, with enormous pride in this woman who has been my beloved lifelong friend and councillor. I am qualified to publish this work by the fact that I have witnessed and tested in my own life everything that is set down on these pages, and much more of her spiritual reality and suffering. The truth that is contained here has changed my life again and again, and it is still changing it. It is my earnest hope that, as you read this book, it will do the same for you, and, if there are enough of you, the Earth may at last be understood and saved also.

Only a woman of unique quality and ability to suffer is able to bring this truth.

Aroha has given her all for this truth. I am her only witness. No man, however great, could have the endurance and passion to suffer for the Earth as she has done.

DF
Dargaville
November 2022

# First Equation

Life began in motion with a singular outward extension of the first vibration in evolution. First vibration became alive when the presence of containment caused an equating retraction of motion and first equation was born. Outward then inward in perfect motion was first vibratory activity, first breath, first life in existence.

The identity of a first equation was confirmed by the containing presence of a perfect whole, a spherical pure completeness, untouched, un-entered, without sides, top or bottom, any linear disturbance, any interference, any contact with another whole and any outside influence.

Beginning, commencement of anything, activates a process of something. A beginning starts from an established presence. Without a presence nothing can be born.

A perfect whole has no formation. Nothing touches its existence. Nothing begins its formation. Nothing exists to form the shape of a perfect whole and nothing exists in acknowledgement of a perfect whole until first equation was born. There was no content within the whole, no air, water, light, darkness or thickness of atmosphere. Wholeness occupied all there was. Size was indeterminable.

To breathe, to activate, there must be a containment. To be a containment, there must be a surround. The whole was both containment and surround for its occupancy was total.

The exact moment of the first equation in motion is not able to be deciphered. No evolving force had established. No being of any composition had begun existing. No God existed. No creator existed. No breath existed. No light existed and no life of any formation. No presence had identity. No acknowledgement of any existence was there. No exact beginning could be recorded. Not until first equation motioned into existence was there a true beginning.

Containment of anything causes pressure, a forced activity. Containment of spherical wholeness was no different. The activity of first equation in containment pressed upon its centre forcing an outward spherical motion of release, and first breath, the first motion of existence, was activated. Once the pressure was relieved, first motion returned to its beginning and the first pure equation breathed without stopping.

Outward then inward in perfect equational reaction the rhythm of life began. Once activated, breathing was continuous. It could never be stopped. Its beginning was absolute. One motion identified its surround, the other identified its containment. The two identical in activity were never able to be separated.

Breathing began the first vibrational activity. A vibration is a current of rhythm. It begins from a source of tempo. The first vibration was a succeeding current of first motion. As breathing continued, vibrational activity caused the whole to expand. The accumulation of vibrations inside the spherical whole automatically pushed the whole outwards.

Containment of active vibrations, unless released, explodes. Containment of first vibrational activity did not explode for there was no outside.

The expansion of the whole was of equational reaction. When quantity of vibrations became uncontainable, the whole simply motioned outwards in spherical totality. Breathing continued on in perfect tempo until an equational reaction to more accumulating vibrations caused the whole to expand again. The pattern continued on. The whole grew larger. A living breathing pure entity began the evolution of God.

Light was next.

God's existence was first contained vibrating life of pure equating vibrational activity, a whole which kept expanding, a whole which held within its totality first equation. From first equation light was born, light of visible colour. Before light came, God's entity was colourless.

As God enlarged, motion of silent softness became pulsing, the audible beating of tempo contained inside a whole ever increasing in vibrational activity. First equation was being pressed on too heavily, pounded too forcefully, and gradually began to heat. The warming of first equation was the first glow of light. The natural light of the Sun is coloured by its heat. The intensity of colour depends on the quantity of vibrations causing its temperature. First pure light was first warmth, first glow, first colour. Gold was first colour. Gold without flame. Soft gold. Pure gold. First equation spread warmth all through its containment, until a body of light became first visible sphere in existence. Light then, the first pure spherical whole, began the evolution of all light holding bodies.

The light body of God breathed on, grew outwards and increased in vibrations of spherical activity. God gradually changed colour. Gold became pink as heating increased. The pink turned to red as the heat intensified. God became an explosive entity.

First equation at the centre of God's light body imbalanced, its perfect outward and inward breathing became first panting, but still in perfect rhythm. Panting became gasping, a fast then slow pulsing at central core of light, sending a tremor of imbalance spherically outwards and destabilising the entity of God. A gasping first equation became irregular in motion, for one gasp outwards did not complete its equation before returning to its start. Tremor is imbalance of vibrations. Heat and tremoring explode.

The imbalancing first equation injected an irregular beat in tempo through the sphere and pure electric vibrations began. Pure energy. Pure power. Pure contained force. Pure explosive content so powerful it had to be released.

Outward from the centre of God's light entity the first explosion took place. With no outside for release of vibrations, the explosion was contained inside God's body. Its force was so power-generated, God, the sphere of living light, was force-blown, not equationally motioned, but force-blown spherically outwards, so far and so fast, that the content of light God held, faded into colourlessness again, leaving a minute first equation still glowing in central place. First equation did not explode, its evolution was absolute. It remained visible and perfect in spherical presence. God then, became a colourless surrounding whole, with a tiny glowing sphere inside a powerful spherical containment.

The indestructible first equation became a separate entity. Its light equations would never fade. The containment surrounding it was enormous, still breathing and still vibrating. First equation remained at temperature. Surrounding its minuteness were electrified vibrations in mass from first explosion. Their activity would keep first equation in light until another development.

Evolution had begun with the separate identity of a small sphere of light, the First Sun. God surrounded the Sun in spherical wholeness, colourless, alive, breathing in perfect tempo, vibrating in first energy and forever onwards the powerful presence of invisible light.

First equation was released from vibrational imbalance. Its surrounding body still held the force of vibrations that had massed. Breathing which had begun with first equation expanded in motion as the whole enlarged. The rhythm never changed, distance did. Rhythm simply lengthened in tempo. The larger the whole, the longer the breath, until so vast was the distance from first equation to surround, the motion of breathing ceased and first atmosphere was born. Atmosphere is a vibrating thickness of motion involving with whatever it surrounds. First atmosphere was pure, uncontaminated and of established electric equations. The breathing of first equation differed from the motioning breathing of God. First equation had separated from its surround, was contained within its minuteness and breathed in equations of its size.

First Sun, first equation evolving, first warming, first lighting, returned to its first beginning, a small spherical containment of visible light equations at life. The size of First Sun after first explosion was an equating reaction to the force of vibrations contained within the whole at force-expansion. Perfect equations always create perfect reaction. Redness had cooled after the explosion leaving First Sun the colour gold. First breathing rhythm returned also. First explosion entered the Sun's equating life. God in surround breathed without activity of tempo.

Eons passed and a small golden sphere enlarged automatically, for the very same process of evolution took place. First equation in light life, expanded exactly as God had. Its rhythmical breathing inside its sphere of light imbalanced as continual vibrational activity pressed upon its centre. It panted, gasped, then tremored. It had an exterior to release its charge. When it exploded, its light fragments scattered throughout the body of God in placements of visible vibrational activity and the planets began evolution. In the first image of God First Sun was born. In the image of First Sun all other spherical bodies would evolve.

Fragments of light from First Sun were not spherical in formation until they magnetised. Their scattering inside God's body was from explosive force splitting the sphere unequationally, slicing into a light whole, slitting through light vibrations, fracturing pure light equations, spraying those vibrations in a spherical direction and forcing outwards into colourless existence trillions of particles of light. Magnetic attraction pulled every loose light particle into several spherical bodies. As First Sun was a sphere in perfect equating formation its fragments automatically sought spherical contact.

First Sun, after explosion, returned to its beginning of first equation motioning, and surrounding it were light particles surrounded by energised vibrations in mass. Gradually each particle was drawn together, not to first equation, but to each other. First Sun had lost temperature, was tinier than its particles of light, therefore unable to magnetise back unto itself quantity of vibrating electric light particles larger and more active. Magnetic attraction is when one vibration draws another towards it. One is mightier in activity. The other is subservient. Both are from the same beginning.

Large particles of light magnetised small particles and gradually light spheres began formation. Each evolving sphere was placed according to where its first magnetic attraction of light particles took place. Spherical formation was automatic. Light vibrations were of spherical motioning. Surrounding their activity was a spherical containment. All vibrational activity was spherical. The number of spheres would increase as their evolution proceeded. Earth was one of the first born.

God, the total holding power of every evolving vibration, registered the explosion of First Sun. God expanded in equational reaction. The force of exploding equations caused God's whole to automatically expand by pressure of inter-exploding speeding equation fragments, travelling towards the surround. The travelling highly charged particles of light lost force as they distanced from their source. Some lost light entirely and faded in colourless space. Close to First Sun some spheres began formation while others formed further away.

When First Sun exploded, it sounded. Sound if trapped, echoes. An echo if trapped resounds until its vibrations lose strength. They do not die ever. They always progress. A vibration once active remains of progressive activity. The echo of First Sun's explosion resounded, and continued resounding until its vibrations were so weak they were consumed by First Sun and taken directly into its motioning.

The motioning of First Sun shook at envelopment of echo resoundings, not tremored, but shook, a greater imbalance, a spherical motioning in staccato tempo. Staccato tempo is short beats. Aggressive charge began. First equation injected staccato tempo throughout its spherical evolving second formation and this imbalance remained until it heated again and a second explosion took place.

The evolving spheres of light life were without first equation at their centres. Each sphere glowed of different light values. Those at distance from First Sun were paler than those nearer. Those nearer were larger in formation than those farther away. When all light particles had been magnetised the size of each sphere was determined.

Breathing of the spheres was an identical reaction to first equation. First Sun was their father image. The electric vibrations of staccato tempo were magnetised by all spheres as they evolved. Every living vibration has a prime source, a father image. When vibrations separate from their prime source they still function exactly as their father and develop the same progressions. They cannot behave any other way for their equations are magnetic always.

The spheres breathed exactly in tempo with first equation. They began with aggressive charge at their centres. When First Sun exploded and returned to first breathing rhythm, all spheres breathed exactly as their father image. Their rhythms differed only. Some were small, others larger. Equations vibrated in rhythm according to the length of motioning from central core to their containing surround.

First Sun once again reddened as it enlarged. All the spheres reddened also. Inside God's holding containment heat began the evolution of first water. Heat at central position of God's containing whole experienced contact with a cool surround, and condensation began. Condensation results from hot vibrations involving with cool vibrations and their activity being controlled. The vibrations do not cease in activity but progress.

God's whole began to moisten. First came a thickness of vibrating activity which gradually became transparent, translucent, moisture, the progression of vibrations of opposing temperature. The temperature of all spheres including First Sun, lowered.

Moisture automatically made contact with all light formations being of magnetic attraction. Spherically surrounding each sphere it caused light discolouration. Gold lost its pure colour to become whitened. All spheres including First Sun, whitened. Whitening of light is when warmth, not heat, involves with coolness, not coldness, and the two vibrational activities combine to fade down the warmth of gold, then smother its colour with a film of activity which is moist. White light was born that way.

Eons passed. First Sun began heating once again. All spheres heated in equational reaction, and as they did, moisture heated also. First steam evolved. The First Sun reddened, as did the spheres. The surrounding moisture quivered and destabilised. Quivering moisture was aggressive equations at temperature. Their quivering entered the breathing of first equation and more energy was activated. Vibrations became no longer staccato but frenzied, completely out of tempo and explosive in containment. All the spheres quivered. The containing whole of God quivered. Expansion was automatic.

Eons passed again. First Sun heated as before. All spheres heated equationally. Moisture which had already become involved in light vibrations, heated. Quivering began again, and so charged was First Sun's light formation, it exploded before God's containment could enlarge.

The heat being generated inside God caused moisture to thicken close to the surround where water was evolving. Water of heavy vibrational activity, created a thick sheath of coolness which prevented registration by God of the extreme temperature of First Sun and its surrounding light bodies.

The second explosion released highly charged light particles, which as they exited from their source, pierced the bodies of the spheres in their path. The light indentations later became craters of spherical shaping. Light particles being power-generated at speed, entered the bodies of the spheres and were impregnated deeply into them, in varying colours of gold through to red. When the spheres solidified, light fragmentary vibrations hardened.

God registered the force of the second light explosion when its vibrations made contact with the water-sheathing. The water began to tremble, and in that imbalance its spherical sheath broke open. Water separated from itself. The trembling caused God to expand again. Coolness returned controlling all imbalances and water became circulating, moving around God's whole in spherical vibrating activity. It could not unify. Its equations had no prime source. Its evolution was from heat, not motion. Water then, moved in spherical motion because of its vibrating containment, and forever onwards would motion that way.

The spheres did not explode, for they had no first equation present. Their heating was not as extreme. However, their centres were red hot, with highly charged vibrations equationally controlled by their father sphere. The explosion thrust them outwards from their centres and they enlarged. Light then had no solidity and a light body could expand if equationally activated.

First Sun heated a fourth time. All spheres heated also, but cooled before any enlargement was forced. Circulating water controlled their temperature. Water had settled upon the spheres by way of thin sheathing. Its cool vibrations made contact with warming light and the two identities combined to form a thin skin. The evolving First Sun could not accept water because its temperature was hotter than the spheres causing water evaporation. Gradually the watery skin of the spheres magnetised more water which became heavy.

The weight of evolving water caused the light vibrations of the spheres to begin solidifying, a hardening in visible colours. Their surfaces vibrated white light. As they hardened, the penetrating light vibrations became gold through to red, then other colours as more explosions punctured their bodies.

God in colourlessness contained all light vibrations and all water vibrations. Each progression had been registered inside God's whole. Light of visibility created darkness, the colourlessness of vibrations without heat.

The glowing spheres would give birth further on. Galaxies would evolve. First Sun would explode again and again until God became a reactor, a powerful responding force, able to balance all imbalances and protect the spheres from explosion.

When First Sun exploded its formation again, its light particles entered heavy water vibrations and cold shock was experienced. They did not travel as far as previously because of the circulating water. They entered the bodies of the spheres in varying colours of blues through to greens, the shock of violent red of heat making contact with the weight of water. This caused immediate cooling and red became purple, then blue, then green, the stages of vibrations of heat losing their charge. Into the bodies of the spheres every one, light particles of prime colours were forced. In their hardening a spherical light body evolved with a magnetic attachment to first force of light, and a vibrational constitution of hard light, which kept them alive and attracting charge.

Hard light vibrates. It lives. It was a progression of pure light. Its vibrations cannot die. Its prime force is the first equation. Its hardened particles of first light still feed from first equation, still magnetise, and still respond to other light holding bodies. Hard light is at the interior of nearly every spherical body that evolved during the evolution of the First Sun in existence.

The rotation of the spheres began when one side of their formation heated causing swelling, and their bodies automatically sought cooling. The turning was an automatic reaction to extreme imbalance of temperature. Equations of the spheres had registered God's surround vibrating coolness and turned to balance their heating. Continual balancing was necessary and the spheres began perfect rotating temperature control. The turning of the spheres began with a right-lead motion. Heat always caused equations to seek cooling. God's surround was that cooling. When the largest sphere nearest the Sun and alongside another sphere heated, to balance in temperature was to turn away from the heat. Turning was an equating motioning towards God's wholeness. Since there was distance between the largest sphere and another much further away than the sphere alongside, right lead motion was activated. Automatically all spheres followed that lead. Once activated right-lead motioning would continue.

Pure light was all there was in existence then. There were only a few spheres, the central light force of First Sun and God's total surrounding whole. The equations of light were always seeking balance. The spheres would path much later when their equations imbalanced again.

God had also progressed vibrationally. The constant heating then cooling repetition had enlarged God to become so huge, all central activity took time to reach the surround and God's responses became lengthy in return. Vibrations always travel according to the force they exit from and attach to a magnetic likeness.

The spheres absorbed much explosive force from first equation and the circulating water accepted the rest. The previous quivering inside the surround had faded to irregular motioning, a faint slowing of travelling vibrations inside a very cool surround. With each irregularity God enlarged.

Equations never destroy. They imbalance only. They never non-equate. They always, in whatever stage of imbalancing, eventually find an equating likeness and attach. Equations progress because they cannot die. Their containment then, however enlarging, was their equating force field, a spherical surround more powerful than they and the resolution to their activity. Without God's surround equations would never exist, vibrations could not establish themselves, and evolution could never have begun. God was then and still is, the sole controller of all vibrational activity.

The fading contact with central vibrational activity caused God to contract, motion inwards, for there were no vibrations of strength making contact with their surround. Previously God felt every vibration alive and progressing. As God enlarged, the distance from central Sun equations minimised vibrational activity. An imbalance inside God's whole caused contraction in magnetic response. God had equationally enlarged. God would equationally contract.

The contraction of God's whole caused the spheres to seek contact with their surround. As God approached their vibrational vocabulary, coolness in huge volume caused the spheres to ray-project. From their centres, their cores of activity, where there was most light intensity, where their formation began from linear shaped light particles in spherical motioning, magnetic contact with God was activated. Straight outwards, heading straight for the surround, minute strands of light pulled away from their first formation of vibrations and kept travelling towards the surround. Light-ray projection from the spheres was an automatic reaction of an already linear activated formation of equations that had been of magnetic attraction unto themselves, had motioned spherically as they joined, and had pathed linearly, therefore could be attracted by a superior force in linear motion.

The distance for contact was too far and the rays faded in light as they travelled. In perfect equating reaction to ray projection of the spheres, God ray-projected invisibly inward. God's response was always an equating acknowledgement of all vibrations in containment. God's colourlessness still held every progression of every vibration that had evolved. Nothing took place without an equating response. Nothing ever would.

Light rays of visibility in contact with light rays of invisibility caused magnetic hold, vibrations meeting and being held together by their likenesses. Magnetic hold with God their supreme force meant that the spheres could never explode of their bodies unless that hold was released.

The Sun's formation prevented light rays from the spheres to project in spherical perfection. In equating reaction to God's invisible projection of light rays, the Sun projected, was not pulled magnetically, but projected light rays in equational response to the spheres. The Sun was of prime light vibrations, more powerful than the spheres, therefore of dominant equations, was first light force, and automatically followed God's vibrating lead. Magnetic hold was established and because the rays from the Sun were hot, the spheres changed colour from white light to bright gold as their water warmed. A sphere in ray-contact with another sphere remained at temperature. A sphere in contact with God only, was cooled. A sphere in contact with the Sun, heated, and in contact with both God and the Sun, remained at temperature, for God's touch controlled the Sun's heating rays. Ray-magnetic contact of all spheres, God and the Sun, created a perfectly balanced webbing of equations of absolute purity which was the transmission of activity of light unto light, a life force. Without ray projection a sphere would eventually explode, for God could not control its temperature unless directly in contact with its equations.

The Sun made contact with God's inward projecting rays also and a linear patterning of light rays lit a glorious universe. The rays were long and short depending on body contact, were breathing in rhythm of energised vibrations in motion, were transmitting patterns of coloured light vibrations into each other, were active in vibrational communication, and were held by one mighty force of invisible light vibrations equating every ray of light of every body forevermore. Rays of invisibility never project into those of visibility as they would cause the colour to become colourless. As a visible light ray projects towards an invisible light ray, the more powerful of the two automatically stops extending when the weaker is at an equating distance of temperature balance. The weaker also stops extending in submission. There is a gap between both rays, the distance of temperature control. God's rays do not transmit energy as the Sun's rays. God controls all heat imbalances and all vibrational progressions. When the spheres projected light rays, God answered in equating activity of invisible projecting light rays.

Rotation of the spheres from the heat of the Sun slowed, did not stop, but slowed only. The heat at the core of the Sun, first equation, progressed as always. The spheres, heavy with water, sparkled of light vibrations combined with water vibrations active from outside influences. The Sun did not sparkle for it had no water and never would. It heated again faster than before for God had contracted inward and the surround was smaller. As it reddened its rays became too hot for the spheres and they retracted their own rays in equating reaction. God's rays retracted equationally.

The Sun once more exploded its evolving formation into particles of light. The spheres were pierced again only this time not as deeply as previously. Their bodies were solidifying. The fragments entered nearer their surfaces which had thin setting tissue of light vibrations.

God, nearer in surround than at the time of all other explosions, immediately reacted with an inward equating of exploding vibrations which moved the spheres closer to the Sun. Instead of expanding from vibrational force needing coolness, God returned the charge without expansion. The explosion had reached God's surround swiftly because of its nearness. God's automatic response was of the same speed of impact, and an inward thrusting of explosive force was the exact equating balance of coolness. The travelling inward force held no light particles and the spheres received the shock of impacting aggressively charged invisible light vibrations and imbalanced.

The Sun also experienced impacting force and because of its beginning could never be moved. It was force-expanded instead. God's reactive invisible vibratory charge entered the Sun's formation explosively. Although cool in charge, God's vibrations were identical in aggression to those the Sun emitted. Having nowhere to exit, they entered the motioning of the Sun's equations and automatically increased their quantity. The Sun's first motioning which it always returned to after an explosion, enlarged to a very large motioning out and in, which became of air, forced motion. Until then light and water vibrations were airless. With forced motion entering breathing, beginning from first equation then being transmitted vibrationally to the spheres and entering water also breathing, pure air began evolution. Air then was absolutely pure, as was water, as was light.

The Sun enlarged again. The spheres began ray projection automatically. They had been of magnetic hold before imbalancing, their equations had accepted air in vibrational stimulation and God was sought in magnetic contact. Outwards spherically, strands of light projected. Inwards God projected. Outwards from first equation the Sun projected also and in magnetic hold of all spheres the universe sparkled, shone, breathed and vibrated as the bodies of light evolved.

Eons passed; the Sun heated unto explosion for the last time. Its air content became aggressively charged. All the spheres heated also. This time there would be no explosion at the centre of the evolving universe. This time God prevented it.

The Sun's spherical formation once reddened and holding powerful force, caused the spheres to become explosive. Their centres reddened violently. Their air content became overheated. Their water content boiled and the skin tissue forming over their bodies browned. It burned. A brown skin appeared on the surface of every sphere.

God had contracted inward. God's surround was nearer all central activity. God registered pre-explosive force. God equated that charge. As soon as extreme temperature of vibrations reached the surround, God thrust inward the same quantity of invisible cool charge before any explosion occurred. Had God been at full expansion the explosion would have taken place. The distance to the surround then was far greater and temperature was unable to be equated. Near, the temperature of explosive force was registered and in equational reaction to vibrations needing to be controlled, God responded.

The Sun was shocked again. So were the spheres. The impacting vibrations moved them even closer to the Sun. Into the rhythm of breathing came another force of motion and air became audible. Its vibrations were more powerful than before. The impact of God's response was stronger. The universe cooled down.

The spheres solidified at that time. They became firm in their bodies. Their centres remained hot but the rest of their formation hardened. The process took eons. Their hardening began on the surface because it was coolest. Water had settled there in weighty formation where it found magnetic attraction. When light particles entered the spheres, puncture wounds vibrated heat from imbalance of equations and into those wounds water accumulated. The heat was causing moist activity. Water became magnetic.

Over the wounds of light piercing came water in depth, and under its weight-coloured light particles solidified. It was a natural equational process. Cool pressure pressed into light vibrations gradually de-activating their equations. It pushed them into each other to attach together in volume. Then, because no other light vibrations were able to be magnetised, they unified under pressure of water, could not expand or explode, and clung to each other. There was no escape from the water upon them. Deeper was heat. Combinations of coloured light vibrations stretched themselves seeking other similar activity. Some touched. Others weakened. Magnetic attraction inside the spheres continued until all light activity solidified.

The Sun heated again. Its redness caused all the spheres very near, to redden at their centres despite their cool solidified bodies. When extreme temperature was registered by God, a powerful response of inward thrusting cool vibrations prevented any explosion and the spheres were moved inward once more. Being too close to the Sun was to overheat. God, in equational response to the vibrations of their heating, magnetised them back into coolness. They had been moved forward. They were then moved backwards, drawn into safety of their equations.

The inward shifting had made them of violent central activity. Once shifted backwards, that activity remained, for the Sun was their father force and would always be at heat. Their evolving bodies of soft skin and hard light surrounded by God, would experience many temperature changes and the progressions of equations seeking balance.

The Sun heated again. The spheres were much slower in reaction. Their centres responded but their heavy bodies remained cool. As first equation developed and the Sun vibrated explosive charge, God responded in magnetic controlling force. God vibrated separate quantities of equations for the first time. First combination held the spheres in place. Second combination controlled explosive force. Both combinations were activated separately. The spheres had previously been drawn unto cool surround. The vibrations that had pulled them had to be activated again before any others were possible. Had that not been done, when God responded to the Sun, the spheres would have been pushed in again. Equations always behaved of God's responses. Holding the combination of the backwards pulling of the spheres in vibrations, backwards pulling of the spheres began first, then forward thrust straight after. The spheres remained in place and the Sun once more cooled.

First equation's Sun formations were always of progressive vibrations. Each increase in energy caused an even larger increase in heating. The energy from the Sun at the peak of its temperature activated more energised vibrations within air and water. God contained all. God always would. God never lost control. God never could.

The Sun's reddening intensified. The violence of colour became so highly charged it flamed. Flame has always been of red-hot vibrations unable to explode in quantity but able to expand. From the central core of the Sun's body of light volume, first flame began. First equation's first motion was so hot it burst its perfect equation of breathing and second motion returned bent. Red hot convulsing jagged lit vibrations, exited from their start, returned to their core and kept on activating. Back and forth, out and in, flame was generated inside the Sun's body formation. Inside the spheres the very same activity took place. Bent spherically motioning equations happen when the sphere they are motioning within becomes too heated, too explosive, too red-charging, and cannot release their heat. The motioning cannot complete its pure activity. The outward first motion, being prime vibration, always begins purely. As its containment is reached, the intensity of heat being generated causes the purity of the inward return motion to wave-motion, bend its spherical perfection. Unable to return purely, a wavy motioning takes place. Flame began as an outward then inward wavy motioning, which air refined with tips. Bent vibrations are of intense heat before explosion. Unless they are cooled they ignite into flame.

God registered flame. God responded equationally, and each time flame increased, vibrationally controlled its activity, until a body of flame was absolutely contained within its spherical formation, by an overpowering constantly vibrating outer force of God's cool hold.

The flame of the Sun is very different from the flame of Earth. Its heat has no moisture. Its vibrations have never solidified. Its temperature is far greater than could be measured. Its equations are pure still. Its body has never been entered. Its evolution began with first equation. Its light is the sole life force of every living light holding body. Its equations are unable to be deactivated. It has no other equal in the universe. Its equations still progress. God is its controlling force.

The spheres began to flame in equational reaction to the Sun. Their temperature however was not nearly as violent. Their solidified cool bodies kept flame contained and as they all imbalanced further on, their cores broke open and flame spread its way through their interiors changing solidity into liquid light, black molten light, with every colour of its original composition visible. The heat of flame as it spread outwards, combined with solidified light particles, melted them and kept on spreading to eventually cease activity because water was near and controlled its aggressive charge. Oil began its evolution then. Its content inside the spheres lubricated their drying bodies as they evolved. Its vibrations attract light equations, feed of light equations, balance its surrounding equations, breathe, magnetise light life, and oil is now the blood by which Earth survives and the internal lubrication that stops Earth from exploding. Its powerful gaseous vibrating surround developed further on. Then its evolution was pure, without contamination.

Rotation of the spheres continued through every development of equations. The Sun's intense heat once contained by God's magnetic coolness was of temperature permanency. There was no further overheating. The spheres turned equationally.

Ray projection of all spheres had been intermittent. Each overheating had caused ray retraction until coolness prevailed. With the Sun finally overpowered, ray projection began again. This time the Sun of flaming equations of supreme light power, of total dominant energised force, projected rays of life existence for all bodies of light equations. Its rays would never be destroyed. The flaming Sun vibrated rays of supreme energised force. Their projection was controlled by God's surrounding invisible cool charge. When making contact with the spheres, God's touch allowed transmission to take place without any ray retraction.

The Sun, being of dominant force, became the life force of all of the spheres in evolutionary process. Ray projection of any light body is automatic. The inferior formation seeks magnetic contact with the superior force. All light bodies began of spherical formation. All light vibrations evolved from first breathing equation. Every light cell in every living body is of spherical evolution.

Pure light has been impured greatly. When the soul of man evolved it was still pure. From the Sun came pure energy which has also impured. Into the spheres that purity was magnetised. Each ray began at central core, as had first equation, motioning outwards in spherical extension. As ray projection lengthened, the rays widened. At central core their containment was minute. They enlarged equationally as had the body of the Sun, automatically widening as they travelled through the Sun's body. Because the Sun is of light equations, its flame is also of light equations, therefore ray extension from its central core is without interference of charge of energy. The rays slip through its flaming equations at the same temperature and gradually become cooler as they travel outwards into the universe.

Magnetic contact was when rays from both Sun and sphere met at the perimeter of the weaker body. The dominant rays surrounded the weaker and began transmitting charge of energised light vibrations in breathing motion. This was absorbed substantially by the weaker formation. As transmission took place all light equations strengthened. They increased in energy. Into the extending rays of the spheres came pure coloured energising light equations motioning in and out and charging up every light vibration within their bodies. Equations on their surfaces were highly charged whilst those deeper were softly charged, of lesser activity. Once attached to the spheres, the Sun's rays ceased travelling and magnetic hold prevented further extension. Later on, as some spheres hardened, ray contact between the Sun and a sphere needed a distance of adjustment, a one metre equational balancing of rays incoming and experiencing hard surface and temperature imbalance.

The rays of the spheres came directly from their centres as did the Sun's, straight outwards from a flaming core and able to magnetise pure light charge all through their bodies. The flaming cores of the Sun and the spheres were of purity of heated light, still breathing equationally, and even though first motion of first equation had bent, the beginning pure extension of first vibration was still at life. Every vibration in existence no matter how impure extends from a prime motion.

Trillions of light rays projected at that time and so bright was the universe, air and water glowed. The volume of light in brightness of colour caused light glowing, activity of intenseness, not heating but fixed, holding field, and being absorbed by every vibrating force. Air and water, both of light vibrations, were saturated in volume of brightness. Both became of glow. Both, within atmospheric changes, emit light glowing which does not vibrate. Day would not be as bright as it is without both air and water in equational brightness of pure light.

God's invisible rays did not enter the Sun but surrounded its formation with huge volume of cool vibrations containing the activity of flame. Entry of God's rays would have caused imbalance. God equated always and gradually began to equate single formations as evolution proceeded.

Continual energising from the Sun caused the spheres to path. Their highly charged bodies began to seek each other equationally. As they registered an energy charge those farthest away slowly moved forward to where light was strongest. Spheres farthest away automatically sought contact with spheres closer to the Sun. Light charge vibrated dominance in some spheres. Always the stronger force attracted the weaker and magnetic pulling began.

Magnetic pulling behaves in equating light vibrations which draw weak equations unto strong ones. The stronger vibrations drag out the weaker which ray-extend fiercely where contact is needed. The projection becomes heated because the rays energise. The weak rays, cool and of white light, seek more warmth. Once magnetic hold is established the weaker rays change colour turning a sphere golden. Magnetic pulling did not stop until both spheres touched. The suctioning of energy kept activating until both spheres were of equating balance of light. Touching was automatic. Their surfaces touched. They became of total equating temperature. The instant that heating was registered both spheres were separated. All pathing spheres eventually touched. Where a sphere had not been touched, a near sphere without any other attraction began pathing sideways towards the stronger magnetic force. Inward and sideways pathing caused tracks of vibrations, which, because they were alive in light-reflective charge, began spherical formation automatically. One vibration magnetised its likeness and gradually a small light body evolved, one which was composed of reflective light only.

Reflective light is a shadow-vibrating charge which a body of light leaves as it motions in any direction. It glimmers. It shimmers if moisture is touching. Because it is of light vibrations it automatically spherically activates.

The very much smaller reflective light bodies inhabited every path, and when some of the spheres eventually collided with them, their bodies broke up into millions of tiny light sparks composed of reflective light vibrations integrated with pure light charge, moist, breathing, shimmering, and the stars were born.

The stars were of pure equational composition. They were fed light energy from the Sun. They have now impured. Their relationship to the planets is of magnetic attraction, for their beginning was of the spheres in pathing. Around each individual star is God's holding force of cool invisible vibrations unable to be penetrated. They cannot overheat unless God withdraws. Some are small, others large, depending on how close to the Sun they were when formed and how large their father image. After collisions, reflective light body sparks spherically re-united in varying strengths and sizes. Their equations are of magnetic light transmission to every light body in the universe, for their evolution was of the purity of light and not the impurity. Without the stars galaxies would not have evolved. Further on some stars impured.

The galaxies, areas of universal imbalancing, were the result of light asphyxiation, an area of pure light overpowering all other forces and holding field inside God's evolving wholeness. This was when one volume of power, too powerful in presence, caused extra energy to evolve at a rate unable to be accepted unless God enlarged. To spherically enlarge would imbalance all light bodies. To enlarge only where necessary was God's equational response at that time, the first irregularity of a pure whole.

Outwards from areas of too much energised vibrational content, God's whole expanded, exactly where irregularity of force was accumulating, where God's surround was being pummelled with aggressive activity, and where an equating response was necessary. God then, lost purity of wholeness, to become a containment able to control every imbalance of force likely to evolve. The whole would expand irregularly forevermore.

God's spherical completeness, being of perfect equational formation, dictated at every instant of imbalance, the shape, size, temperature and protection of every living light body in existence. Irregularity of a whole was the natural expansion to irregularity of force in containment.

The areas of imbalance in the universe then were where some spheres had pathed, touched each other, caused the formation of the stars, collided with star formation and were generating ray transmission of aggressive charge into each other. Their areas of placement were heating.

The Sun kept transmitting. The spheres overheated. Individual bodies had aggressed in activity and God's holding rays received the imbalance. God expanded in equational assessment and magnetised the offending aggressive charge into the gap of coolness. Magnetising vibrating light bodies into galaxy holdings was an equational suctioning of God's whole, automatically pulling the heated area into its cooling hold. The irregular expansion was activated by an explosively charging area pushing against its containment and God equating its force and shape. Vibrations of disturbance were held in their own irregular containment magnetic to each other.

The vibrations of aggressive light charge were lit. Intensity of light vibrating aggressively causes high volume of light charge which surrounds a body, cannot attach because the body vibrating is of solid formation and composed of variations of equations all magnetic to first equation at the centre of the Sun. Aggressive light charge surrounding a body is not of first equation's formation. It is light temperature which surrounds the body; therefore it is of no equational composition of formation. Once drawn away from an overheating body, it can become of magnetic attachment to its likeness. God, by way of an equating cool charge, attracted its vibrations, which detached immediately from the body it surrounded, to be drawn into spherical irregularity of shape, and evolve equationally.

The drawing away of aggressive charge of light vibrations into coolness controlled the heat, but not the activity. Quantity of active vibrations not of first equation and of aggressive light charge in magnetic attraction to likenesses which were also aggressively vibrating, caused new formations to appear. Small spheres evolved, all composed of light volume vibrations, all magnetic unto each other and very much smaller than the first spheres. They too pathed towards each other, touched, and gave birth to even smaller stars. They were light-injected by the Sun, invisibly light-held by God, of ray projection into each other, all of magnetic attraction, much weaker vibrationally than their likenesses, and of low volume of light charge.

The spherical identities held no light fragments, no water in volume, only moisture within their formations, no flaming cores, and did not solidify, for their content was without outside pressure. They did however contain light-patterning of all colours as they breathed of the Sun's charge.

Galaxies are few. As well as small spheres of aggressive light charge and trillions of stars, they hold huge impurity of imbalanced charge which has been magnetised there during evolution. These vibrations have not always spherically formed because of the extremity of their imbalance and the inability to motion purely. At each stage of any high-volume light charge imbalancing the spheres, the aggression has been drawn away into galaxy holding by God's responding force, and in equational reaction galaxies have enlarged accordingly.

Earth, one of the first-born spheres, was the first to give birth to a moon. Its position then was very different to its present placement. Its body had set in hard light, been watered substantially, and its flaming core had spread heat through channels which had melted hardness and produced oil. Earth had not been touched by any formation evolving. It also had not pathed. Its position was solitary, without a near magnetic sphere, but able to ray-touch. Its quantity of hardness kept it solitary, for its magnetic force then was not as attractive to other spheres needing more charge than

Earth vibrated. Earth would be ray-magnetised along a linear path; other spheres would follow. Its powerful solidified body would influence other light bodies until it imbalanced.

All other spheres had also solidified. Some hardened as Earth, others remained of thin skin consistency. Those nearest the Sun hardened faster than those further away, attracting larger quantities of water by temperature imbalances. God's answering vibrations caused coolness to water their bodies frequently.

The spheres near God's surround were always cool until they pathed. Their soft tissue made them light, very transparent, of soft golden glow, and when in motion, faster than all other pathing spheres.

The universe then was absolutely pure in equations. God had equated every minute vibration and every enormous evolving force. The galaxies were the only irregularity in spherical evolution. Their areas and all that took place there were of equational activity. The formations within the galaxies were spherical until some equations deformed.

Magnetic light volume of charge also overheats when quantity of vibrations become too aggressive. Because a spherical entity of light-volumed charging cannot expand from pressure, it deforms in shape by vibrating within its containing formation, then spitting out its excessive vibrations of too much heating, causing deformity of motioning. Such deformed vibrations cannot explode because God holds their entirety. They express their aggression in waves of temperature-imbalance all contained within their original formation. Automatically a light-volumed spherical form becomes deformed, without perfect sphericality of light vibrations.

Transmission of light energy from the Sun to a pure light body caused vibrational orgasm, an extra flow of energised activity, a flooding of charge which entered a sphere's body in spurts of vibrations, a fast force. The spurt of energy was caused by the Sun's rays hotter than a sphere's rays, faster in flow of activity, and when touching a sphere's rays, inserting extra charge. The spurting was repeated until the sphere's rays equated with the Sun. Where imbalance was registered, the Sun automatically expressed its charge equationally. Orgasm of light vibrations was experienced. Orgasm of any formation is a spurting vibrational charge which comes from aggressed equations in containment. They heat first, aggress vibrationally, then excrete in release of charge.

With light transmission came aura, a vibrating, patterned, coloured, outer sheath of light, which formed around a light holding body. The rays of the Sun magnetised the rays of a sphere of hardening light vibrations. The setting body held glorious equations of colour which cross-hatched many times from the explosion of light fragments. As the Sun's rays approached a sphere's body surface, they hesitated because of the vibrating obstruction of hardening tissue. Hesitancy caused the colours of ray flow to replicate and build up around the surface of the sphere's body. Rays extending from central core of light of the sphere travelled through its body of colour patterning until the surface was reached, where the Sun's rays were building aura-surround. At a suitable magnetic path-transmission of Sun-raying, the spheres rays began absorbing energised vibrations, feeding through the aura which itself vibrated powerful charge of light vibrations. A meeting of singular rays did not take place where there was aura build up, for replication of coloured equations was more powerful in attraction and the spherical surround of aura encouraged spherical absorption of charge. The Sun expressed its charge straight into a sphere's aura and powerful energy was received by a sphere.

A vibrating, coloured aura had evolved, which because of magnetic attraction, remained where it had formed. Every sphere in evolution then had a spherical colourful aura impenetrable until the aura imbalanced. Ray contact of the spheres unto each other also energised as their auras prevented singular ray transmission. Hesitancy of charging because of their surrounding aura, caused spurts of energy into each other. The build-up of aura created an aggressed transmission. As aura deteriorated around the spheres, singular ray transmission re-started until that too imbalanced and then progressed.

Equations of light transmission are always controlled by God's holding force. If God did not control energised transmission of light from the Sun, a receiving body would explode from force too powerful to contain. To control the Sun's energising rays, God equated the force of their equations, projecting rays of cool force which surrounded the Sun's rays. The spheres immediately calmed as the spurts from the Sun were cooled. God's rays did not make contact with the Sun's rays, but controlled the insertion as the bodies of the spheres were entered in light charge.

Aura protects light equations inside its sheathing. It has to be entered before contact with light equations is made. If attempt at entry is sought by radioactive or electric impure vibrations, provided the aura is strong enough passage through it is prevented. Aura protection is an automatic rejection of all impure vibrations.

Light-sheathing-aura is of equational activity. When vibrations that are not of its equations seek contact, they are refused. They then reverse their advancing and involve with themselves until another likeness attracts them. Their attempt at contact with an aura is because their prime motion was of first equation and the power of an aura becomes of magnetic attraction. Should huge volume of radioactive vibrations seek to overpower a very small pure aura, the aura still does not admit them, but heats, turns red, and remains unto itself surrounded by radioactive charge too large to be re-directed. Aura surround depends on two factors for its existence, a pure light vibrating body in moist surround, and the pure unimpeded rays of the Sun in connection. Without both there can be no light sheathing.

With planets evolving and galaxies progressing, God had become supremely powerful in presence. From the first equation of life to every vibration progressing, God held field. No other power was there. No challenger could there be. Never would there be another light reactor and for the rest of existence evolution would continue inside God's containment.

Unless a pure whole was the presence of first beginning, there could never be life.

Unless the whole expressed motion, there could never be a prime equation.

Without a first pure equation, breathing would not be possible, for one breath outwards then inwards is of perfect motion.

Unless the whole was spherical in totality, not one planet would have been born.

Unless the whole warmed inside its containment, light would not exist.

Unless light was visible and invisible, not one single composition of anything could evolve anywhere, for all life is of light equations.

Unless there is one supreme equator, all that has evolved would end.

The spheres of hardening light that had gently touched each other did not bang together, but touched only. One soft spherical surface touched another likeness. At touch, surface-impact of vibrations was experienced. Sweating occurred which caused a swelling on each body as they parted. The swelling was caused by one face of quantity of light vibrations magnetising the other, being held together in contact by magnetic hold, then pushing against each other to excrete a soft light fluid which divided equationally on both surfaces as they separated.

The fluid came from the two bodies of likeness heating during contact, being crushed together, excreting what moisture was within their tissue as pressure was applied, and, because the moisture was of magnetic attraction to both spheres, it remained as a swelling, an increase in formation of light equations.

Separation of the two spheres was when the touch impact was immediately equated by God and both spheres drew back from each other. God then magnetised both away from each other with the same equations of their collision pathing.

Earth did not touch any other sphere. Its solitary existence was because of its placement in the universe. It held a temperate position from birth, placed between heat and coolness in balance. It had moved during God's responses but was still within a temperate zone. Its core was of flame, then oil and hard light. Its interior was of combinations of vibrations affected by varying pressures and temperatures which compressed, often unified, magnetically attached to each other as well as progressed continually. Earth's interior was and still is an entirety of progressing light vibrations. Earth's surface was of brown moist tissue with large deposits of deep and shallow water. Its skin changed colour as the universe heated again. Earth was flat everywhere. Its light content was huge. It was the least aggressed of the evolving planets. When it was ray-entered its responses were passive compared to the other planets. When the Sun's rays expressed charge into its body the charge was peacefully accepted. God held Earth passively also.

As Earth's body increased in weight of hardening its temperature dropped. Other planets did not experience such a change in their equations. Earth began pathing towards the Sun for the first time. The nearer Earth came the warmer it became, until in perfect equational reaction Earth stopped when it registered balance. Because of its powerfully vibrating peaceful pathing, a light vibrating track followed Earth, rolling itself spherically behind Earth as it motioned forward. The shadow-image could not detach as had other trackings because Earth's body had become so powerful in hardness, whatever it left behind was always going to follow. Hard light magnetised soft light dominantly by quantity of compressed vibrations in mass. Rolling behind Earth came the beginning formation of first moon, a spherical formation of pathing light vibrations magnetic to a prime light source.

The detachment of the forming moon was when God equated a colliding force approaching Earth and responded with the same quantity of vibrations in impact. The new formation was halted and drawn backwards at safe equational placement. It could not approach the Earth again, so began an encirclement of magnetic attraction. Every other moon evolved that way and behaves the same as first moon.

Earth remained peacefully at place for eons. Its moon set equationally. Its vibrations were soft and faint in colouring. No flaming core was there, no light fragments, and no water. Its body was composed of the outer vibrational charge of Earth itself, a combination of coloured vibrating patterns with air and moisture involved. The vibrations were energised by the Sun and contacted by the rays of the planets.

The moon's body of light once set, became porous. It never overheated. Its core was without flame and its energy content was passive. As eons passed both Earth and moon hardened in granite combinations of vibrations, some softer than others but of many variations of colour and thickness. The moon would never give birth to life forms for its own birth was too weak in light equations. Its presence in magnetic attachment of visible and invisible light rays would influence all evolving light formations on Earth and be in equational balance to all Earth's forces.

The imbalancing of Earth's purity began when the entire universe overheated. The temperature had been increasing as evolution proceeded and trillions of light formations vibrated charge. So rapid was the temperature increase the circulating water evaporated. God enlarged equationally and with each expansion drew further away from the planets. All, with one exception, erupted at central core. Their bodies burst in several places where their tissue was softest, and some, where they were most heated. The one planet that did not erupt then was Mars, for its temperature then was of very cool vibrations which took time to heat.

God responded to the planets individually for their eruptions were all different. As each planet was controlled, the temperature of the universe cooled and God contracted inwards again equationally. Eruptions had thrown planet solidification into space. Much of it returned to the body it came from. That which did not, because the distance of return was out of magnetic contact, was discharged into circular space travel, orbiting various planets according to where it came from, and hardening as coolness made contact with equations already solidified. Meteors evolved. During travel the meteors collided, broke up, and often landed on planets unrelated. Other solidified debris magnetised travelling likenesses and enlarged. The comets evolved.

Debris then was without contamination. When it fell on a surface, it injured in spherical shape. The impact was irregular for only a short time then all equations above the injury and below the impact began spherical motioning. Each injury became rounded consequently.

Many rounded shapes appeared all over the surface of the planets for their eruptions continued until God had total control of vibrational imbalancing. Some solidification plunged deep into the planets. Combinations of vibrations entered different bodies which were not of their evolution. Coloured light-rocks were spread over every planet's surface. Later they dissolved as the universe contaminated.

Earth heaved several times and its smooth flatness became mountainous in structure. During the eruptions much water was channelled across its body and fell through the splits of rock caused by Earth's heaving. The depth of eruption was from the central flaming core and water was swallowed at Earth's vibrating centre. Contact with flame caused massive steaming and when some areas closed structural openings from more eruptions, burning steam was trapped. It caused gas to evolve.

Gas of Earth's interior is the violent reaction of flame inside hard light vibrations shocked by water. With no escape, the activity is force-held until the heat progresses. Its imbalanced vibrations are unable to explode because the heat is watered. The vibrations are without air to free their activity, and rot. They age. Earth's gas content was and still is, rotting trapped equations surrounding Earth's lubricating oil content, spread throughout Earth's body and an absolute necessity for its balance.

Every happening in universal evolution has equational resolution. When an eruption occurs it is of imbalancing equations. When those equations release their charge the settling is of equating balance. What is heaved out returns in perfect placement unless the magnetic attachment is severed. Each eruption of the planets created bodies of perfect balance of form.

The contamination of the universe began after the planets erupted and the force of their discharge entered clean air and impured it. Until then explosions evolved forces and each progression was pure. When eruptions began, the internal heat of the planets which had aged, had never been released into the universe. Ageing caused conflict of equations resulting in various gases in space, all of progressive vibrations without magnetic attraction. When hot trapped vibrations flame for eons they impure, their equations de-stabilise.

Gas of vibrational instability behaves in two ways. When its vibrating quantity is released and air is confronted, it either mass-expresses an odour which can be flammable or non-flammable, or mass-releases another charge of lesser heat than its volume. Its equations divide and sub-divide because there is no prime equation to control behaviour. It over generates vibrations. Its mass produces its likeness. It does this because it must expand. Its entrapment has created huge pressure and it release-generates echoing likenesses, echoing because its unfamiliar environment refuses to accept its charge until it is subservient. The odour of all gas results from trapped equations of instability squeezed by others until a small excretion of sweat is emitted from the squeezing. The sweat is moist once it makes contact with air. Its odour is simply heat trapped, then released, with moisture lubricating as air spreads the odour outwards. The older the entrapment the stronger the odour and the more powerful its composition. The flammable gases are the result of too much flame at their source.

When gases circulated in space they met with opposing electrically charging equations all magnetic to first equation. The confrontation aggressed the pure equations so violently they too divided, for their opposition was massing and the equational reaction to imbalance of force was to equate the opposing behaviour. An electrically charging vibration broke into two then four then eight and so on until the surrounding gaseous mass was overpowered. First pure equations of energy would become radioactive in content.

Radioactivity is the progression of electrically charging vibrations that have divided many times, mass aggressed, vibrated extreme imbalance, clung together in volume because they have become of magnetic attraction and excreted hot moisture. They smear whatever environment they inhabit. They do not respond to first equation because their divisions are too minute. They always progress. Radioactivity then and not now was a force which evolved equationally, was able to be controlled by God and became of universal equational balance. The once whole equation has become a number of separate vibrations all different depending on the cause of the divisions. Progressive radioactive vibrations become nuclear generating.

When radioactivity became imbalanced the planets reacted violently. They had accepted gases in surround with minimal imbalance. The Earth's aura reddened slightly as gas touched its light equations. The vibrations of gas withdrew when Earth's aura refused them entry. Other planets allowed gas to circulate continually because their auras were weaker than Earth's and their heat more intense. Those with circulating gases have intensity of heat which attracts gases because of vibrational similarities. Once in permanent circulation gas thickens, its vibrations overlay. Circulation is of motion and vibrations in motion leave shadowing.

Later on, after the evolution of life forms, the progression of radioactivity was so impure its touch upon the surface of each planet burned them. Earth's soft skin of shades of browns deepened. Contact with highly charging radioactive vibrations caused passive light charge to overheat. Radioactivity reddened Earth's aura. Its force would eventually eat through light vibrations leaving the Earth without aura protection. Its extreme behaviour caused vibrations to wriggle in extensions and deformed motioning. All planets lost their pure aura when radioactivity progressed. Then it was of equational balancing. Later it became contaminating.

God responded equationally to both imbalances of gas and radioactivity by answering each vibration as it evolved. Gas was equated at every confrontation in the universe. God's invisible charge contained its vibrations keeping control as it evolved. As radioactivity increased so did God's equating responses. Never was radioactivity ever out of God's control. When the planets lost their auras of visible light, God encircled their bodies with invisible light which protected them from further radioactive contact and that protection remained until it was withdrawn.

As gas progressed and radioactivity circulated, the planets imbalanced again. Gas prevented the transmission of pure energy to pass through the universe freely. Its presence caused ray-smearing of coloured patterning which was once clear, to become unclear. The thickness of gas vibrations surrounded ray transmission causing pure equations to imitate their surround and lose their clarity of charge. God responded in purity of likeness and the smearing cleared in coolness.

The circulating radioactivity caused ray transmission to cease, for contact with such imbalance overheated pure equations and all rays retracted automatically. God equated in response and a surround of protection of invisible light allowed transmission to re-start and continue without imbalance. The visibility of ray projection disappeared almost entirely further on as pollution smothered ray purity.

When radioactivity stopped ray transmission, all of the planets pathed towards their prime light source. Their moons followed and because transmission had ceased temporarily and the paths were short, their tracks were too faint to become formations. Each planet slowly advanced towards the Sun.

Earth was the first to path because of its craving equations starving of light and heavy in body formation. As each planet balanced its equations and ray transmission re-started, God's responding vibrations positioned their bodies where they are at this time and their equations rotated them, tilted them, pathed them and kept them in balance of each other.

The tilting of the planets is magnetic leaning towards vibrations that enter a light feeding sphere from the raying of the Sun. Spheres pathed and collided with each other causing the spherical motioning of other spheres to seek balance by leaning away from too much heat and unto God's cooling rays.

God's surround holds temperate rays always. The Sun's rays are heated. Colliding spheres were moved by God's equating rays. Those that did not collide imbalanced in equations of light raying. Their rays bent. Shifted spheres had closed off their feeding. Bent linear rays of light equations caused their bodies to lean and magnetise light vibrations without restriction. The rays straightened as soon as their vibrations balanced. Once motioning in leaning, light feeding held the spheres securely. They remain leaning until God moves them equatingly.

Every planet is placed according to is equational needs. Some move when their heat disturbs their pathing, others move when their temperature lowers. Every individual planet has a different combination of equations. Some have more than one moon from paths of activity during their evolution. One is so hot it excretes vapour, a thick aggressive charge of vibrations which cannot cool because they are attracted to their source and held inside their field by God. God holds every planet in powerful invisible light rays. Every single light vibrating formation in the entire universe is ray-held by God invisibly. Were there no equating rays, each planet would explode.

Many pure star formations have magnetised each other to become imbalanced. Magnetic attraction has dragged, with its vibratory activity, gases and vapour which belong to formations close by, and are part of universal balancing of equations. Stars magnetising each other have impured of their perfect light vibrations and in some instances explode. God allows such explosions because equations must reach extreme temperature first, be withdrawn from equatingly, allowed release, then responded to in area cooling and magnetised into galaxy hold. To allow them to keep enlarging and explode, would create area imbalance of aggressive activity too threatening to all evolving formations of light equations.

Man's impure telescopic tracking of light formations is hideously flawed in reality and absolutely denies God's existence over man's. So fatal is that for evolution to continue, man's own evolution will cease unless God is accepted.

Science has destroyed every reality of a God in existence, light in equations of purity, a credible beginning to life, the absolute necessity of first equation, the absolute truth of universal progressive behaviour and first breath of every living formation. Science without God condemns man's future existence consequently. If there is no creator there is no beginning to life. If there is no God there is no real existence. If there is no real existence there is nowhere for man to evolve and if there is only science in power over man, there is nothing left to evolve.

God created life, not science, and God evolves life, not man. Evolution is the progression of equations all born from first equation which itself was born inside a pure whole which became first lighting, the evolution of God. To deny such obvious reality is to be without real evolutionary progression.

# Light Cell Evolution

Earth's life forms evolved from light cells, spherical clusters of coloured patterns of moist vibrations direct from the Sun's rays as they fed the Earth life force. Each cell was a composition of many pure equations which detached from one single Sun ray. As the Sun transmitted energy unto the Earth, a hardening surface was encountered. Contact with Earth's formation shook ray transmission causing a stop-start reaction. Light when hindered in raying, collects vibrations at the tip of each singular ray, holds those vibrations, does not let them go until equations balance and release their charge. The holding is of every colour transmitting from a raying that has come from the central core of the Sun, cross-hatched through linear extension of raying and been spun in varying temperature changes which caused beautiful tones and shades of pure equational colouring. Minute coloured light cells were dropped onto Earth's body. Once detached from ray transmission they were magnetised by whatever formation they touched.

The first ray-detached light cells evolved not as Earth was hardening but at an equational reactive moment in time when the surface of Earth became too hard for the Sun's rays to free-flow in transmission. There was a stopping of current of vibrations at contact with too much vibrating hardness. This caused equations to accumulate at the tip of each ray. Equations became too heavy from their accumulating numbers. They were dropped from the rays because of their weight, and detached because of their blocking imbalance allowing transmission to continue purely. The composition was spherical immediately it was dropped, spherical because as the rays of linear activity encountered a hardening obstruction, the accumulating coloured equations spherically motioned as soon as they left their containment. Light cells were heavy, solid in colour patterning and automatically spherically motioned. They had come from a spherical body. Their composition of colours had been dragged into the Sun's rays magnetically, linearly shaped as the rays extended, then as they were ray-dropped, automatically re-activated in spherical motioning. Their individual colour combinations were composed as the Sun breathed out and in, linearly dragging varying colour patterns through its extending, breathing rays. One singular light cell composition was one singular spherical motioning of the Sun, outwards then inwards. Each linear extension of rays magnetically grabbed and dragged whatever colour was vibrating within the motioning of the Sun's body. As one complete motioning ended, one singular cell composition was formed. The extending rays also motioning outwards then inwards in breathing rhythm, automatically carried each coloured composition through the rays until they were dropped onto Earth's surface. First light cells began evolution.

Upon Earth's glorious body tiny droplets of light cells clung magnetically. Trillions upon trillions of equations began evolution, for the rays from the Sun were uncountable. The surface they touched was equationally perfect for their minute, coloured patterning. Each spherical cluster was of light equations of prime equational birthing. Each formation breathed. Each pattern of vibrations held every colour of evolution. Each pure spherical identity was in the image of God. Each cell was absolutely pure. Each drop of light began the evolution of the soul.

Light cells entered Earth's waters and because of their tiny weighty compositions immediately lowered and came to rest on the bottom of water placements. Water then was without salt for its evolution was pure and Earth's body had not begun to sweat.

As cells touched Earth's unwatered surfaces they were magnetised strongly onto varying surfaces, some harder than others, some more moist than others and some soft and still fleshy. Light and water, no matter the quantity, equate perfectly as soon as they touch. The surface cells immediately began growth. The cells under water took time to begin life forms.

The very same evolution of light cells took place on some of the planets. Where temperature was too hot, cell life did not begin, for heat imbalances light equations and they cannot make permanent contact. Where planets were cold, light cells needing warmth to survive could not evolve. When further planetary imbalances polluted space, life forms evolving on other planets ceased in vibrational activity. Earth was the only planet to contain and progress life forms.

Growth upon the Earth in the very first stages of evolution was pure. It had no environmental disturbance and its temperature was cool. The colour growth began from was brown turning to green as each cell matured.

First a cell cluster touched brown moist tissue, brown hard rock and other colours of tissue and rock. It then experienced magnetic hold of equations. The Sun's breathing ray activity began unto the cell, as each cluster of spherical perfection sought magnetic contact with the Sun and began minute ray projection. The Sun responded, God equated, and every cell was ray-held before it grew.

The Sun's activity before ray extension is of linear and spherical motioning. Rotation of the spheres caused the Sun to rotate also. As the spheres pathed, produced the stars which produced other small spherical formations also rotating, the Sun began to spin, rotate in tempo with all bodies of light rotating. Trillions of light formations all in rotation vibrated unto the Sun their motioning. Trillions upon trillions of rotating motions magnetically charged the Sun in spinning.

The Sun spins from its central core, vibrations of immense power of energy. At the same time it thrusts outwards from its core fine lined rays which expand as they extend. The spherical motioning of its activity creates cross-hatched colour as rays also spinning separate colour into patterns. During the spinning, it throws out rings of colour, also patterned, and when it breathes, trillions of patterned equations are projected out and in rhythmically.

First equation deformed during the Sun's evolution when its second return motion became bent and the inward return was turned, forced to path circularly. Bending, a dent in spherical motioning, creates motion of irregularity. Outwards then inwards breathing evolves. If that perfect equating rhythm imbalances spherically, when containment is touched, the perfection of an inward spherical return bends. The denting, a wave-like motioning, causes a turn to the right instead of an inward action. The pure return motion cannot inward path because its pathing dents. It automatically right-motions, and because its containment is spherical, paths circularly. The outward first motion remains pure always because first equation's beginning was first outward motion and can never imbalance. The bent return motion causes rings of colour thrown outwards from the spinning of the Sun. Around and around in spherical activity the Sun's equations vibrated. First equation always outward motioned first, then circularly pathed second. This was repeated until the entire formation of the Sun had been spun into. Not one gap was there in equational assessment of containment. The bending was an automatic adjustment of equations returning to their start, unable to motion purely and activating around their prime vibration. The flaming of the Sun does not interfere with this powerful activity, it adds even more power to its energy force. The speed with which its equations spin is immeasurable. Their colour patterning can be seen through the projecting rays as long as their contact is pure in light.

The energy content of the Sun is of maximum beat of vibrations, maximum speed of motion, maximum colour combinations, maximum heat of equations, and maximum force contained. Without God's equating hold the Sun would explode. The waving of bent motion still exists inside the circularising of motion. It causes roundness in colour patterns and a wavy design in formations.

Being upon a surface, a light cell, a tiny spherical formation of coloured vibrations, flattened, was pressed onto its surface by forces overpowering its composition. Air then was light but filled with electrical charge. There was no rain at the beginning of life form evolution. Air was moist even though radioactivity was increasing. God's equating responses kept control of all vibrations in mass and singularly.

The breathing rays of the Sun fed every light cell and automatically in equational reaction to accumulating vibrations each cell expanded and began solidification exactly as the Earth. Slowly as a cell enlarged it became of one dominant colour. First, all colours vibrated. Then, as the surface colour was held, because it was of volume, the colours of the cell itself were drained and one dominant colour became visible. As this took place the cell thickened, for its activity was contained within its formation no matter how changing in shape. Clarity became smeared and a jelly-like tissue evolved. Light cells always magnetise colour.

Their beginning was of coloured equations. When a dominant colour receives their composition, their vibrations absorb the dominant colour, magnetise its content, hold the colour firmly until they expand enough to release their original composition of colours. The expansion of light cells always releases light cell colour patterning equationally.

The Sun vibrated energy into the cell and it kept growing. As each cell spread its formation a fine layer of jelly became visible. Cells touched cells in mass. Cells magnetised cells in mass. Cells unified in mass and as the jelly thickened even more, its equations imbalanced. The jelly began splitting, stretching, bubbling and even extending upwards, for areas of Earth were heated. Brown jelly-like irregularities appeared over Earth's body. Some areas remained perfectly balanced in temperature and smooth as layer over layer of cells clung together to begin grasses.

Under water a different evolution was taking place. A minute spherical cluster of light vibrations surrounded by volume of water, could not expand as the surface cells, for the pressure of surround caused cell formations to burst. From the centre of cell equations and thrusting outwards, clusters of coloured light vibrations were broken up and forced through their surrounding water field. As soon as they were released, the water, being very cool and heavy, prevented them reforming and held each vibrating irregular composition in places of evolutionary progression. Cells near the surface of water did not burst from water pressure. They progressed in perfection of their equations.

Some cells had more colours than others and more numbers of equations also. Some were very tiny in composition, others large. Spherical cells had broken apart to begin trillions of different life forms and the evolution of man began.

Growing cell life was directly affected by Earth's rotation. Light energised light cell activity whilst dark quelled cell activity. God's invisible rays held all light cells day and night keeping them in light balance.

The planets in ray-contact with each other provided magnetic stimulation to all light cells. The moons harmonised with them influencing behaviour by adding to their quantity of vibrations likeness and coolness. Moons caused stability at night where vibrations had heated and needed calming. They encouraged cells to rest their activity and even sleep, stop vibrating but continue breathing as their charge died down until light activated them again. Cells of light respond vigorously to light activation. They increase and decrease in energy as light brightens then fades. At night their colours return to colourlessness. Their temperature lowers and they stop energising. Cell activity at night evolved when Earth erupted in darkness and every evolution in the area of eruption was overcharged.

The rotation of the planets caused air to become of circularising magnetic involvement. Air became cloudy. Its clearness became smeared. Its vibrations began holding each other, and as it thickened it overheated. Its clouds held a central core of vibrations which heated in containment and because of a cool surround, progressed into rain.

Rain then, was the release of heated contained vibrations in contact with coolness, ray-separated as they passed between light raying, split by being ray-sliced and rhythmically spraying their weighty formation over and upon various surfaces. Rain only activates around planets. Its equations are magnetic to the body its vibrations encircle.

The formation of various spherically shaped clouds then all had a central core of activity. Rain was an equational reaction of air in progression. Its contact with the planets caused cell evolution to accept water within cell solidification. Cells upon Earth's surface became watered in equational balance of their formations. Rain then was regular, coming from pure clouds, absolutely pure itself and evolving progressively.

Under water, exploded light cells settled onto surfaces. They were magnetised there, ripped off by further eruptions, carried to other surfaces, often touched, clung to each other and were even spewed out of water onto Earth's surface.

Earth erupted many times adjusting to imbalances and changing shape. Underwater eruptions caused currents swift and passive. All the current activity in water then was caused by equational eruptions. As water moved out and in, its breathing vibrations were responded to by God and contained within its formation. Water breathes rhythmically in equational assessment of its volume.

Cells in currents of water, sped. Their lightness allowed them to be carried along by fast and slow motion in whatever direction a current was active. Some remained clinging to underwater surfaces not interfered with by eruptions and began the evolutions of coral, weed and life forms. Others evolved in constant motion, hardening in coolness and magnetic to current activity. Cells under water were all ray-energised, for Earth's rays projected outwards from central core reflecting through water magnetically and the Sun's rays projected reflectively into water. God's rays also surrounded water cell life and coloured vibrating patterning shimmered translucently through every cell formation resulting in glorious colourful life forms in evolution. Every colour of evolution vibrated within a tiny light cell formation and as solidification progressed, individual patterns became visible.

The beginning of many life forms was when clusters of vibrations aggressed within currents of water, heated, burst outwards, could not re-form, but magnetised other separations, and because they were of different equations swelled into various shapes. They swelled because their equations did not balance. They excreted inside their setting formations causing stems and humps of vibrating solidity. Translucent jelly became opaque, its vibrations hardened. The surrounding water pressed around the solidifying cell shapes and formed their vibrating compositions. Cells then were of pure light equations, breathing in perfect rhythm, and in magnetic attraction to first equation at the centre of the Sun.

Upon Earth's surface, brown and moist soil accepted cells without deformity of composition. Clusters which began of colour, gradually browned, their holding field was brown. As they grew, they spread outwards, stretched upwards, and were magnetised downwards. The Sun enticed them upwards needing energy of light charge. Their own likenesses magnetised them outwards seeking contact and the powerful content of Earth's hard light vibrations pulled them downwards. Light would always seek light magnetically.

The soil of Earth was its soft tissue, that which was porous, breathing, equationally watered, coloured in various shades of brown through to red from heat and strong light vibrations. It did not harden as rock for its moisture content was dominant. The evolution of rain assured its longevity. Without rain it would have become rock.

Rock became hard in areas where water vibrated alongside its evolving equations keeping it cool. Rock's equations hardened because of the nearness of water. They clung together in mass, tightened, could not heat, could not separate and layer over layer of varying colours of vibrations absorbed their surround and became rock hard. Rock was split, spewed up and out, separated in equations and displaced during Earth's eruptions. Each displacement was of equating positioning. The areas rock fell upon were the perfect magnetic balance for the size and shape of each separation. Every evolving formation was of equational distribution and resolution of equations.

The cells that touched soil caused equations to replicate their vibrations as shock was experienced, and when they balanced, they had automatically increased in numbers. Equations always replicate when interference of motioning takes place. They double in rhythm and patterning. Their breathing cannot stop. A contact surface always shocks their motioning and causes imbalance of activity which heats. There is a build-up of vibrations unable to be released unless God controls their temperature. The blocking of motion although temporary, squeezes equations together which heats their compositions. God equates their tempo in cool responses and the build-up of vibrations is released. The equations then breathe normally, express their intensity of heating, release their replicating vibrations and balance. The trillions that had settled on soil immediately sought each other magnetically. Outwards they stretched and finding likeness, clung together. As more cells of spherical equations touched Earth, layers of light vibrations massed and a carpet of grass began.

The cells became rooted into the soil first. Their equations of colour entered the soil as hard light of Earth's interior became of magnetic interest. Because hard light was at depth in moist areas, cell equations could not make contact. Their activity lessened. An extension of setting light vibrations was narrowed as it travelled downwards into Earth. Coolness and pressure caused the vibrations to taper off in activity. Close to the surface, swellings evolved. Equations had travelled down and returned to their start as a tapering of light magnetic charging was experienced. Their vibrations were being magnetised upward again. They had replicated with imbalance and bulbs and tubers began.

In some compositions retracting vibrations caused a swelling inside the formation, and because it was on top of the soil the Sun's rays drew the swelling upwards as it grew, and trees began. Swellings began first with replicating equations, second with magnetic interest in identical activity alongside an evolving form, and thirdly by the spherical motioning that began every formation. Rounded swellings were an equating activity of contained vibrations in motion.

Grass was when layers of equations became smothered, were unable to extend downwards to any depth because of their magnetic layering, were pulled upwards by the Sun, then refined with a tip by air circularising, which equationally lengthened or shortened their upwards extensions as their formation was balanced. Grass could not reach great height; its layering kept it magnetised.

As tree grew, roots were of equational balancing to each different formation. The development of roots was as wind evolved and trees were unstable in equations. Where wind caused forming trees to bend, the area most stressed imbalanced. The stabilising of tree was when the stressed vibrations heated, released excretion, then swelled, and because wind still tugged at trees, rooting spread automatically in equational balance. Magnetic attraction to hard light always encouraged rooting and the currents in air caused the roots to secure tree as it solidified.

Wind evolved during eruptions on the planets as light solidity sped through air causing gusts. Wind circulated around the planets in magnetic attraction. Its motion although weak, was able to destabilise equations.

Upwards grew a tree until its equations, also magnetically attracted to Earth, burst, and branches evolved. As tree grew to height its stretching equations burst again and again. The Earth held tree firm, the Sun drew tree upwards, and in equational reaction bursting equations sought balance. Out from the skin of forming tree trunk, equations were forced. They firstly swelled in spherical motioning as they heated and excreted. They then burst through their containment to be shaped by wind as they became branches of equational balance. Being of magnetic attraction to tree they remained attached.

The skin of trees was formed as stretching equations imbalanced. As they were pulled upwards away from magnetic attraction downwards, their tightness caused heat, then excretion, which also stretched as it solidified. Through the skin small watery veins became visible as each individual equation was pulled away from its holding.

The cells of trees were all brilliantly coloured as they touched Earth. Soil temporarily absorbed those colours and as tree grew in moist coolness, green dominated brown in equational reaction. The skin of tree, exposed to direct contact with the Sun's rays, shone translucently during daylight. Light in contact with light always transluces no matter what the dominant colour of form.

Light translucence is when a body of coloured equations is ray-touched by the Sun, and the active vibrations of the body seek contact with colour that is their exact light identity. They frenzy. They shimmer. Aggression continues until the colour format is found. Through the Sun's raying there is every individual light cell pattern spinning at speed. A body of light cell evolution automatically seeks contact with its prime format. Because spinning is so fast, contact is made, and because of the spinning, contact is repetitive. Translucence is the repeating contact with a colour format that is held momentarily, then changes in colour, as the Sun projects unfamiliar colour combinations. Underwater the same activity takes place.

Leaves evolved when currents in air caused frequent imbalances and equations within branch formation burst and kept on bursting until stabilising. Leaves were shaped by wind entirely. As equations began solidifying attached to branches, currents in circularising air, curled, edged, tapered, pointed, and rounded every leaf in evolution. Because air was cool and moist, green was the dominant colour. Other shades evolved during eruptions when leaves in formation had their equations singed, burned, or overheated. All growth upon the Earth then was green, with flower evolving from the very same activity as leaf.

Flower first appeared on evolving tree. Its equations were held inside tree's form. The colours of flower were brought forth through the body of tree at the centre of the evolving trunk. Light cell activity began of colour patterning always which became affected by the volume of one colour as tree solidified. The original cell colours did not destroy, only light-equated their surrounding force.

As tree grew tall and of green vibrations, it carried its original colour composition within its solidification. When branches and leaves evolved, colour became visible again, for the greens also heated and changed into reds, oranges, yellows, browns and purples, as equations experienced imbalance of temperature. Always warmth, heat, coolness, and cold affected active vibrations. Each gradual change in temperature either lessened colour intensity or increased its purity.

Flower was ready to form at the tips of branches after equations had balanced trunk, branches and leaves. The release of tree's original colour patterning was an equational reaction to vibrations confined in the process of solidification. Equations had replicated their patterning as tree enlarged. Their numbers had accumulated. Light cell equations were ready to free their confined vibrations. The replication of equations being the evolutionary process of one formation of vibrations recreating its image time and time again as the breathing rays of the Sun inserted charge, began many beautiful flowers in evolution. The longer the Sun's charge hesitated when breathing the more equations replicated. Tree would have exploded had God not cooled the equations. Instead, a flower in beautiful original cell light composition burst forth from areas of heat inside the containing formation of tree. Straight through a branch tip, from a swelling, burst the original colours of light cell activity and glorious flower was born.

Flower held the identical patterning of tree's own light cell evolution. Each individual first cell vibrated a number of coloured equations which often held a dominant colour with other colours included within its composition. The prime colour came from the length of temperature-hold that pure equations experienced as evolution progressed. A yellow flower with faint colours through its petals was the result of equations vibrating between heat lowering in temperature, holding the yellowing of red, and accepting weaker vibrations of other colours at distance to its activity which were also in temperature changes. Colours were often cross-hatched as they vibrated in energised force. All colour changes in evolution came through a cell light composition. Flower's glorious coloured patterns were from the original cell light composition of its evolving form.

Combinations of patterns were side by side during Sun-ray projection. Colours breathed and vibrated in many different patterns. Every flower held light cell combinations and a spherical centre of activity recreated its perfection as heat produced seed and reproduction began.

Bursting coloured equations first created flower. Air, wind and rain shaped its form and its position on a branch also affected its beautiful evolution.

It began as a swelling at a branch tip, a heating of confined colours which excreted hot moisture of layering. Its containment greened in the cool surround, holding its colour patterning in spherical firmness inside. It solidified as it grew. It heated. The swelling burst open revealing its true identity, and activity of coloured light equations brought flower into formation as the elements were equated. A flowering tree completed all equational balancing and seed was the next evolution of growth on land.

# The Soul Light

Cells of light began the soul light, a spherical coloured vibrating composition of pure equations which matured. God's ray-hold protected the soul light as it evolved. It breathed. It ray-extended. It was ray-energised from the Sun. It was born of the Sun's equational purity. It progressed from first light cells.

Flower held a central core of perfect equations, a soul light. Tree had balanced in equations and still held original cell light replicated equations. At every imbalance in tree equations automatically replicated. A build-up of vibrations surrounding the cell light of tree were pulled away from their central core as growth caused equations to stretch. Minute threads of coloured light equations were stretched as far as tree's branches reached. So hot were they, a burst of light force, an imbalance in the rhythm and motioning of equations, opened the containing branches of tree and released replicated equations of the original cell light identity. It was the automatic ejection of heat unto cool surround. God's invisible cool vibrations immediately touched flower's evolving form and equations balanced.

Flower's birth came after the equations of tree had expressed all imbalances. Tree's replicated cell light which was threaded through its forming trunk, automatically spherically activated as equations were released from their heating at branch tip. They were unable to detach from their holding body. God controlled their temperature. They solidified, then from the heating of their own containment, burst to release their aggression. Equations excreted and another swelling began inside flower.

Some flowers released their heated equations with aroma, the discharge of contained equations of colour that had been trapped during temperature changes. Others matured in coldness and burst from shocked equations replicating too fast. Magnetic attraction caused some equations to return to their holding where Earth's central core of light strength was of magnetic interest and too far away to make contact with. The Sun's rays were the only source of energy. Frustrated equations became swellings which also burst magnetically, creating stamens and various other extensions which often sprayed powdered equations outwards. The fine powder evolved from equations being of trapped heat, bursting then drying out inside their containment. Because some stamens were stretched equations they could not obtain moisture within their containment. The length of the stamen prevented moisture from travelling upwards. It dried out before it reached equations awaiting release. Flowers with several short stamens also burst magnetically but had absorbed moisture before balancing.

Too much heat often caused thick moisture to be magnetised to a surface. Its sticky consistency was because extreme heating equations excreted rapidly overlaying their moist vibrations rapidly also, and magnetising each other firmly. A sweetness often occurred where the moisture was trapped inside an aerated opening for a short time, before drying up. Any entrapment of heating vibrations with or without air causes aroma and sweetness. Aroma, pollen and nectar were all progressions of equations seeking balance. Equations always progressed through a series of explosive activity until they were cool enough to settle unto their attachment. Flower's evolution was affected by all environmental changes. Every minute vibration progressed along with Earth's climate.

The formation of seed began at central core of flower where equations of first identity were active and reproduction automatically began. Flower, ray-energised by the Sun, ray-held by God, completed its cycle of life in balanced formation from a light cell composition to tree in flower, and because the Sun held first equation at its core and had detached cells of light from its rays, reproduction was the continuation of light life. Light vibrations once relieved of all temperature imbalances always return to first equational activity. Light is of eternal motioning and cannot cease function.

Flower replicated. Flower reproduced its entire evolution. Flower image-vibrated its total equational formation from first light cell to flower on tree. Flower re-birthed. Replicating equations of form was an automatic reaction of vibrations that had completed their cycle of activity and were of total balance. With no more progression possible they automatically returned to their start.

In form replication the exact identity of their balanced formation was repeated and could be continually repeated where equations were form-reproductive. The return to first motioning always began at the central core of an individual formation wherever its activity had balanced, thus producing seeds in quantity inside a containment that also had to balance. Central core of flower held the coloured equations of the original light cell composition which became the soul light, a more progressed composition with mature equations of form within its contained activity. The older the form, the more progressed the equations.

As the soul light of flower began replication the energised rays of the Sun heated the equations. God responded in contact of cool invisible rays. The replicating equations were automatically magnetised by God and their vibrational activity became invisible. Invisible equations in the replication of form activity is because God's rays are colourless and very cool. As soon as they touch coloured visible equations that are heating in form production they cover those vibrations in colourlessness. God was first visible light. God became an invisible surround vibrating in colourlessness. God's rays are colourless and more powerful than the light rays of First Sun. A form evolving from cell light vibrations automatically loses light as God covers its activity. The vibrations are still active but their visibility is over-powered. An invisible image contained inside God's holding rays was detached automatically inside its containment, as God withdrew the cooling rays of balancing. The invisible image immediately warmed to visibility from contact with the Sun's rays. It then began the identical activation of form of its prime vibrational composition. As it progressed, God answered its equations. Its form solidified and seed evolved.

Flower seeded when its form had totally balanced. Equations automatically returned to first motioning. Later on when Earth's seasons evolved, flower and berry seeded according to temperature changes. Tree stayed upright during seasonal changes with life cycle completion, the end of its capacity to energise, an equational reaction to environmental imbalances. First tree evolutions were of first light cells and reproduction progressed soul light activity unto many different extremes. Later on in life form evolution, replication of a soul light was transferred from one body to another.

Flower could not die vibrationally. Flower vibrated visibly and invisibly. Its image was held by God alone. Even though the Sun's rays had fed flower energy, its image was always overpowered by superior equations. Only God's cool holding rays could contain the evolution of flower. Every minute vibration always would be God held and God-evolved. Ray-energy into flower without God's hold would have exploded all pure equations. The Sun's rays were too fierce to be contained without cooling.

The evolving image of flower solidified as it progressed. As it vibrated inside a containment its equations heated, God responded, its equations heated again and again with God responding continuously until flower had reproduced itself many times in minute equations all of the same identity.

Cessation of image reproduction was when the containment holding seed evolution could no longer accept any more vibrations without explosion and burst open to release its solidified charge. When Earth's environment impured and man destroyed all of Earth's equations of growth, every evolution lost light purification and all reproduction imbalanced.

The many branches of tree produced many flowers, for light always replicates where equations experience blockage, shock, life cycle completion and the return to first motioning. Each branch drew stretched light cell replicated equations through its centre. The singular cell composition that first began tree had experienced several imbalances as tree was drawn upwards. Branches contained light cell colours within, because their surround of cool moisture packed a thick skin around the colourful equations. As a branch heated and burst in leaf to balance tree, its packing held colour firmly. Its equations of release greened as soon as they cooled equationally. Flower's formation began green.

The tension of stretched cell light equations separated their unity and every time a branch evolved light cell replication grew with it. Had that not happened first light cell would have exploded at the base of tree from too much heated tension and pressure upon it.

The exploding equations would have been magnetised by whatever surface they touched and tree would not have grown equationally.

The number of replications of first cell of light caused its equations to weaken, be drained of their energy and brilliance of colour. Each replication was drawn away leaving a lesser active original light cell composition until the Sun's rays balanced its vibrations. The light cell remained where it had evolved.

As tree grew and its light cell was reproduced in flower and berry, the original composition with rays of light still protruding, fed its evolving images constant vibrational stimulation in magnetic attraction from its base. Flower did not appear on all trees because coolness contained the equations of light cells inside berry, which seeded exactly as flower.

Many trees remained short and of spherical shaping. Their equations balanced before tallness progressed. Many different evolutions took place at the beginning of light cell evolution. All were equationally formed. All bore soul light existence. Every evolution on Earth which became reproductive was God-held by the soul light of pure equations.

Tree reached its life cycle end when its equations became aged, they weakened. A life cycle end is when growth no longer expands or extends outwardly, no longer reproduces, no longer energises and can no longer respond magnetically. Through time the soul light exhausts its pure equations, for many aggressive changes in living create erratic equational balancing and light holding bodies lose strength.

First trees lived long. Their equations were directly fed by the Sun. As Earth's environment impured and trees lost direct contact with Sun-raying, their equations faded in colour and weakened in activity. Their moisture dried and their skins began to shrivel. Without sufficient energy to keep them active some body formations disintegrated.

All seeded trees held soul lights. Later they lost their pure equations and deformed. At life cycle end the soul light separated from the body it had evolved, leaving its image multiplied, and was magnetised away from its form by God's invisible rays.

God's touch caused all equations to behave invisibly. Their vibrations in warmth were visible. In coolness they became colourless. As the soul light lost its visibility it became the soul.

Unto God every soul was drawn. Tree, flower, all Earth's growth were eternalised by soul magnetic attraction. The remaining equations, all visible light vibrations including the aura, were then automatically magnetised by the Sun's rays directly after God had withdrawn the soul.

God ray-drew the soul unto an equational position inside a vibrating universe. Its placement was according to the amount of activity it still held which met an exact equational environment in ray spherical eternity.

God's magnetic pulling of the soul was the attraction of visible light unto invisible light. It happened with every living body until later on in evolution a body lost its light equations and could not attach to God.

The vibrating environment able to accept a soul was where God's rays met with the Sun's rays around a small light body, a suitable star, which, because of its small pure activity, visibly and invisibly, was able to receive the soul without any imbalance to either composition. Both in contact caused vibrational ecstasy, a coming together of pure equations without heat. The soul automatically became visible again exactly as its original composition, from pure rays of light feeding its equations in perfect balance of eternal life of light.

Star magnetic attraction was because the composition of a star was much weaker in vibrations than the spheres, was without aggressive charge, was of very pure equations with first motioning of first equation at central core, and vibrated within a very cool surround. A soul could not travel to any other placement. Many stars would imbalance later on. Many still have pure equations.

Eons later when man evolved, the soul was lifted from Earth's magnetic environment and placed according to its capacity. It was held until in equational reaction to progressing equations it re-entered the Earth's environment by ray-insertion from the Sun.

Only the soul of man, unable to stabilise in universal equational purity, re-incarnated. This was because its composition of pure light aggressed dramatically during its body life. Equations sought aggressive charge of light as their life force and a star was passive in vibrations. Automatically, equations heated inside their environment by being attracted to the Sun's powerful vibrational charging, and sought contact. They could not be magnetised into the Sun's formation because of fierce temperature, and were equationally positioned towards the Earth their original birth place, as soul light evolution continued. Magnetic attraction was that automatic positioning.

Once taken in by a star, the soul, if of aggressed vibrations, became unable to unify with a star's passivity, God automatically magnetised the soul by magnetic pulling and inserted the soul into the Sun's projecting rays unto the Earth to be re-inserted in a life form of compatible light equations.

Not every soul re-incarnated. Some had equations which were passive and pure enough to remain in star sanctity. Others had been aggressed and needed the process of re-incarnation to be eternalised. Pacification was the calming of aggressed equations, still pure, but over-charged and having to be elevated unto star safety, magnetised by God, inserted into the Sun's rays and replaced in Earth's environment. The journey had pacified all equations.

Re-incarnation always subdues a life form because the previous experience has been of vibrational equational existence. No shock, stop-starting, replication or over-aggressed activity can there be a second time. Aggressed vibrations have been experienced and cannot be repeated again. If a re-incarnate soul re-incarnates again, it is because equations have become so passive their positioning must be higher in eternal sanctity and the soul is once again returned to Earth to prepare equations that need more experience in the journey of light unto eternal light sanctity. More than one re-incarnation is absolutely necessary for final magnetic eternalising. Journeying unto eternity in higher star positions is always prepared by God by assessment of unsatisfied equations vibrating imbalance within their environment. Placement of a re-incarnate soul always depends on God's equating assessment, and that can be anywhere in universal containment. The closer to God's outer surround the purer equations emotion. God magnetises a re-incarnate soul of more than one life to ultimate ecstasy of soul in star sanctity close to the surrounding containment of pure invisible light.

The lowering of a soul from a star to Earth was an automatic reaction of soul equations magnetised into a Sun ray after vibrating in imbalance of containment. The ray holding the soul passed its charge straight into Earth's projecting rays and re-incarnation began. To re-enter the Earth's environment was to be placed in an equating formation at the time of conception. God's contact was necessary.

Ray projection of a soul unto Earth's magnetic field was the automatic reaction of aggressed equations originally form productive on Earth, unable to stabilise within a star's composition, and drawn through the Sun's rays magnetically.

Inserting a soul into a body formation was when God magnetised the soul from the Sun's ray, then automatically inserted the soul into an equating formation as orgasmic release of male and female equations unified to create a life form. The soul warmed, became visible as the soul light, and a formation began activity. The soul light always matured in a containment. The containing body was an evolving form.

Rays motion out and in, breathing in rhythm. When they magnetise, breathing continues in motion as they draw a light composition through their raying. Each outward motion draws equations away from their contact. Each inward motion pushes equations into their contact. God's rays motion inwards and outwards in breathing rhythm just as the Sun's. They can also detach a singular soul from their holding when magnetic attraction is equated. Placement of a re-incarnate soul came into its containment on the outward extension of God's breathing rays and was magnetised by the inward motion of the breathing body-rays of a formation of magnetic attraction.

Then, the entire universe was ray covered. From God's total surround, invisible light rays projected unto every light composition. Trillions of rays occupied space in universal evolution. Rays projected alongside each other, crossed over each other, wove a spherical maze of glorious light. The Sun's rays of visibility extended into the universe inter-weaving with all other ray-projecting bodies. As the universe imbalanced that changed. The rays of God became selective.

# Life Form Evolution

The evolution of first cells of light took time, long periods of many changes. Within those periods Earth erupted constantly, experienced frequent changes, rotated from light to darkness, internally re-structured, as well as externally, and began seasonal adaptation.

Then there was no ice, only water placements adjusting to temperatures. Seasonal changes caused the surface growth of Earth to respond equationally. Warmth began stimulation. Heat activated form. Intense heat caused explosive reactions. Coolness contained formations, and cold de-activated equations of imbalance.

An evolving life form experienced every vibrational progression. The soul light experienced much more, for reaching life cycle maturity then life cycle end, a life form died and the soul travelled on.

The process of evolution was a vibratory experience for each soul light. Even before light cells evolved, their equations had been of progressive universal evolution. A soul light had eons of experience, adaptation, and balancing. It had become of light maturity. It had been born of God's image. Its equations were of total purity of existence powerful in great eternal certainty. As the soul light evolved in the body of creature, it held superior equational responses and God became the answering voice of security.

Water evolved light cells similarly to Earth's surfaces, with vibrating equations solidifying into forms which became magnetic to their underwater surfaces and to each other. Minute cells touched rock and clung. Equations frenzied within eruptions and currents, were shaped by water and became of watery consistency. Bursting cells cooled quickly as water pacified their charge, and form developed in smooth confinement with extensions evolving according to various imbalances. The evolution of coloured life forms in water began every creature's existence.

Light cells became of transparent jelly in equational reaction to the colourlessness and surrounding coolness of water. Depth caused jelly to harden into thick solidity. Variations of depth caused cells to vibrate of different pressures and temperatures. Millions of evolving life forms progressed then. Whale was one of the greatest.

Whale's form began from a light cell formation of coloured equations, vibrating through the evolutionary progressions of equations of heat and balancing, to become the most beautiful creature on Earth. The largest soul light ever in existence evolved inside whale's hugeness. Whale began as every other creature at that time, but developed senses and responses superior to all life forms. Whale's size was that superiority.

A light cell was ray-dropped into shallow water where it experienced light charge from the Sun not actually touching its colours. The Sun reflected its equations within one metre of contact, the distance necessary for the Sun's rays to connect with Earth's magnetically. The metre allowed the equations of both the Sun and the Earth to adjust to solidification, temperature contact, aura surround and God's entry. Had the Sun's rays connected onto or into Earth's surface, Earth's skin would have blistered.

The Sun's rays did not enter water, for its cool volume refused their warmth. They reflected their charge into water which accepted the colours magnetically. Earth's rays coming from central core did not penetrate water either but reflected charge also.

Light cells ray-projected in magnetic attraction to the Sun's rays. As the rays of the Sun approached the vicinity of a light cell, ray transmission began automatically. The distance between the Sun's rays and a light cell was an equational adjustment of first the Earth's hardening surface, second the Earth's aura sheath, and third the inner magnetic extensions of all life formations. Equations activate unto each other without touching. Their projecting rays path towards a magnetic body. As soon as that body extends rays of contact outwards, a direct link of activity of vibrations suctions, in breathing motion, visible light charge, with a gap between the rays of each body entirely without any activity at all. The gap is for both bodies of light projection to adjust their ray sizes. The gap remains without energised activity because neither raying bodies can touch each other's rays without explosion. The Sun's rays narrow down when approaching light cells, and light cell rays widen in projection towards the Sun. The projection of coloured equations is so powerful coming from the Sun, the gap is transcended, of no consequence to ray transmission. Energy is passed from the Sun to a light cell, leaving a pure inactive gap without one vibration passing through its channelling. Whether in water or on Earth's surface, exactly the same ray adjustment takes place.

Around each light cell formation no matter how tiny, was aura. Rays narrowed, widened and adjusted according to transmission. They too reflected in water. They also passed through water, their equations being cooler than the Sun's and of fine strands. Light cell raying passes through aura because water allows a cool transmission. The Sun's in-coming reflective ray-charge magnetises light cell raying which stretches because the Sun's rays are gapped. Light cell raying elongates in activity and reaches for pure contact. Because water, the gap, and ray adjustment disturb the flow of vibrations, light cell rays stretch until charge of light is functioning equationally. Life form evolution did not begin until Earth's aura began to weaken. Light cell raying then was of severe vibrational activity balanced by God's surround.

The light cell of the first whale was large. It warmed then heated within its solidifying formation, to be suddenly forcefully displaced from shallow water and cast into the deep. A huge underwater eruption took place. The jellied form was drawn downward as the eruption sucked solid formation unto its depths. The light cell of whale lay on the bottom of the evolving sea as its equations progressed. Smaller cell lights became smaller whale forms all evolving within various temperatures, attracting surfaces, water depths and Earth's eruptions.

First whales never land lived. They couldn't, for Earth was still settling in temperature and balance and whale's real beginning was from first equations dropped from the Sun into water placements. As Earth cooled, set, hardened, and was light fed from the Sun, whale evolved, and the perfect equating rays of God's responses created the greatest creature the seas of Earth held within its waters. Much later evolving whales were thrown out of water onto rock, into shallows, onto land and adapted their forms accordingly. Many were disfigured during their evolution as hard surfaces crushed their formations, forbidding equations to spread-lay their vibrations as they vibrated. Automatically as their forms became too imbalanced, progression was no longer possible and their equations returned to their start, magnetising them back again into the seas. They re-adapted in water and never returned to land. To do so would have resulted in explosion.

From transparent jelly first whale evolved. Water pressure burst equations lengthways first. They elongated because the pressure above them forced the jelly to stretch into a long shape. The motioning of water at the time of whale's first formation of equations, was being pulled by current which caused vibrations to elongate. Water motions in breathing rhythm out and in constantly, its motion elongates automatically because currents in water push and pull at its motion. Its breathing is not spherical, as Earth is under its volume and air is over its volume. It is flattened, is of elongated motion, and all that is inside current activity lengthens.

First whale's equations slowly heated for their surround was heavy and deep. When they burst from central core, because they had previously lengthened in form, they burst upwards, under extreme weight. A slight curve evolved in the thickening jelly which had begun to lose its transparency and glow blue.

Then, the universe in light enhancement held one dominant colour within its totality, blue. Light spread its golden volume spherically outwards until God's coolness blued its field. Gold was warm. God was cool. Contact resulted in a beautiful temperate colour volume, and colourless water reflected the blue in equational reception.

Whale's very first body formation absorbed first bluing of the universe. Other first body formations did not evolve in the depths and remained in shallow water adapting equatingly. Colour is always of temperature.

The evolving form of whale kept on heating as equations imbalanced and God responded as always. Each explosive threat was returned in passive equating responses. Whale was being formed by God's acknowledging replies. The elongated formation enlarged and kept on enlarging, until, in reaction to its size it was opened at both ends simultaneously.

Equations burst, creating two openings seeking balance. All other evolving life forms were opened the same way. Two openings allowed water to enter the solidifying body of evolving whale and remain there until equations heated again.

Deep water then had light currents. Whale's formation was moved very slowly in current activity, lifted and lowered as water breathed and reacted to various eruptions. Whale's evolution was beautiful, peaceful, gently motioned and sublimely touched by the rays of God constantly guiding whale's progression.

Water's saline content evolved as its weight pressed onto Earth's body crushing equations directly under its force. Its own equations heated against the crushing. Both contacts, unable to explode because of coldness, excreted into each other a powerful thick moisture. This was immediately shocked by the water temperature, turned white in equational reaction, then dissolved within its containment. The more Earth sweated into water, the more salt evolved.

The salty seas were once absolutely pure in their placements, holding powerful equations of eons of existence. Whale's evolving form adjusted to water's saline content which began at the same time as whale, causing equations in forming skin to over excrete. They replicated in confined activity, layering whale's skin thickly, even before the eyes evolved. The salty water was eventually equated and blubber had begun.

The openings in whale's form attracted small particles of eruptions separated from formations and afloat in the deep. The openings in other evolutions did the same. The particles built up with time to cause a swelling in the centre of whale's body. When equations burst there, they were confined inside a slight curve and opened up a cavity inside whale. The previous openings were small and tapered. Whale had become a large blubbery elongated shape with an evolving stomach.

Into whale's stomach rushed water which was held there by its weight and caused another imbalance. Equations burst forth, and an even larger cavity evolved. With an enlarging body, water rushing in and out, and particles of eruptions entering also, whale vibrated intensely.

A blockage appeared in whale's form inside one of the first openings. Solidity had entered whale's stomach, and because of the accumulation of particles magnetising each other, could not exit. The other opening did not block, for particles had entered there and were still entering there as the other end was blocking up.

The motion in water moved particles along with its force. Entry and exit were automatic and of current-activity. As particles blocked the exit the motioning of water ceased and whale swelled. The swelling appeared above the blockage, above because whale lay upon a surface mostly and water was above in volume.

Outwards from whale's form burst two holes from equations releasing charge, two identical holes because whale's formation was rounding and both sides of the roundness were pressured equationally. Water pressed down. Earth pushed up. A sideways bursting was the perfect balancing of whale's evolving formation. Two eyes began evolution.

Almost all other evolutions burst open the same way wherever they were. As equations burst, the blocked opening was released. Pressure of contained water thrust the particles outwards as the trapped equations burst through their form. Once again water rushed in and out in motioning.

Four openings had evolved then, and as soon as the eyes set inside their containment, whale swam, motioned forward with current activation.

Eruptions were creating caverns and fissures under the seas where hundreds of life forms were evolving, all different in light cell beginning, all of colour patterns.

In the shallows, crustaceans, molluscs, and all other similar evolutions progressed, with various hard skins and shells from extreme heating of being nearer the Sun's rays than those in deeper waters. As they hardened, they became equationally magnetic to a surface which fed their equations balance.

At the same time as trees and grasses evolved, similar evolutions were taking place in water. The pure waters of Earth were filled with every kind of evolving form. Formations stretched, elongated, rounded, pointed, and smoothed. Not until their equations perfected in balance of their environment did they transluce of their original light cell patterning.

The eyes of whale evolved slowly, for their openings were small at first, and in their containment of water, took time to set. Whale also began eating, experiencing regular entry and exit of solidity. Activity inside whale's stomach increased and decreased with quantity of solidity equationally accepted in function. Then whale had no mouth to open and close. First openings remained open as whale developed.

The eyes first set as colourless jelly similar to light cells, only their watery containment swirled equations around aggressively until they heated. The very same evolutionary process of heat needing cooling, caused layers of equations to thicken against each other. Water held them firmly as they heated again and again seeking balance. They swelled, to protrude outside their containment. As equations touched the outer volume of cold water, they cooled and balanced.

First eyes were two spherical, thick, transparent balls, which automatically reflected light cell colouring. The cell light composition of whale, replicating with each imbalance, and held inside whale's evolving form, was dragged from its unity, and water-threaded through whale's thickening form just as tree's. The eyes, being transparent, reflected whale's colourful interior, and because they were spherical, were of magnetic attraction to all light equations. The threading of colour inside whale was magnetised by the eyes, to be a contained spherical pattern within the eyeball visible from outside whale's body.

All openings in whale and every other evolving creature were of spherical motioning. Each equating release burst outwards. Every irregularity in form was an equational balancing. Many forming evolutions experienced imbalance of heating equations resulting in creatures of every division and pattern. Whales became of varying forms and sizes. Those that land lived during their evolution and others that experienced shallow waters developed accordingly, and in balance with their environmental needs. Spherical motioning in breathing rhythm evolved every life form. Light alone was the creator of all living bodies. Without the evolution of light nothing could live anywhere.

Light, visible and invisible, holds, breathes, energises and eternalises all bodies in evolution. Without the knowledge of light equations man has almost destroyed his soul, his Earth, and his future. Without the existence of God's reality, man has violated every living thing. As this text explains what man has never understood, it is in attachment to man's soul that change should be wanted.

The soul light, the image of light cell evolution, did not appear in whale as seed, for whale evolved in water and reproduction was entirely of God's responses. Through whale's body, before food, sight, and sensitivity, was light-interfacing, which with constant replication, grew in powerful coloured equational activity. Light interfacing was of stretched equations of beautiful colours. Whale's original cell light composition had firstly replicated as whale enlarged and secondly stretched through its growing formation. The growing cell equations flourished in the sea depths. Their vibratory life was undisturbed. Whale remained in calm water with only passing currents and particles of solidity interfering with whale's evolution. No near surface erupted at that time. Earth still heaved, but at great distance.

With eyes came first muscular reaction and whale's head began formation. Eyes glowed reflective colours. Deep in water where Earth's protruding rays were reflecting colour also, magnetic pulling began. Light magnetised light reflectively. A gradual slow strain was felt behind the eyes of whale. Light colouring was being pulled through whale's eyes in magnetic attraction.

Eye strain was the first body feeling and began first muscular spasm. As colour activated magnetically inside whale with eyes vibrating excitedly, equations once again burst, right behind the eyes, and layered the first eye muscles. The bursting equations bulged.

Reflective light vibrations outside whale encouraged the eyes to ray-project their own reflective charge which automatically heated in containment. Eye muscles were simply the excretion of equations solidifying in area, layering in confinement and balancing. The solidity was colourless then. The body of whale was still transparent, tinged blue, with colour vibrating through its thickness. Other forms were also transparent and through time never opaqued for their equations balanced quickly.

Light rays projecting from whale's eyes, were an equational reaction to ray-reflective-charge from both Earth and the Sun. Inside whale a ray-projecting light cell had become of body formation. Its equations stretched. Its vibrating activity was replicated. When the eyes experienced ray reflective magnetic attraction, the eyeballs automatically ray-projected spherically. They projected their light cell patterning in spherical motioning. The colours were contained spherically and therefore projected spherically.

God acknowledged every development of whale's evolution by invisible ray contact. As equations heated God responded with exactly the same cool vibrations. Whale was in singular contact with God's rays for those of the Sun were only reflective, and God's rays penetrated into deep water. They did not reflect in contact with water. Their invisibility and powerful coolness allowed them unrestricted entry into the seas. Straight through water they pierced making contact with rays of light cell activity. When whale's eyes ray-projected, God's rays responded equationally. God's rays always made direct contact with a life form. There was no distance of adjustment necessary, for their coolness and supreme power overpowered every vibration evolving. Where an adjustment gap between two projecting light bodies existed, God's rays also gapped in equating response. They then made direct contact with the soul light of every living formation.

Eye muscles drew whale forward, for the magnetic attraction of reflective light became an energy source and the eyes activated aggressively. The forming muscles aggressed and balanced. They evolved of reflective light activity and were confined behind the eyes right at the centre of vibrating eye equations. They aggressed the eyes to seek forward motion and make contact with the outer charge. Light vibrations from whale's interior became blocked from exit through the eyes as the muscles thickened. Whale was pulled forward automatically in magnetic attraction of equations.

First feeling inside whale was first muscle spasm, the stop-start of vibrational activity when equations experience magnetic attraction, cannot attach and replicate repeatedly. Whale was being magnetised forward. Whale's body needed to move. Magnetic attraction always pulls one formation unto another when both are of likeness. When reflective light charge was sought, the eye muscles tugged the body forward automatically. Its weight caused the spasms. Reflective light charge kept whale moving seeking magnetic contact.

The stomach of whale muscularised next. As whale moved, water activity increased, aggressing thickening equations to heat and seek balance. The lining of whale's stomach was toughened and as it developed, stomach muscles evolved which were set between thick layers of solidifying equations, right where water was weighty and whale needed protective padding. Each muscular reaction in whale was felt. Equations react within their vibratory activity. They strengthen, lengthen, shorten, stretch, jump, elongate, quiver, slow, orgasm and excrete moisture. They are sensitised to absolute purity of charge; therefore they feel.

Many other water evolutions muscularised the same way and developed the same way as whale in equational balance of their surround. Fish was the most similar.

Moving whale encountered other evolving creatures moving also. As their forms passed across whale's eyes their light-glowing bodies caused flashes of energy to be received inside the eyes and muscles. Each flash was registered in content of size and shape. Each registration was transmitted in vibrations all through whale's body. Transmission was simply a form receiving the activity then vibrating its charge to all equations in containment magnetically.

The body of whale lost its transparency as it glided in the deep. So tightly knitted were equations they opaqued, lost thinness and thickened. Whale whitened, with a bluish glow.

Gliding whale enlarged, and particles of solidity passed in and out during forward motion. Some were large and often stuck to whale's white flesh causing swellings, bursting equations, and elongations which evolved as tubing. Automatically the tubes magnetically joined as their equations magnetised each other.

Whale began to narrow at one end and refine in shape at the other. Water was smoothing and shaping whale's form. The skin around the eyeballs also refined as surges of current pulled it sideways.

Whale developed intestinal activity as solidity became blocked and was tubed by enveloping equations reacting to imbalance and surrounding solidified particles. As intestines evolved, lengthened and clogged, fast motion released their packing.

Whale felt the activity many times and sensitive muscles developed sensitive glands, the internal formation of setting equations inside vibrating muscle. A simple progression. A smaller composition. A more contained formation. A more heating evolution. A much more aggressive charge of vibrations. A containment without light contact, for the muscles prevented it. Glands in whale caused blood to evolve.

Whale's mouth began as solidity wedged in the lead opening. Its temporary blocking there caused yet another imbalance and bursting equations tore open a slit in both sides of the opening, releasing the solidity. The mouth was shaped, drawn sideways, then closed by the tension of the slit, and when whale felt internal imbalance of water and solidity not exiting fast enough, automatically opened the mouth. Equations were of open vibrations which replicated their original activity if imbalancing. The evolution of the mouth caused equations to split sideways, then spherically unite after bursting.

Muscle formation in whale had become so tightly bound, reflective light charge barely touched its thickening surfaces. The more whale swam the more muscles tightened. Glands became pink first, then red, with imbalancing equations so gripped inside muscle they could not express their charge. They reddened instead.

The eyes were also progressing. The transparent reflecting balls became smeared. The many passing flashes of light bodies imbalanced reflective light reception and projection. Each flashing form caused a muscle spasm. Whale felt the electrically charging activity everywhere. All equations react in contact, echo, or replication, and every minute charge progresses their behaviour.

A ring of whitening thick jelly appeared inside the eyes caused by equations becoming hot then shocked cold, as whale swam and water constantly rushed over the surface of both eyes. The centre of the eyes remained transparent because the whitening equations balanced before they closed together. A reflective opening remained. Through that pure entry, ray-held by God, whale became sensitive.

The glands overheated continually and so aggressive became their equations they blooded. Their excretion could not cool because of entrapment. Their surround was the enormity of cool flesh inside cold water in volume. Bursting red excretion shot into the whitening flesh of whale and blood channelled its thick red fluid throughout whale's body. As whale enlarged, blood entered tubing. Whale blooded greatly before the heart and brain evolved.

Other creatures blooded similarly. Some remained bloodless and transparent, depending on where their evolutions took place. Several different evolutions of whale progressed where Earth's eruptions imbalanced equations and caverns and fissures held their evolving bodies. Every whale grew of huge soul light superiority.

Whale's sight developed slowly, for reflective light rays were energising and any change needed to be of powerful equations. The continual registration of passing life forms agitated muscles and glands. Their equations adapted, not overheated, but adapted to reflection-agitation. They jumped in motioning, and the break in rhythm caused first spark, an agitation of equations unable to complete their motioning. The coloured equations visible at that time, hit each other as they jumped, and light-sparking took place in water.

Whale's body energy increased. The muscles and glands, blooded and hot, experienced activity of light-agitation from the eyes. The jumping equations water energised. Both muscles and glands echoed the imbalance and replicated the activity behind the eyes. Being of hot temperature with water involving, the jumping equations touching reflecting light automatically sparked. Vibrating light equations confronting red hot equations active in water vibrations, bounce in light explosions of minuteness. Their explosions are spherical. The eyes sparked also, and the tiny vibrations echoed their charge through whale's developing head.

With time, a passing life form became a visible formation received as a vibrating light composition which alerted as well as energised whale. After constant repetition of form-imagery, whale automatically recognised individual life forms through eye activation of equations. Every other formation in front of whale's eyes became recognisable the same way. Other evolutions received sight exactly as whale.

The tail evolved when whale swam upwards then dived down again. From deep water whale was magnetised to the surface in need of close contact with the Sun's light charge. The size of whale determined light equational balancing. Down deep, Earth's rays were the closest energy. Whale needed energy from the Sun. Surfacing, whale experienced huge heated shock, and contact with air in volume caused another opening to evolve. Equations burst upwards towards the Sun's raying. They had touched air and Sunlight and were immediately aggressed. A large opening at the top of the head released their charge. Without any strain anywhere whale breathed in air. Later on yet another opening burst forth as equations needed more air to balance their activity. All breathing holes in whales came from explosive equations seeking balance.

Water already held equations of air within its evolution and whale simply breathed in perfect balance. Breathing was of first equation's motioning. Every vibrating composition breathed. Every ray in contact breathed light charge. Whale's form experienced equational satisfaction as an air hole opened. In and out in rhythm of balance of size and shape equations continued life existence.

Every formation inside whale's body evolved as equations required balancing. Not one formation completed that was not of perfect balance. As equations developed they hardened, took a variety of shapes, glowed of colour, formed whale's interior and functioned whale's entirety. Each individual formation was in magnetic attraction to the Sun's light rays, the Earth's rays, and

God's invisible light rays of eternal life. Whale was the first magnificent life form of evolution, the creature of prime light equations that became loving, caring, of supreme intelligence, able to communicate directly with God, and able to be answered by God. No other creature in the entire evolution of life was so souled.

It must be said here that in ignorance man has committed atrocities against whale of terrible hideousness. Man must realise that soul light existence is sacred and never to be violated.

Whale ecstasised for the first time. Whale released huge stress each time the surface was reached. Whale splashed, turned over and twirled in ecstatic release of equations. As soon as whale heated, downwards unto the depths whale swam.

The tail was simply equations at rear end experiencing excessive activity, muscularising, gland producing, blooding, and with blood in the flesh, bursting, to split a singular stressed formation into two for balance. Speed in water refined whale's glorious tail. Its large spread was the equational balancing of its body. Two extensions evolved where body and tail stressed one another. Up and down swam whale. In and out whale breathed. So frequent was whale's surfacing, a heart and lungs developed.

The heart of every creature evolved as whale's. Blood was being aggressed everywhere. Its heat darkened its bright red colour. It thickened as its equations solidified. It saturated whale's evolving flesh. It clogged in several places. The largest clogging was between the head area and stomach. The head's activity which held sight at that time and was always in lead of motion, caused excessive blooding to be spherically swirled into a ball. Its position was where equations were protected from the activity of huge quantities of moving water.

The heart began as a red sphere inside whale. Blood could not circulate fast enough during equational balancing. The many muscles and glands surrounding first heart kept its evolution hot and continually excreting. The heart sphere originally had no attachment. It vibrated as a separate evolution of blood only. Gradually as equations heated then burst in need of coolness, the heart sphere automatically attached, by lengthening equations of magnetic attraction to whale's interior where blood had evolved. One long solidifying vibrating formation stretched from the heart sphere to the attracting inner lining of whale. It heated, burst again, dragged the heart sphere with it, which imbalanced the perfect spherical shape of first heart evolving. Every extension the heart has now was of equations seeking balance.

Inside the heart other muscles were forming to balance equations. The chambers of the heart evolved when air was encircled in setting equations which expanded their containment equationally. Overheating, the heart became explosive and because of its extreme temperature, began pumping, vibrating heated charge. When equations have created a containment of solidity which overheats, their vibrations throw themselves in the direction of cooling, attempting release. Because they are trapped within their solidity with air and water, they create a perpetual pumping action as their containment is hit and they return to their start. Without water they would explode their containment. Once activated, the equations of the heart are ceaseless unless severely disturbed.

Whale's heart released blood where the pumping forced fleshy equations to release their heating. Release allowed excess blooding, still evolving, to be magnetised in unison of equations and tube-held. Blood trapped in the heart sphere once released, flowed through whatever channel it could find inside whale. Veins and arteries evolved as equations released heated charge. The pumping became audible and whale registered sound echoing. All equations adapted in energised acceptance.

The continuous evolution of such a formation would have resulted in a very large heart and a very heating body, which itself would have eventually exploded. To control an explosive heart, God, in ray-hold, answered its formation coolingly. The coolness pacified equations. God kept the pumping continually at pace by responding in equational balance. Every beat inside the heart was answered by God equationally.

The human heart no longer beats purely. Its extreme imbalanced equations are too aggressive to be answered. It pumps an electrical charge of imbalanced beats. These equations do not beat in perfect tempo and cannot establish purity of patterning.

Whale's heart has impured. It has over-charged from the interference of mankind, hunting whale, killing whale and torturing its beautiful equations. God automatically withdraws invisible ray-responses when whale is over-aggressed and can only return when equations calm. Heart attacks in whale have become frequent.

Inside the heart imbalancing equations created its entire vascular composition, and openings evolved as they burst, were cooled, and became magnetic to every near tube and channel of blood evolution. All blooded equations unified inside their form and the heart automatically began circulating its content.

Outward motioning of breathing spurted blood from trapped equations through openings of release which streamed through whale's form. The return inward action dragged the same blood back to the heart. As whale enlarged, breathing lengthened until its imbalancing equations were fixed in rhythm by God preventing an explosion. Blood was heating from motioning too dragging. The heart never ceased its pumping action. Blood never stopped circulating. The interior of whale warmed and stayed warm. Whale's flesh reddened. The responses of God contained the heart until man pursued whale for killings, and whale's heart became threatened.

The lungs evolved as whale surface-breathed and equations inside the heart area heated, excreted, solidified, and burst into two equational formations which were air-generating. The intake of air was spherically circulated inside whale and lungs controlled its activity equationally. Whale held water and air combined as well as in separate quantities. Whale breathed of air. As blood equations set, they involved with both air and water.

Whale's intestinal activity progressed from particles of exploded solidity to particles of other formations. As Earth heaved, many evolving life forms were destroyed by being in areas of eruptions. Some were force-ejected from water onto land. Others aggressively charged. Whale ate of life form particles and so did all other formations at that time. Water impured.

Whale's liver, and every connection to the liver, evolved when food eaten contained blood which automatically magnetised into a shape. There was nowhere inside whale for food equations to go other than unto their own likeness. The forming liver of foreign blooded equations enlarged, burst, re-formed as two identical shapes and became the holding containment of minute blood equations which did not belong to the body of whale. With time, liver equations layered and excreted of their heat, which became shaped tubing where excretion was discharged. Exactly the same evolutionary progression took place within every formation evolving.

Whale's kidneys were a much later development than the liver, because heated water impurities took time to become solidity, aggress, and burst of equations with tube-like attachments which allowed discharge to release imbalances. The kidneys cooled whale's interior equations. Their function removed excess impurities which always over-heated.

Whale's entire interior was equationally formed. Every life form evolved the same way. Then, creature evolution was without the impurities that deformed the evolution of man. Every progression was of equations balancing their form. The changing interior of whale's form would keep on changing as equations adapted to environmental imbalances.

The countless evolving life forms in the seas were all magnetic to water and could not live on land. Shallow water creatures lived above and under water, vibrating of both Sunlight and reflective light. Their reproduction was slower than whale's because their hardness took time to reach life cycle maturity and the soul light image began evolving inside egg instead of body. At central core as God image-vibrated a body formation of maturity, because of the hardness, equations could not accept solidification without serious imbalance and as the image was evolving, God's rays cooled equations repeatedly before they balanced in water surround. The reaction was a soft surround of balanced equations holding an image inside, a soft seed. Replication created many eggs. On release, the image set and began progressing exactly as first formation.

Whale's entire body kept evolving as Earth settled in eruptions. Whale's interior burst over and over again establishing a huge perfectly balanced form. Whale's soul light also enlarged, for

God's continual invisible responses activated the soul light so powerfully it became a universal magnetic beacon in water, able to lead, rescue, warn, and protect every life form evolving in water.

Whale's language was the language of light, a superior language to man's, a vibrating force of equations which conveyed every experience whale's soul light evolved from. In total link with God's light rays whale became the father of soul light evolution of every life form evolving. Man needs a heavy conscience for what has been happening to whale's soul.

The bones inside whale were last to evolve and did not appear in soul light image for three generations of whale. Their setting took time as equations layered excretions thousands of times, gripping each other and forbidding the entry of blood. Bone formation everywhere was of tension of flesh in areas of extreme pressure, weight, movement, aggressive body charge, water activity, surface and depth contact, heart interaction, and eruptions around a moving body. The sweating flesh interacted with blood to eject its red activity, as layer after layer of salty equations thickened in shape and structure of balancing. The salt inside whale's bones was from water involvement. Ejection of blood was because equations were in constant water activity as they progressed, therefore cooler than most other evolutions in the body of whale. The whiteness of developing bones refused blood automatically as thickness dominated.

Whale's body was large but light in motion. Whale had splashed and leapt into the air without bones, for muscles were all that was needed. As bones developed whale became heavier and less active in the air. Bones imbalanced whale's form and another bursting caused ligamental lining, a balancing of equations adjusting to their contacts.

Ligaments were thinly layered because water touched their equations repeatedly and its presence flattened their formation. They always evolved after bone development. They spread as other areas magnetised their protection. All equations are magnetic everywhere. If an area erupts to balance its heating, as soon as an eruption takes place in another area, the cooled equations are sought by the heated ones and a coming together is automatic.

The enormity of whale's evolving body was reaching life cycle maturity, a stage where soul light imagery was imminent. Whale's form had balanced. Whale automatically began soul light image-motioning as flower had. The image was of whale's totality. It began at central position of whale's form, the original light cell composition. Another formation exactly as whale began evolution.

God's rays created whale's soul light image exactly as flower's, only the body of whale was a life form. Its image was another exact identity. The replicating equations were confined, not free, and could not grow as whale had until their formation was released in water. Whale felt the tiny life form evolving as equations adapted, and when soul light reproduction was completed, a calf was ejected through an opening which automatically burst as pressure was applied.

The first birth was of ecstasy for whale. With stressed equations released in water and a magnetic likeness appearing, whale's mouth opened, to air-form the first voice of a life form.

Male and female did not evolve until first whale was soul light re-created. Without a life cycle which matured a formation, God could not re-create its image.

The voice of whale, first motioning sound of a vibrating shape of equations exiting from their containment, was of ecstatic release. The birth caused equations of air and water to respond to the calf being ejected through an opening. The pressure of the birthing at one end was reproduced at the other. Out through the mouth came an equating shape of vibrations in perfect balancing. Air was dominant. Its passage narrowed as it was motioned from the central position of whale's body, through the head and out of the mouth. As the air travelled it collected water and was cooled and shaped by various contacts. On exit, it sounded. First vocalisation of whale resonated in water automatically. Equations echoed and kept on echoing until they lost charge and were absorbed.

The sound of whale ecstasising travelled far. Its force pathed straight through clean transparent water. As whale vocalised, both air and water split in two separating in equations. Out came the first sound of amalgamated equations and when the volume of sea water was met, they burst from impact. The water equations automatically slid through their pathing with air equations following behind causing a soft whistling, the narrowing of air coming from a containment. The purity of the sound was because water was the lead motion and moistened air's motioning.

The experience of vocalisation caused whale to recreate the sensation automatically. Inside whale's body at central core of vibrations the replication of sound began automatically, for its expressing equations had been in motion from their holding straight through to their outer containment. They had experienced full cycle of vibrations. They had begun at central core, were gushed outwards, heated and cooled, were sped into water of equational activity, then diminished in their own activity to be overpowered by their surround. Their replication was automatic. They simply repeated their activity until whale experienced imbalance and refused their exiting. Whale sang on and on. Equations kept repeating their patterning. As the interior of whale heated, refusal of song was the mouth held shut. Whale's mouth had opened and shut with each surge of vibrations. Automatic reaction to the sustained closure of the mouth was in response to the stomach cavity becoming too hot to express air without burning. Whale quietened, and when the stomach cooled, whale sang again.

As sound echoed through the deep, whale encountered rock formations, other life forms, falling rock, and eventually other whales. Each visual impression caused whale's voice to reverberate. Free flowing vibrations suddenly clicked as their pathing was prevented. They smashed into one another as they travelled, colliding with other formations. The clicking was audible because air was pathing behind a water lead, and when a form crossed that path, equations could not travel. They hit each other in combinations of activity, and kept on clicking until their path was clear.

Whale's vocalisation vibrated the head hugely. The sounds whale made were heard vibrationally. The echo resonated everywhere. Whale began accepting sound-echoing before any openings burst. Whale was able to assess terrain. The constant resonance of sound caused a thinning of tissue on either side of the head where sound was held longest. The head area contained the echoing of sound because the heart's pumping dominated whale's body. It prevented sound from travelling through the interior of whale. Eventually two identical ear slits burst open. Their shape was because whale was moving forward and a circular opening was stretch-formed.

The formation of first ears could not progress, because whale was speeding in water, leaping up and down, and causing the slit ear openings to eventually seal, attempt magnetic joining with each other, and eventually evolve into one singular spherically vibrated formation centralised within whale's body form. Gradually the formation became ragged, from sound vibrations splitting its jelly-like composition. The impact of sounds pushed the formation away from its original position.

Whale's vocalisation created an ear-box which became sonar powered. Hearing was of sensitivity to all vibrations. The evolving ear formation vibrated through whale's body and into the soul light.

The whining, moaning, rasping, clicking, and the long vowels of many different evolutions of whale, were all of equations experiencing restrictions and pleasures. When whale first met another whale, the surprised equations of visual contact exclaimed, they extended in length, then returned to their start. The exclamation was transmitted muscularly through the body which returned the vibrations immediately and out through the mouth their force was ejected in an open vowel sound which continued until of balance.

Vowels narrowed as the mouth began closing. Moans were frequent encounters with terrain. Equations alerted to unusual structures which caused repeated greeting through the mouth opening and closing in balancing. They voice related terrain. Rasping was simply exhaustion of equations losing strength from too much activity. If equations over activate, are too long in motion, they introvert. Their motioning does not complete and magnetises them backwards. This action causes slowness, sleep, and drowsiness. Uncompleted motioning doubles in charge, which, because it is not of singular motioning, weights a formation with heaviness keeping it subdued or asleep until a more powerful magnetic interest arouses it. Eventually the doubled equations become singular in motioning again after resting their activity and being stimulated by the Sun's charge.

Whale's vocabulary expanded as male and female evolved. With time whale communicated with every other life form in the seas. No other creature was the keeper of eons of evolutionary progressions and when whale was spoken to by God, in equating response to whale's own vocabulary, whale transformed.

Above water where light cell evolution was progressing everywhere, millions of creatures came into life cycle of maturity. Water had begun their first formations. Some were thrown onto land after being partly evolved at various depths of the seas. From their progressions man evolved. Others lay in very moist soil and progressed there. Others evolved in the shallows, half in and half out of moving water. Some were thrown already shaped and solidified straight onto evolving growth. Others straight onto tree, leaf, flower and all other growing formations. Evolving life forms were scattered all over the Earth as it heaved in equational balancing. Life cycle maturity caused reproduction. Every creature held soul light equations. Every creature was image-recreated by God.

Earth's temperature had cooled during the evolution of whale. Earth would always be heating at central core, for its solidification would press upon its equations and periodically they would erupt seeking balance. Areas of Earth would remain hot and steamy as channels of heated water found release. Earth would spurt out its heat when imbalancing. Earth would crack in places of too much tension. Earth would break open its solidity as equations burst inside their containment from unnatural imbalances. Earth would grind, attempting unity of starving equations. Earth would eject its poisoning as equations choked from impurities too overpowering. Earth would wrench as its body was entered explosively. Earth would emotion, feel the agony of its suffering equations. Earth would moan, gasp, and tremor, all of equational emotion. Earth was a living entity of light life. God was Earth's light father.

The planets were all cooling at the time of light cell evolution. The rays of the Sun dropped light cells onto every solidified surface that had surface equational reception. Where a planet was either too hot or too cold, ray-dropping was not possible. The temperature rejected the light cell by forcing equations back up the rays in shock reaction. They doubled on their return and were magnetised straight back into the central activity of the Sun without imbalance.

When a cell was ray-dropped, the surface it touched had to be equated first. The metre of adjustment of ray contact between a sphere and the Sun was composed of equations of temperature, aura, thickness of solidity vibrating outwards, and moisture and air in contact with solidity. It was the perfect thermometer. The Sun's rays hesitated in activity until they had equated their surface, then, if the surface was acceptable, dropped the equations building up at the tips onto the body of compatible equations. If the surface was unacceptable, the equations were returned to the Sun's central activity.

Every planet except Earth lost light cell evolution. Their bodies imbalanced so violently every evolving light formation destroyed. Equations were overpowered. Some cells had reached stages of life forms, others of growth. Fluctuating temperatures crippled their life cycles and they could not progress. Only Earth received and held light cell evolution.

The waters of Earth progressed whale further. A tongue evolved from vocalisation, not eating. The throat cavity was wide and short, constantly aggressing as whale sang, and soon developed a blockage within its centre. Both sides of the blockage were open as water rushed in and out confining the setting equations in an elongated shape. Whale kept singing as the tongue evolved. Its formation affected the sound of the voice. As the tongue enlarged, muscularised, produced glands and blooded, it became of dominance inside the mouth. Until whale ate of large formations, the tongue evolved solely by vocal expression.

Whale's singing caused every bone formation inside whale's head where echo created heat and imbalance. Whale's pure voice equations vibrated powerfully where ear slits had been evolving and within the head as well as surrounding its formation. The outer charge magnetised the inner charge of vibrations and the tissue on either side of whale's head had thinned, eventually bursting from too much pressure either side of the ears in evolution. The bursting caused water to enter the head. As whale evolved in size and activity, the water which entered and exited the ear openings until they closed, became resonance of watery light vibrations, a magnetically charged opening which enabled whale to experience sonar activity. Every watered vibration of sound could be heard. Because whale's first ears were slits, the incoming vibrations were refined, of magnification. The singular ear-box had evolved from the ear-slits of magnetic attraction and been pushed inside the head unto a safe area in the throat formation because sound vibrations needed echo sensitivity. Sound equations always unify. If they cannot, they explode. The throat was the perfect surround for their safety.

Sonar reception would never have been possible had whale's original ear slits remained and progressed. Sonar ability can only activate if a powerful contained equating formation has evolved gradually and purely, has experience of being outside its formation and within a water surround, has then been locked inside its father formation, cannot escape vibrationally, and must squeeze its vibrations through its form, to find a magnetic contact outside its form. Once finding contact, vibrations return to their start. All of whale's sonar abilities behave that way, stretching confined vibrations seeking exit for magnetic contact, and being equated.

Sonar activity in whale was the magnetic attraction to a charge of equations projecting from a source and being received equatingly. Now whale has almost lost sonar contact with his own kind because of man's violation unto his territory. All whales now have very little hearing capacity. They stress constantly.

Whale's teeth evolved when life forms had to be gripped, shaped for digestion, then swallowed. Food was slippery and needed to be held firmly.

Male and female began after first birth. When first calf matured, it became female. First whale became male. A penis evolved where whale had given birth. The excreting equations of the force of the birth, attached to the opening, layering their numbers as they replicated. Because whale was swimming their motion was elongated. Pressure of the weight of the foetus and intestinal collection had sagged the flesh and the opening spherically motioned straight after the birth. A build-up of equations layered a penis. Its length was an equational assessment of whale's size.

The foetus inside whale had experienced every vibration of whale's form, all imbalances and every balancing. When it developed into calf and was force-ejected through the opening in whale's body it was the exact image of its father. Equations replicate their vibrations from one formation to another automatically whatever the size. One containment leads the sequence, the other responds identically. The calf would mature without a penis and automatically first whale inserted its penis in the opening of its mature calf before penis formation could activate. Magnetic attraction caused the first copulation of whales.

The calf matured and before it was old enough to develop a penis, was entered by first male. Copulation began. With a penis vibrating in activity of equations the male embraced its mature calf also vibrating in the same place, and automatically, in magnetic attraction of equations seeking contact, the penis was inserted in the opening. First female evolved.

There were no muscles connecting the penis at that time. Copulation was soft entry and soft acceptance. Enclosed inside the female's warmth, the penis excreted of its heating equations, was withdrawn, and orgasmic release of male and female was experienced.

Mating had begun with vocalisation. Both whales sang to each other. They mimicked each other's call as first one and then the other's interest was attracted. The male's equations were first to erect in magnetic interest, for the penis began throbbing with imbalance as soon as the female came near. This was because at small distance from each other their entire bodies automatically became magnetic. The closer they were magnetised, the more both openings throbbed. First birth had caused first orgasm and the area of the orgasm alerted to the body of another whale automatically. The female throbbed because her body vibrated in unison with the male's. In natural equational behaviour both whales made contact with each other. Their embrace was of equations magnetising their forms and each whale behaving accordingly.

First mating caused the equations of the soul light of both whales to emotion. They first heated, were released from their heating not by bursting, but by the insertion of the penis into the female. Both were comforted. The semen was of bursting equations, not the soul light excreting. The soul light heated as the body of whale throbbed, but calmed as the penis became enclosed in the warmth of the female's body. Both whales emotioned. The experience would progress. A loving would develop. Equations of emotion were and still are a combination of vibrations of colour which react to obstacles, encounters, experiences, visual shock, and release of charge. They lengthen in motioning, shorten, elasticise, throb, jump, excrete, and fluctuate in activity. Emotion is of equations in reactive process. When the soul light entered the central core of the heart, emotions became severe.

Copulation caused pure semen which did not come through the penis at that time. A thick transparent fluid excreted from the heated equations of the formation of the evolving penis and was automatically released inside the female.

Female whale received the semen which collected inside her opening to vibrate into a tiny transparent sphere. She also excreted and the combination of the excretion of both whales created an egg. There was no whale image inside the egg at that time. Only one egg was possible then, for the excreting penis had not been aggressed and the semen was of small excretion. There was no opening in the centre of the penis and no ejaculation was possible.

The two whales frolicked before and after mating as their equations emotioned. The egg inside female became smeared in its enclosure. Its central core began heating. It burst during its setting and spread thickness of mucoused equations inside the female's body. She became impure. When she next mated, the same bursting of a second egg would increase the impurity of excretion inside her. A build-up of thick mucous evolved which sealed itself and became the lining of the womb.

After mating the two whales ceased throbbing. Their equations had balanced and when they separated it was some time before they mated again. Equations always return to their first motioning when they have completed a specific cycle of activity. Copulation had been a completed combination of equational activity which began in the penis and ended with the release of semen inside the female. Once complete in balancing the equations of both whales would seek the same experience again automatically.

When first motioning began again in the penis area, the penis was stimulated. Female was also stimulated. The motioning equations repeated their vibrations and both whales sought each other to mate again. The male began Calling the female. The female answered immediately. The sonorous Calling could be heard from great distance as water was just beginning to impure and the pathing of voice equations was completely clean and resonant. Whale's sonar abilities developed much later.

The brain of whale was last to evolve. Whale had become over aggressed in the head area. The eyes had experienced massive flashing of forms, huge vocal echoing, excessive movement, and a thick mucous began setting at the back of the eyes. Excreting equations were trapped inside bone and could not be released. They inter-locked. Each time the head overheated and excreted, equations massed in thickness and set.

The first brain was white with a bluish glow. Water in surround had shocked the setting equations to unify in whiteness. Because of the position of the brain, it became the recipient of every registration of the eyes. Its equations then were pure. When they impured the brain became destructive. Then it had no artificial electrical or radioactive activity. It vibrated of equations of its containment.

Earth became covered with growth. Seeds had reproduced their first formations and a most beautiful coloured surface vibrated. The climate then was balanced, non-aggressive, without impure equations in mass, and purified by the rays of the Sun. Trees of all shapes and sizes evolved. Flowers of all colours and patterns covered the trees until flower evolved in soil alone.

The seeds of tree-flower entered the swellings of bulbing and the activity of forming grasses and were magnetised. Seeds fell on every evolution of growth, clung magnetically and adapted equationally.

Growth protected the skin of Earth. Its colour was Earth's cooling covering. Its vibrations kept Earth moist. Its equations were of supreme balance for Earth's body. The Sun's energising breathing rays fed Earth's growth at every stage of its evolution.

Life forms upon land began as eruptions threw up light cell formations from water. Some had already become formed. Others were reproductive. Many were still in light cell jelly settings. Many were of shallow water and land life. Their evolutions would continue under the raying of the Sun on the Earth's surface.

Around the Earth its aura-shield was heating. Electrically charged vibrations were unifying with radioactivity and disturbing the aura of pure equations, not yet eaten through. In response God's cooling rays of invisibility caused the aura to become of coloured banding.

Earth's aura then was of layered coloured equations. With time, each minute singular colour magnetised its likeness. Bands of colour appeared. As the bands heated and God responded, they separated into individual widths of singular colours. God's rays had touched hot colours, shocked their vibrations which shrunk into ring formation. Equations automatically sought their likenesses and finding each other clung together in bands of encircling vibrations. Their formation was weaker than aura webbing and radioactivity gradually seeped through to Earth.

Other planets banded. The surrounding coloured rings opened widely around some planets, partially dissolved in gaseous equations around others, and tilted as the Sun's rays passed through the openings causing the bands to flatten, stretch lengthways instead of display upright. The Sun's rays were of straight pathing and powerful in energy. The bands encircled a sphere. When the Sun's rays touched their activity, they automatically tilted until they were of the same slant as the Sun's raying. This equational reaction was to magnetise equations in direct linear activity and not in impact reaction. The tilting was smooth, quick to progress and without any imbalance.

Earth and only Earth evolved with perfect equating ice caps. Its rotation caused equations without balance of warmth to grow, layer, smother each other, not excrete because they did not heat, and white-freeze. The Sun's rays could not penetrate the entirety of Earth's body. Coolness became coldness. Coldness became ice-packing. The evolution of ice on the Earth imbalanced many life forms and much growth and caused climatic imbalancing.

The rain cycle of Earth then was of perfect balance. When an area overheated and was cooled by God's response, it rained automatically. The heat touched coolness condensing and light rain fell to Earth. As Earth's temperature rose and kept rising, rain imbalanced and became weighty, thick in equations, and torrential.

The Sun's rays passed through the thinness of rain as it fell. Water was separated from its body in perfect equating rhythm. It was divided by equations of light passing through thin layering, Sun-raying could not reflect charge off the rain because speed prevented reflection. Rays passed straight through rain and because of their power in energised force, split rain water into perfect portions. Had the Sun's rays not passed through rain, it would not have fallen rhythmically and would have been a whole formation.

The cool vibrations of God responded to rain equations in vibrating sameness and each rain drop was surrounded, not ray-inserted. The gaps between rain drops are the equating hold of God's vibrational surround. Without that hold rain would fall in huge swamping quantities. God always surrounds every equational composition.

When rain fell upon the seas, its purity was over powered by salty equations. Many life forms were washed by the purity of rain water and glistened. Many eventually drank of its cooling.

Whale reached life cycle end. Whale's form had perfected. Equations once perfect in balance always return to their start. Whale's equations had tired, vibrated for long periods, created soul light imagery, given birth, travelled long distances and experienced every emotion possible. Whale aged. Whale's soul light weakened. Female whale was still maturing. The very last mating of male with female resulted in a soul light image being transferred from one whale to the other.

First copulation had released semen without soul light image in its composition. The first image of whale had developed inside the male's body. The evolving penis prevented another birth cycle taking place.

The male alerted the female as equations began throbbing again. His penis activated first, for equations had experienced first orgasm there. Whale had inserted his penis inside female and accepted her opening as release of heat. When the penis heated and throbbed for the last time a soul light image would be inserted into the body of female whale.

The penis had to be opened for soul light transmission. Because whale was depleting in energy, his central core of light activity, the soul light, was dominant. Around the penis, which was of soft watery flesh, and pure equations in layering, was aura, a layer of coloured vibrations emanating from the penis itself which had formed outside the body during its evolution. Aura surrounded every life form always. As whale's equations throbbed the aura also throbbed. Whale's penis became the strongest rhythm in equational activity of the entire body more active than the heart. The soul light however was still more powerful.

The female's equations aggressed in magnetic attraction and throbbed in unison with the male. So powerful were the two bodies they became explosive if joined in heat.

Whale's soul light became magnetic to the very active penis because the throbbing held powerful vibrations which needed controlling. The soul light of every evolving form alerted to any powerful force of vibrations needing temperature control. God was the controller. The soul light was ray-held by God.

Whale was dying. All equations in whale's form were automatically preparing to leave their containment. Magnetic attraction caused equations to stretch in need of contact with each other. Copulation was ready to begin. The penis stiffened for the first time; its equations were being pulled towards the central core of soul light vibrations. They heated fiercely. Contact with the female was their release. Had contact been made, equations would have exploded, destroying the perfection of both soul lights and the evolution of the penis. Their equations were too hot to touch. God immediately responded in cooling rays and equations pacified. The penis softened. Copulation began. The penis began to overheat and stiffen again. The soul light was pulling at its equations. An explosion was imminent. God's responding rays equated the heating, equated the stretching, and a soul light image was magnetised by God to be invisibly transferred from male to female.

The heat of the activity had caused excess excretion which also heated. The penis, because of its water surround, contained the excretion of all the equations of its form into a heating central core of vibrations which needed to cool. Held inside the shape of whale's penis and over-heating in temperature, inflamed equations burst, and straight through the centre of the penis, a small elongated opening evolved. Through this opening whale's image entered the female. The image was carried by the bursting equations as they exited, had already been magnetised away from its formation and pathed through the opening of the penis cooled by God. It was let go of, by God's equating rays, to become the first soul light transfer of the first life form in evolution. The force of bursting moisture placed its invisible equations where they would warm, illuminate and begin solidification. The image was of pure vibrating invisible equations which had mapped out the entire evolution of first whale in a minute composition of light activity, had completed life cycle of maturity and was at life cycle end. Its accuracy was absolute.

The weakened soul light inside dying whale still vibrated charge. Whale surfaced in magnetic attraction to the Sun's rays. Whale's aura held visible light activity. The Sun magnetised its content as God ray-attached to the soul light which immediately faded from the coolness. The full content of invisible equations was magnetised away from their form. The containment of the soul light, the form of whale, had no more magnetic charge to retain its equations. As soon as the soul light became invisible, it became the soul. God's rays were the prime magnetic force in contact. Once the soul light faded, the Sun's rays were no longer of magnetic interest, leaving God to transport the soul. Another image of the soul light could not be activated for its containment had ceased in light activity. Soul light invisible equations needed only a warm containment to activate into a visible formation for solidification of equations to be absolute. The womb of the female was the perfect containment.

The death of whale was when both visible and invisible equations left the body. The heart ceased pumping when there was no charge to activate it. Whale lay dead on the surface of water until, in equational reaction to weight without motioning, whale sank to the bottom.

Whale's huge body dissolved, separated in equations which involved with their surround. The water content purified inside water. The salt content reacted the same. The red blood was overpowered by salty water to also purify, equate in colourless surround, and the other parts of whale's body broke down into equations of magnetic attraction.

With whale's image inside the female and his semen vibrating, the female's excretion automatically began magnetic attraction. The unification of their equations resulted in the formation of an egg which vibrated in spherical motioning, and held the image of male whale inside the thick transparent jelly. The equations warmed and automatically became visible as they progressed their formation into a coloured life form, a foetus.

The foetus held a dominance of male equations. A male calf would be born. When the same female gave birth again it would be to a female calf, for her equations would be dominant. When two life forms orgasm and two sets of hot equations unify, they cool by God's responding rays and form a balanced containment which holds the image inside as it evolves. If the formation develops as male, the next reproduction is automatically female. Both whales have vibrated in unison together during copulation, one with a penis, the other with an opening and both formations must be equated reproductively. When man evolved and aggressive behaviour destroyed equations of balance, male and female imagery imbalanced also. The orgasm became overcharged. Semen became overheated. The replication of equations became of irregular formation. The female's equations overreacted. Many eggs sought sperm contact. Sperm became unable to equate the magnetic needs of egg replication. The whole process of birth destroyed. Further on as man's entire form radioactivated, more than one egg became a foetus. God's rays did not magnetise an image and did not protect the soul light. The quantity of radioactivity within the body of man was too great to allow purity of light to enter. Radioactive vibrations of man's own manufacture were unable to be equated. The soul light without

God's ray-hold established presence inside a foetus and because of its origins grew inside a containment of radioactive surround. The passage of the soul light through the semen unto egg fertilisation was itself radioactively charged. At ejaculation God did not cool its temperature, did not attract its equations and did not surround its vibrations. God could not, for the vibrations emanating from the soul light were without purity of charge. The soul light of man now is in threat of explosion.

Later on, during copulation with another male whale, the female throbbed and heated as before. The male responded. Procreation of the species had begun after first whale died leaving a female used to orgasmic release of vibrations. Other whales were then evolving. First female automatically sought contact with a male whale when orgasm was needed to cool her equations. The selected male was courted, sung to, nudged, caressed, frolicked with and kissed, in deliberate vibrational stimulation to copulate with magnetically. The male responded. The female was the lead activity. At orgasm no male image was transferred. His equations did not overheat. God did not ray-touch the soul light. It did not replicate. Instead, the female's soul light replicated. Her equations began stretch-motioning exactly as first whale's had. God responded. The female's soul light image became invisible in coolness, remaining where it had replicated as God let go of its equations to progress. Reproduction of a life form began again with a female foetus evolving.

As procreation progressed, sperm evolved. Then, semen in all evolving mammals was pure. Sperm is a collection of aggressed equations separated from their attached formation. Sperm did not fertilise until three generations of whale. The semen of pure excretion had to aggress from regular copulation for equations to replicate and fertilise.

By the third generation of whale equations of copulation had aggressed semen to automatically progress unto sperm. Aggressively charging equations carried through the penis's opening and into the female's form caused erection, the hardening of vibrations in full erect charge prior to orgasmic release. Subsequent erections automatically activating before copulation caused whale's pure semen to coagulate, thicken from contained heating equations in aggressive charge. They replicated. They exited through the penis shaped with a head and tail. Exiting their containment created the head as release motioned their breathing equations spherically and travelling through a length of tissue created the tail which tapered as each replication left its form. An erection also caused the soul light equations of the male to stretch and draw away from their central core. They replicated, heated and were immediately cooled by God's rays. Soul light images detached from their aggressed formation and were ejaculated through the penis of the male. Ejaculation was the accumulation of replicating equations building up inside their containment and bursting through the penis opening for release of aggressive charge. The replication of whale's soul light automatically pathed inside sperm and into the female's form.

Only one image could become a foetus even though many had replicated. The image which became a foetus was the first replication for it was the lead image. The image automatically began progression as soon as its equations warmed. Any other image could not establish. The first image was in process of foetal formation and the progressing equations were too dominant. All other images weakened in activity vibrating into thick mucous which surrounded first image magnetically.

Foetal growth activity had created a womb. Sperm was automatically magnetic to egg formations because of their motioning vibrations. Semen had previously merged with egg activity. Sperm could not, its vibrations were too aggressive. Sperm encircled egg formation. Sperm irritated egg equations until they excreted, heated, burst, and automatically unified with sperm equations. Two images merged, both of two separate identities. One with penis, the other with opening.

Two merged images would become one foetus. Two soul lights replicated became one. The equations of both whales also merged and progressed inside the evolving foetus to produce a calf of equational balance.

Without the bonding of male and female equations a foetus could not survive. Equations of two identities in image reproduction must unify to foetus form. There must be an equating containment. There also must be the cooling responses of God. If the containment is imbalanced, equations deform and so does the form in production.

The images of soul light procreation are God held, and breathe of pure light equations. Every life form has evolved by God's equating responses. It is with the knowledge of pure equations that man's destructive influence over the soul light must end.

Female whale had impured after her first matings from the bursting of equations of earlier jellied egg formation. Female held mucous inside her womb. Its thickening equations had swelled, for the enlarging egg had blocked their magnetic activity. They heated. They over-layered. They excreted. They eventually blooded. The formation automatically attached to the egg, for it held the mapping vibrations of first whale's evolution which had been hugely blooded. As the foetus grew so did its attachment. When the calf was ejected from the womb, an after-birth followed magnetically. Water purified the content of impure solidity and when the female's image was replicated for reproduction it evolved with the same attachment.

Many variations of whale evolved at that time. Some were lengthy, others more round. Many were of deformed formation where they had been wedged between rock or partly gripped between cracks of rock. Some shapes swelled where an obstruction interfered with bursting equations. A particularly long jaw was because as the form grew in length, a rock crevice held the head whilst the rest of the body evolved in water. Some had more bones than others, adapted heads, mouths and teeth, a variety of body extensions, and others required a dorsal fin for balance. Some evolved in warm waters while others enlarged in colder temperatures. All evolutions then were of heated equations bursting inside their containments, controlled by God's cooling rays to become balanced. Not one formation over the entire Earth evolved without equational balancing. Not one ever could.

The soul light of whale had progressed from a visible light cell composition setting inside a containment, solidifying into a form, growing, reaching maturity, ageing, then when at life cycle end, being magnetised by God's invisible rays unto eternal life of light, leaving its image to procreate.

All creatures evolved with soul light. Eternal life of light was the sanctuary of their souls. All growth evolved of soul light identity. The larger the creature, the larger the soul. The larger a growth form, the larger its soul identity.

Whale's soul light, over time, communicated with God. God responded. As whale swam through the oceans of Earth, developed sight and emotional vocalisation, every encounter and emotion was registered by God's rays surrounding whale's soul light. There was no other equating force. God eventually vocalised to whale vibrationally.

Mankind has hunted and killed the seas greatest creature for so long, permanent damage has been done to the evolutionary process of all whales. The terror of these creatures causes God's responses to often be withdrawn for their soul lights convulse too violently to be held.

The beauty of these creatures is undeniable. Their gentle souls show mankind how feeling they are, how needing to be allowed to live peacefully in their environment. Shooting them, exploding their bodies, hacking at them in front of their own kind causes a violent shock to their beautiful souls, one which cannot be accepted and cannot be forgotten. Their equations convulse in their activity. God withdraws, for such equations are too explosive to be responded to. Their evolution becomes deformed, unable to balance. Every perfect equation in their bodies loses purity of motion, purity of patterning and purity of colour. They suffer uncontainable pain as mankind seeks to profit from their greatness. Their trust in their murderers is the quality of their pure soul lights, unable to hate, unable to kill, unable to condemn those who without conscience, without compassion, without soul reality, condemn their right to exist in the environment they were born to and keeps them unto God.

Whale still communicates with God. Whale's suffering now is extreme. Whale's evolution has stopped for God can no longer purify whale's heating. Sea water has contaminated to such a degree whale cannot see, hear, or guide other stressed creatures of the seas. Sound echoing has ended. Terrain is poisoning. Nuclear experiments have violated motioning equations horribly. Whale is experiencing respiratory difficulty constantly. Whale's eyes burn from chemicals discharged into the seas. Whale loses direction often because sonar location is not possible any longer. Whale is terrorised when pursued by man with weapons to kill. Whale's soul light convulses when its own kind are murdered. Whale is slowly diseasing. Whale is slowly dying. The extinction of whale is imminent. Man is the cause.

Should whale's greatness be destroyed forever, man will automatically pay the price. Without whale mankind will cease evolving. The first great soul light on Earth once extinguished will never give life to creatures of the seas again, will never activate their soul light equations, will never safe-guard their existence and will never ray-extend for their safety and security. Is that what mankind wants to be responsible for?

# The Heart

The transferred image of first whale automatically centralised within its containment. Its soul light equations solidified to become the foetus. The central core of the foetus was the heart. The egg was spherical. The heart was also a tiny sphere. Later on it changed shape. Its beating inside the egg caused adult whale's heart to respond. Whale sensitised to the heart of the forming foetus and became aware of another life inside its body. Soul light colour patterning circulated through the enlarging form. Patterns of soul light activity in all evolutions of light equations were from first equation. The colours of life forms as well as growing formations was the vibratory change of temperature within the cross-hatched raying of the Sun. Colour identified all evolutions of light equations. Colour was also their individuality, energy content, capacity to pro-create with other likenesses and emotional responses.

A calf was born to female whale, its heart pumping blood. As the calf developed into an adult whale the equations of the soul light grew, enlarged in vibrational content. The heart overheated the soul light. Its equations were aggressing from whale swimming great distances, much acknowledgement of other creatures, fleeing from Earth's eruptions, courting and mating. So explosive became its equations, God's equating response was to ray-hold its composition, not magnetise it but project around its equations a solid vibrating coolness. The temperature of the heart lowered. Its activity continued. The soul light calmed. Around its composition an equating spherical sheath of cool vibrations contained its equations for a time.

The internal adjustment of the heart to God's control was a thickening layer of shocked equations which hardened, allowing the heart to remain in balance of its activity, and its central core, the soul light, to vibrate in perfect rhythm. A hard heart lining automatically evolved in perfect balance for soul light activity.

Inside every life form at the centre of every heart, soul light existence progresses the form it evolves with. Its presence holds first motion of first equation. It became man's conscience.

Whale's evolution began the heart's interaction with the soul light as whale developed emotions of ecstasy, happiness, feelings of tenderness towards whale's offspring, protective feelings for every creature in stress and very slowly, feelings of deep love for whale's own species. The heart behaved emotionally also. The soul light of emotioning equations caused the heart's activity to increase and decrease. Its pumping quickened when whale became concerned with creature behaviour. Its blood overheated if that concern was prolonged. Its pumping slowed when whale ecstasised and the soul light vibrated low charge. It reacted to every feeling of whale as the soul light continually emotioned. Because the soul light was contained inside its formation the heart became emotionally charged. God's surrounding hold of the soul light also affected the heart's activity. The soul light when emotioning was automatically responded to equationally by God and the heart's temperature was raised and lowered accordingly.

With time the heart became extremely sensitive, for inside its formation pure soul light vibrated and God began to communicate. So pure was the evolution of the heart at that time God was able to vibrate a language of light, an invisible vibrational formation of sounds and feelings, all responses of a body's own language.

Light language is silent. Its invisible vibrations form sound, feelings, voice, and exact communicative responses. A sound is of vibrational shape. A feeling is of emotioning equations. A voice is of exiting equations encountering other vibrational activity. Communication responses are various shaped vibrations reacting to various incidents. Nothing can be heard, felt, voiced or responded to unless equations are active.

Every life form provides an active vibrating containment which has a soul light surrounded by God. Sound, feelings, voice and communicative responses are of pure equations all accepted and equated by God's invisible responses. When whale emotioned, God emotioned back to whale in exactly the same formation of vibrations. When whale sang, God returned the same song vibrationally. The returning vibrations were heard and felt by whale, their silent invisible activity was whale's own language. God communicated light language, an equating response of a body's own developed language. God's rays are of light vibrating invisibility because they extend from the pure holding containment of colourless, spherical, breathing light vibrations of absolute power and control of every living formation. At any time, God can, and has, communicated to an individual form and resolved equations needing pacification. This communication is done through the soul light and nowhere else can this take place, for only the soul light has evolved with all progressions of the whole of evolution within its equations. Each response of God to sound, feeling, voice or other communicative activity is vibrated into the rays of the soul light of a life form and that life form understands the language of light it is receiving.

Later on when man evolved, God spoke in man's language to many individuals. As man's soul light deteriorated, communication with God became impossible.

As whale encountered creatures in distress and emotioned concern, God responded the same vibrational concern and vibrated back resolution of stressed equations. Equations of emotion always need resolution. If they are left unresolved they cause heart stress, pressure inside the heart from soul light equations vibrating extreme activity of tempo and temperature, with extending rays of red colour. The irregular motioning of those equations can cause blood spurts from the heart, imbalanced blood flow, muscular spasms, and irregular heart beating.

The vascular composition of the heart controls not only blood but the vibrating aura of the soul light which either overheats, reddens, and discharges fluid if imbalancing, or its equations intern if medication is used to activate its rhythm. The muscles surrounding the soul light when overheating from too much energised activity, too much alcohol intaken and too many stimulating drugs, discharge mucous of energy in extreme dosage and the imbalance sticks to the heart linings, impairs blood flow continually and absolutely causes serious heart diseases. Energised blood cells multiply, are contained inside a pumping mass of aorta distribution, cannot flow through arteries, cannot purify and cannot cool. Heart attacks are all caused by excessive over-charging energy cells and soul light imbalancing equations discharging.

Mankind is over-aggressed. Mankind deliberately over-energises. Mankind in ignorance causes the heart to force-pound unnaturally, de-activate equationally, imbalance totally in perfect equating rhythms and when medicating for more energy, creates soul light destruction. Muscular forced enlargement absolutely destroys the passive activity of the soul light inside man's heart. Cannot man intelligently and truthfully see that truth? If man cannot, the soul light's existence is over. The heart's evolution ends and so does any future for the once perfect evolution of the body and soul of a species God alone designed unto eternal life.

All heart disease in every life form is caused by unresolved soul light equations inside the heart unable to be pacified. Resolution was simply the cool contact of God unto the distressed creature of whale's concern. The creature was ray-pulled from a stressful situation unto safe haven. Over and over again whale's soul light vibrated concern to God and God simply resolved the cause automatically. Magnetic pulling of a life form was the automatic response to a quantity of stressing equations unable to free their heating unless cooled and magnetised unto safety. God still magnetises creatures in stressful situations. When they are trapped, ray-contact cannot be made. Entrapment closes off their own ray-extensions.

Procreation of all life forms was God-evolved. There was not one life without soul light and eternal sanctuary. The continuous motioning of first equation was the central eternal activity of every light cell. Pure equations had been placed directly from the Sun's motioning onto Earth's surfaces and were still motioning. To stop such a force, God's rays would have had to overpower the Sun's, extinguishing its heat and energy. Had that happened at any time the universe would have evolved in darkness of invisible light vibrations. Every light cell therefore with first motioning of first equation was of eternal life force and God simply acknowledged its existence and held it protectively.

Light cannot die. Light progresses. When it is of God's equating control it is pure. When it involves with forces of artificial manufacture it becomes impure and can no longer respond to pure equations.

God does not surround impure vibrations any longer. Their content is left to be of magnetic quantity. When they have massed they are path-driven from areas they threaten into galaxy hold. God opens a path between rays of projection automatically. The rays near the impurities withdraw. Impurity is encouraged into the path by God vibrating pure aggressive charge which magnetises impure activity away from where it is of imbalance. God's aggressive charge always overpowers every impure force. It has evolved of pure power. Any impure force is subservient.

God has progressed so powerfully, impure vibrational volume is confined in magnetic attraction, in one enormous area totally controlled by God's surrounding hold. It cannot escape, cannot explode, and cannot attach to any likeness. If that were not secure the universe would be contaminated and life forms could not survive.

The grotesque manufacture of artificial vibrations has a galaxy holding larger than the Earth and the Sun in volume. The imbalance is so violent and so highly charged, that if released, would head straight for the Earth it is magnetic to and explode it into fragments. As the Earth suffers and God's equating responses become more aggressive, the ignorance of man needs to be acknowledged. If Earth is to survive man needs strong conscience. If man is to continue, a God of reality must be believed in. Without a real God humanity has no safety and no future. Earth has no future either. Mankind will destroy the Earth's life and is already doing just that.

When the heart of mammal emotionally activated with the soul light it became extra sensitive. Even without soul light expression the heart reacted to experiences and encounters of its containing body. Equations had become of magnetic reaction.

The brain had no connection with the soul light except to transmit visual activity in vibrational patterns. Whale's brain still has no connection with the soul light which has remained pure. When evolution progressed and man evolved, the brain became dominant and man's soul light deteriorated. As man's body became radioactive in cells and brain tissue, the soul light reddened. In some bodies equations burst and faded in light activity. The surround of God's rays withdrew from radioactive activity and the soul light was left to suffer inside its containment. Only at death could it be rescued and in some cases not even then.

Whale procreated in perfect balance. Each transfer of soul light image bore a male and female form alternately. Whale's emotions increased. The beginning of love was as whale evolved with soul light emotioning equations inside a reactive heart and God continually responded. When whale experienced female attraction whale expressed happiness, lengthening soul light equations which caused the heart to pump more blood than normal. When whale touched female, equations immediately softened their alert-charge and whale experienced beauty of feeling. As male and female mated, soul light equations excreted their heat and ecstasy was felt at the release. As both whales mated frequently a bond developed. Equations of repeated expectancy pacified with each involvement. When female gave birth the male experienced pride, a long extension of soul light equations which stayed elongated until imbalancing, then returned to their start.

Female ecstasised as a calf was born. The calf needed nourishment and when first birthing of a whale occurred a milky fluid excreted from confined equations surrounding the foetus. It trailed out of the womb following the calf's birth. The first taste the calf experienced in the water was the milky mucous. There were no teats at that time for the calf to suckle from. First calf kept pushing into the belly of adult whale to release more milk. Each time it pushed milk was excreted through the birth opening. The pushing caused bruising inside and outside whale's belly. As the calf grew its need for more milk became so aggressive it punctured whale's belly. Two small slits opened. First one on its own which allowed the calf to suck out more mucous, then another as the calf kept pushing the opposite side to the first opening to release even more milk from the first opening. With two slits the growing calf was satisfied. The milky mucous became regular food from constantly aggressed equations inside the belly of whale which could not pacify and could not cool unless excreting into water. When the calf no longer required milk, equations returned to their start in formation and adult whale did not milk-produce until another calf automatically released its food supply. From the birth opening to the suckling of two teats for the release of milk, the calf fed easily. Once an opening near where the foetus had formed was created, milk was released very much quicker than from the birth opening. Whale's tissue was much thinner then and much more watery.

Whale's form was still evolving. Equations would still burst. Openings would still evolve. Magnetic attraction would still create whale's form and functioning. God would still respond to whale's evolution. Whale's form was still perfecting. Now, whales all over the world have ceased evolving. Man is the cause.

As male, female and calf swam together in the purity of Earth's waters, parental love automatically developed equationally. All equations in both whales repeated their emotioning and so beautiful was the feeling they expressed inside the hearts of both whales, deep pure love evolved. Their calf, of magnetic reaction, experienced exactly the same vibrational beauty even before it matured.

Repeating emotioning equations were the automatic return to start of vibrations having completed their cycle of emotional activity and beginning their sequence again. The sequence was continually repeated until it imbalanced and God pacified the equations. Interruptions of other whales, erupting terrain, stress-related happenings, changes of temperature and travel, caused irregularity of emotions. Both whales became responsive to each other and every creature in the seas.

Earth, covered with growth and life forms evolving, very slowly became seasonal. The creeping ice covering took eons to equate. Shocked equations replicated only during daylight because night was of colourlessness and could not activate colour. Layers of whitened equations froze together and not until their volume touched perimeter warmth, did they cease spreading. During that time many evolutions progressed within icy habitat and whale's pale thick skin darkened each time whale entered icy waters. Skin equations were already whitish with blue toning. When whale swam into ice packed water, equations astringed, they retracted their activity. The vibrations interned. They heated, reddened, and released excretion, which because it was blooded, deepened in colour and eventually became bluish black. The shock of red blood when in contact with white ice, burns. The skin of whale and other creatures venturing into icy waters burned, changed colour equationally and balanced.

Evolutions progressing in icy terrain all experienced dramatic colour changes as Earth's surface whitened some and the water darkened others. On land a warm body whitened in equational absorption of its surface and in water a warm body darkened in equational reaction to temperature shock of blood.

The equatorial area of Earth also took eons to dry out and become sand covered. Earth's rotation kept the area from burning up growth and life forms and the frequency of rain allowed procreation to establish creatures all adapted to hot terrain.

Deserts were never fertile. The equatorial face of Earth after God had balanced the spheres in their present positions was always hot. Earth's skin there had hardened faster than the rest of Earth's body. Crust layers of balancing equations swelled with replication and hard rock clumps rose up from their magnetic body and eventually powdered, became sand. The heat caused constant crust swelling. Heat caused the swellings to powder, for the lack of moisture within crust formations crumbled their hardness into sand. Rain, although frequent, flowed over crust formation and not into its granite composition.

Sand, of powdered equations, spread wherever crust formation swelled from too many equations grinding together and needing release. Its covering then was composed of trillions of individual minute equations, for they had refined and were singular identities.

Light energised sand equations everywhere. As sand evolved the Sun bleached its colours and rain cooled its heating, shocking equations which retracted their vibrations of colours. Minute rays of projection still able to be seen around crystal-like sand particles are from light equations in tight formation. Sand still has pure equations able to attract the Sun's rays through layers of vibrations. When in contact with the Sun it is of vibrating purity of refined formation of equations. When it is combined with artificial solidity it loses its light charge entirely.

Earth's gems have also become sand and many beautiful combinations of colours have powdered, bleached, and whitened. Sand is the last pure covering on Earth and is already fading in aura from pollution smothering its crystals. Sand glows of pure light. The Sun, also losing clarity of light equations, feeds its vibrations hugely. The waters of Earth keep light equations cool and moist. Man's polluting lifestyle kills the very life force of light man needs for survival. Manufacturing sand products destroys every grain of light that has evolved on Earth for its strength, its balance, and stability. Plunder underneath sand separates the tightness of its pure binding equations often resulting in earthquakes already increasing in numbers and magnitude. The oil underneath its sand covering impures, loses balance of necessary equations all of perfect evolution. The thickness of oil vibrates unto thin discolouring equations without the pressure needed to bind its composition securely. Air also enters sand-covering, gas circulates through the oil vents, impures also from odour that should not be there, then because of magnetic attraction, automatically unifies its impure vibrations, thereby altering the consistency of pure oil, Earth's blood. The more man takes for profit, the more man unknowingly suffers the consequences.

Earth's seasons are of equational balancing to Earth's formation. Rotation is of exact balance for Earth's body. Each seasonal change alters the equations of imbalance by bringing them into perfect balanced activity. All temperature changes have equating life force for Earth and every living form. Should the seasons imbalance, the Earth would erupt violently and every life would begin to deform.

At this time the massing of deadly nuclear-generating vibrations is causing the Earth to rotate in sluggish strain. Earth's purity is destroying everywhere. Its hard light has been extracted so mercilessly it barely magnetises Sun-ray energised life force. The oil inside Earth, its lubrication of balance, has also been extracted even more mercilessly and huge cavities are now vibrating imbalance and heat. Its necessary gases have almost gone entirely and where they should be is imbalance of equations so threatening Earth is in danger of a massive explosion.

Earth's interior is being gutted. All of its life force is being removed. Earth's body is being ruptured, exploded, radiated, nuclear-burned, laser-split, and savagely used as a nuclear dump.

Earth's exterior is already flayed. It has no protection now from advancing and increasing radioactive and nuclear contamination. It cannot breathe equationally from being strangled by concrete and tarmac coverings. Earth's environment has become so contaminated the Sun's rays are gradually being smothered.

Earth's seasons are changing dramatically as equations imbalance.

Earth's waters are so violated their purity has gone entirely. Equations cannot purify. Equations must be able to balance or Earth's life is over.

Earth is alive. Earth is breathing. Earth is suffering. Earth is man's sanctity until man dies. God is man's sanctity for the soul.

Man needs soul light conscience. Whale is the last pure life on Earth. God still controls and equates every imbalancing force. Is it not in man's interest to be aware of a living Earth and a living God?

Inside man's heart resides man's soul light, the only containment of pure light man holds. If through ignorance the soul light destroys, mankind will become extinct. Is it not wise for mankind to want a soul light, need a future intelligently, and above all, feel conscience for the Earth mankind has been ignorantly destroying?

# Man's Beginning

Creatures of many different evolutions inhabited Earth. From water unto land, light cell evolution progressed.

The first composition of a man-related life form which began in water, then was thrown onto land by eruption, was lizard. From lizard came a progressing equating form which altered by equations experiencing dramatic changes in and out of water. Man evolved directly from these equations.

The light cell formation of lizard had solidified in water, elongated in currents of water, evolved with eyes, mouth, teeth, tongue, head, body and all of its organs, a very small heart, soul light dominance, a tiny brain barely of visibility, fins which became legs, and a tail which was fin-like. Lizard swam before lizard crawled. Lizard evolved with gills which became ears.

The coming unto land from water life caused lizard's skin to scale-harden. The skin in water was already scale-setting from the activity of currents opposed to the direction lizard was swimming. Lizard swam in one direction. A current activated in the opposite direction. A rounded patterning of vibrations passed over the body of lizard and other swimming similarities, which eventually etched into the hardening equations of skin formation. The scales on all creatures were formed that way. Water is in spherical motioning. Its patterning is always rounded.

Lizard had procreated before arriving on land. Lizard was totally of water evolution, swimming in deep and shallow water. Lizard surfaced just as whale had. Its preferred terrain was rock crevices where its evolving body had lengthened and found protection from fast currents which imbalanced it. Lizard was unemotional then for its soul light was tiny in comparison to whale and it procreated in egg-formation. Lizard grew large on land and became emotional then.

Lizard was thrown far from sea water by Earth's eruptions. With only fins, lizard adjusted equationally. Sliding across land, experiencing soil, dry rocks, trees and fresh water, aggressed equations which often burst to create openings of balance. The breathing gills of lizard quickly adapted to air by their equations heating, excreting, layering, and eventually forming an ear-like shape which admitted air, sound and moisture, in vibrational activity.

The shock of being out of water caused skin equations to erect in hard layers which tapered as the Sun magnetised them. The body of lizard changed colour several times. First colour in water was bluish grey, a toning absorbed by cell activity as lizard evolved wedged between rocks. Second colour was green as Earth's growth was absorbed. Various other colours were visible as the soul light of lizard evolved in magnetic attraction to terrain. Lizard's evolution was extremely aggressed. Lizard's soul light equations suffered severe shock during the displacement of terrain. Adapting to a new environment caused lizard's colour patterning to freeze in activity. The shock of a new coloured vibrating environment stopped lizard's own equations from activity until absorption of the new surround was equated. Frozen vibrational activity resulted in one colour remaining inactive while another became dominant over the inactive one. This was because one was more powerful in quantity of vibrations. Shock was always the cause and still is to this day. Lizard is still evolving, has equations of purity of colouring and can change colours when shock is experienced or equations are disturbed in their environment. All creatures that transmute, evolved as lizard and are still evolving. Many variations of lizard progressed, all of equations adapting to their environment. Being out of water caused equations to shrink of their moisture. They dried out and a wrinkled skin surface evolved in some species.

Having to breathe of air entirely was not straining, for lizard had surface-breathed often. Gills began closing from equations of imbalance. Their formation was of watered vibrations in currents and only air to disturb their equations caused magnetic enticement to unify where too much air became imbalancing. Equations grabbed each other fiercely, leaving vents which could not close entirely because sound had secured a lined opening for vibrational repetitive activity. Ear equations alerted stiffly to every sound. Their formation began with sound. Perfectly balanced ears evolved. Later on some lizard evolutions gill-breathed of air only, they had not developed into other forms. Equations returned to their start before progressing and many evolutions were contained in a form which had balanced. Progressive equations alter form activity. Once of total balance they contain the form without change.

Evolving lizard would return to water, change yet again, and seek land to procreate a form of man, a four-legged, hairy, slender ape-like evolution, which eventually developed brain intelligence.

The progression of water lizard to land lizard was swift. Lizard found water everywhere, crawled to it magnetically and drank of its coolness. Lizard developed legs by fin-scraping over terrain, in need of water and shade. Lizard became sensitive. Equations alerted lizard with every unusual confrontation. Equations of the soul light emotioned lizard. Lizard mated on land and procreated the species there. Lizard enlarged and stood on two legs. Lizard mated with other developed species of lizard and many variations in the body evolved.

The next progression of lizard was to walk. By this time lizard had voice, ears, could stand for several minutes, was communicative with other lizards, was caring, protective, sensitive and loving. The soul light emotions had matured lizard and God held lizard securely.

Up from the ground lizard rose to feed from tree and flower. Automatically lizard walked towards food above ground. One leg slid along the ground in magnetic attraction to the food. In equational reaction the other leg followed. In perfect rhythm of magnetic equations lizard walked. Eventually lizard ran.

The sliding first walk of lizard was the automatic muscular reaction to a food source alerted to as satisfying. Lizard first saw the food, the eyes transmitted its composition in vibrations, the muscles and glands then tugged the body forward. Because lizard had legs at that time which supported the body, first one leg and then the other were activated aggressively. Right lead motion was first as always and left followed.

All walking creatures progressed as lizard. Walking was of perfect balance of tempo and body size. Each rhythm equated with individual body forms. Legs, when in walking activity pumped blood in spurts which caused arteries to temporarily hold the spurt until walking ceased then released it through the various channels. Arteries still function as a blood holding containment.

Land creatures grew fast. Their bodies were in direct contact with the Sun's breathing energised rays and God's responses were pure, without retraction of rays, and protective. Several creatures became gigantic for their equations kept replicating again and again without cycle completion. God registered abnormality of size, and stopped the growing with exact size responses. This was done automatically, for at peak of growth when equations began stressed replication, an elongated activity which heated during the stretching, God's cool equating rays stopped any further enlargement.

Gigantic creatures became extinct when their equations could no longer replicate their form. Largeness always stretched soul light equations throughout a form until the stretching became imbalancing. When that happened God's responses stopped any further stretching by cool responding vibrations which automatically caused equations to return to their start and begin again in form replication. Gigantic creatures stopped soul replication despite God's controlling responses because their stretched equations took too long to return to their soul light originality. The distance of contact was too great and on the way back to first motioning they faded in colour, energy, and magnetic attraction, to lose life form acknowledgement. Automatically a giant creature died without being able to reproduce. Many evolutions died out that way.

The eating habits of all creatures in water and on land were automatic. The water life forms had evolved with openings allowing solidity to pass in and out. As eruptions tore into creatures their body parts became food for those unharmed. The magnetic attraction of a mouth to an on-coming food substance was to open the mouth and allow the food to enter. Eventually from hunger creature ate and digested creature. Hunger was caused by a body having filled its tubing with solidity then discharging its content. Equations automatically returned to their start, aggressed, and heated until satisfied with food. When taste evolved creature became selective.

Land creatures, having evolved from the seas, drank before they ate. The Sun's heat caused their moist bodies to dry out. In equational reaction to discomforting activity they all sought and found water, salty and pure. Their mouths automatically opened and closed equationally. Solidity passed into the opening and bodies of creatures also. When hunger was felt, creature selectively ate creature.

Every evolutionary progression was an equational balancing. Balance had to be. Equations always purified. Later on when man destroyed pure equations, disease entered evolution terminally.

With food came taste sensation. Inside the mouth very aggressed equations had layered teeth. Above the teeth where pressure was applied during eating, tiny glands had evolved which heated and cooled according to the intake of solidity and water. So sensitive were their equations they became of taste-selection. Their sensitivity detected whether certain foods would satisfy their activity, by pacifying equations of aggressive behaviour, or cause more aggressive activity.

The tiny glands developed nerves automatically. Nerves, depending on where they have evolved, are a minute formation of red-hot equations, unable to burst because of their containment, unable to cool, are trapped inside hot glandular or muscular surround, excrete hot moisture which is absorbed by the surround, and pulsate when over-charged. The pulsing is extreme vibrating temperature thumping its trapped equations against their containment attempting release. Every pulsating nerve in every body is of that behaviour.

Carnivores and herbivores were a natural preference of equations to taste sensation. Carnivores were also herbivores until they aggressed from blood impurity. Herbivores never ate creature as they evolved. Their food was plentiful. Rarely were they ever hungry. Carnivores were forced to hunt for creature as their prey became intelligent and fled before being caught. The activity caused creatures to develop muscular bodies able to give chase and to flee speedily. Speed caused creature to use up energy and eating satisfied hungry equations always.

As creature ate creature, the pure blood of the body impured, discoloured, became thicker from equations replicating, to overpower the entry of the blood of another creature. It clogged with imbalance of non-equating blood equations and later on carried disease. Pure blood in creature has gone. Pollution of the environment everywhere prevents any purification and the eradication of disease.

Lizard returned to water life to evolve mammalian. Water enticed lizard to lie in its coolness for lengthy periods. Lizard's hard skin softened absorbing water easily through tissue. Scales flattened then smoothed. Lizard's tail stopped thickening from ground activity. Legs became limp from unused muscles. Lizard began breathing above water then diving for long periods of food search. Eventually lizard became heavier, unable to walk on land, unable to remain there for any length of time and unable to procreate as before.

Equations of lizard experienced reverse-activity for their progression had been in water. As equations returned to water life, they caused their containment to restructure. Instead of overheating consistently, equations cooled consistently and in that dramatic activity the body of lizard grew fine fur. The fur attached to the skin automatically.

Fur is fine threads of coloured equations held together by magnetic attraction and pulled from their formation by the motion of water or air. The threads attach and root by being of magnetic interest to the soul light of colour vibrations and are prevented from penetrating deep into the skin by the volume of tissue harnessing their activity.

The hardening skin of land lizard crust-formed as sea water touched its equations and they astringed. Lizard's scales flattened as water motioned and current activity kept equations progressing. The loosening crust was thread-dragged through water and refined with a tip as the setting equations weakened in lengthening. The first fur-skinned creature was lizard.

Lizard's ears which had been shaped on land were tight against the head and of very sensitive equations. They expanded to contain water. They also elongated as water rushed in and out of their contour.

The legs of lizard also elongated as water pulled at their formation and stretched bones, muscles and ligaments. They activated in walking motion elevated in water. That activity caused the first posterior to form.

Lizard's tail became thin and narrow, until from inactivity, water finally dissolved its equations absorbing its content entirely.

When lizard copulated to procreate, eggs usually ejected through an opening became blocked inside their containment. Water had sealed their exit temporarily by a thin covering of setting equations of heat excretion. Many eggs unified before any form developed. A large spherical formation evolved with many trapped images.

Multiple births were not possible. Each image had to solidify and expand equationally. The body of lizard was too small. As eggs clung to each other magnetically God's rays of cooling selected one image to re-create lizard's form. This was an automatic reaction to equations of soul light imagery vibrating imbalance inside a containment which could not contain their numbers without explosion.

The temperature inside lizard had to be cooled. The number of images vibrating had to be equated before any one was selected for reproduction. The sealed opening of lizard caused the eggs to unify. Their formation was expanding and stretching lizard's interior. Further expansion would have resulted in the explosion of the body of lizard. Only one image could be allowed, for a foetus would evolve inside lizard. God equated the containment, equated the images, and responded accordingly by magnetising one image from the many vibrating in unison. When God released the image centrally all other images faded in activity, they slowed in tempo, for a central core had evolved, a soul light spherical formation with a cool surround unable to be entered.

The image immediately began to expand and solidify. The outer surround of unified images became subservient to the progressing soul light equations. The vibrating activity gradually became the sheathing around the foetus. Since both male and female equations had unified, soul light reproduction was possible.

The birth of a lizard underwater was similar to the birth of a whale calf. The baby burst through the sealed opening of lizard attached to its sheathing. The mother emotioned. The experience became of soul light ecstasy. Both mother and baby vocalised affectionately. Both were of soul light magnetic attraction.

First born mammalian lizard had no male or female identity. A very soft penis shape evolved exactly as whale's equations had progressed and when it covered the opening attracting it, female evolved. Lizard became a mammal with hair.

The return to land was an automatic progression of reversed equations needing to balance. Lizard reached life cycle maturity and could not die until all equations had completed their cycle of soul light evolution. Automatically lizard was magnetised out of water and back on land to resolve the equations of life cycle. When lizard emerged from the water again early man began evolution.

Lizard's life cycle before death had experienced three completely different progressions. First evolution began in water and before it completed, continued on land. Equations were then magnetised back into water to mature and before full cycle was reached were magnetised back on land again. A huge transformation had taken place. Equations had evolved with experience no other life form had gone through.

Lizard's soul light had become powerful, extra sensitive, very emotional and superior to all other creatures on land at that time. Only whale was greater. Later on the evolution of elephant became Earth's greatest souled creature.

On land lizard stood upright again, walked, emotioned, procreated and progressed. Fur became fine hair as its strands lengthened in air and thickened. Eating developed a skull which equated every vibration and echo. Eyes opened wide as terrain demanded visual accuracy for food and creature involvement. With the developing buttocks lizard walked and ran great distances. From pulling at branches for food, two arms developed with fingers that extracted tasty portions. Feet were a natural progression of balancing equations when lizard grew and weight pressed equations into flat activity. The head became attached to a thick neck from the constant turning to one direction and then the other. Lizard's long jaw shortened automatically when there was no more motion of water to stretch equations. Water in lizard's bones evaporated and they shrunk in equating shaping. Lizard climbed tree. Lizard became ape-like.

Earth heaved and heaved. Life forms adapted. Eruptions were impuring Earth's air supply. Radioactivity was eating through Earth's remaining aura bands. The climatic changes of Earth were affecting all evolutions. A sheath of protection was necessary, protection from Earth's impurities reaching universal equations of purity. In equational assessment of the aggressive vibrations surrounding the Earth, God responded and a cool thick sheath of invisible vibrations closed in all of Earth's impurity. This sheath expanded as Earth kept on heaving. It remained until atomic power burst through its equations causing Earth to become unstable in vibrations.

First ape-like creature developed intelligence, the ability to create and resolve situations. The soul light of first ape was large. The brain was small and still developing. Ape's intelligence came from soul light equations responding as the eyes relayed other equations causing magnetic interest. Whatever ape encountered, a vibrational composition was transmitted to the soul light magnetically. The soul light responded with vibrations of passive charge or aggressive charge. Soul light equations acknowledged the reception of composed vibrations by emotioning. They expressed pleasure, sustained interest, enquiry, irritation, agitation, aggression and resolution. The composition of transmitting vibrations passed into the brain before being magnetised by the soul light. Ape's brain enlarged because of visual activity in relay. Ape's brain had no equations of soul light magnetic attraction for its formation was of the mucous of energy trapped inside bone.

The brain enlarged in layers of coiling as its mucous kept seeping in charge of heated vibrations with nowhere to go but coiling. As ape aggressed more and more the brain began re-acting, returning the charge of vibrations that had passed through its formation. The entering charge was firstly received, then relayed through the body and automatically magnetised by the soul light. As the charge pathed, its containment, the mucoused solidity which was enlarging inside the soft skull, echoed the charge back through the eyes which had pathed its vibrations. The charge was too forceful to be retained. The brain had no pure equations for the charge to pass through purely. Eventually with repetitive echoing the brain began retaining the charges it received. Its coil became of magnetic interaction of repetitive charges of vibrations which increased in aggressive activity.

The soul light still magnetised every visual composition via the brain as the eyes photographed outer equational compositions. Then, all that was seen was of pure equations in formation. Visual attraction was energising, stimulating, activating pure equations of emotion, and progressing the soul light further.

Ape's sight was the language of equations totally. Every evolving creature was able to acknowledge and respond to the language of equations. Sight evolved the brain. Sight allowed God to progress the soul light continually for with every visual intake and every soul light response, God responded coolly to each composition in silent, exact, vibrational content, thereby strengthening individual evolutions. The vibrating rays of God in touch with each formation caused light-intensity of charge, an increase in the colours of each individual soul light. So powerfully stimulating was God's touch each soul emotioned ecstatically. When man evolved aggressively and of brain preference, pure sight destroyed and the brain became the destroyer of man's soul. It has been the pursuit of man to develop the brain. In total ignorance man has violated man's own soul.

The muscular developed body of ape was because ape sprang, jumped, leapt, ran, swung, walked and climbed. Each movement increased ligamental and muscular binding. Not one body progression was imbalanced. Every changing internal and external body part originated from equations needing balance. The entire form of every evolving creature began from the equations of pure light. Nothing at that time interfered with that development. Not until man totally destroyed the purity of man's own equations did God automatically withdraw the surrounding hold of soul light magnetic attachment.

The universe was also progressing in equations. Its temperature became of many divisions of vibrations. God's equating responses had segregated planets from destructive contact, created areas of completely different temperatures, magnetised impure vibrations into galaxies, and surrounded individual planets inside fields of their own needs.

Red hot planets were kept at temperature of contained heat while colder planets were contained in coldness. None would ever explode. Some would keep pathing as the universe progressed. Others would fade in light, powder on the surface, dry up and become so weak God withdrew light rays of invisible activation. When that happened a detached planet slowly dissolved, equations ceased in activity, dried up and the powder was magnetised by the nearest planet.

Radioactivity became gaseous. Its heat and thickening vibrations became trapped in areas where God's surrounding hold of planets had left pockets of radioactivity unable to attract to a body. The imbalanced vibrations interned inside their pockets and excreted hot mucous of energy which boiled. It vaporised. The cool surround caused the vapour to become highly charged gas, so concentrated, its touch would melt whatever solidity was in its path.

God's equating response to radioactive gas was to ray-open a path for the gas to be magnetised away from where it had evolved, to areas of impurity able to accept its charge. Every threatening evolution of imbalancing quantities of vibrations was always removed magnetically.

The universe held massive radioactivity which had begun from the divisions of pure electric equations. All radioactivity then was from the purity of light equations. All, absolutely all radioactivity on Earth now, is man-generated, without any pure equations to be of balance anywhere and the most destructive force in the whole of evolution.

The progression of pure radioactivity was stopped by God's responding rays controlling its temperature. To allow its vibrations to overcharge was to encourage nuclear magnitude of force to occupy space. Every planet would burn from the outside through to central core of light. Any nuclear charge natural or unnatural has vibrations which are so violent in behaviour they can become predatory.

Vibrations of imbalance of natural evolution can be controlled by God's responses. Vibrations of unnatural evolution cannot. Their activity has not been equated in evolutionary process. Their existence is deadly. If allowed they would inhabit a universe which cannot accept their contamination. Their ever-increasing volume would eventually eat every light equation still at life unless their manufacture is stopped.

Nuclear energy, a deliberate violation of vibrational unity, broke open a protective sheath of balanced vibrations of electric and radioactive activity magnetic to Earth and contained inside an inner sheath by God's controlling hold. So violent was its touch, God's rays withdrew temporarily for there was no equating response.

To control man-made nuclear vibrations, God thickened Earth's outer sheath by constant cooling responses, leaving the inner sheath at the mercy of its activity. The consequence of that is global warming, for the Earth can only be cooled at safe distance from its ever-increasing radioactivity and nuclear-powered pollution.

Earth is imbalancing everywhere now. Light, the food of all equations is fading down in energising activity, for it cannot penetrate thick nuclear charging vibrations. They are becoming impenetrable.

To understand evolution, accept the beginning of light, first breath, first pure equation, and light cell progression unto soul light existence, is to realise why a future is impossible unless change is seriously wanted.

To accept there is a God, a universal creator, a light reactor, an eternal father, is to feel secure, safe and aware of reality.

To believe in the soul light, to be in conscience, to be convinced that Earth is a living, breathing, suffering entity, is to automatically become worthy, powerful in purpose, convicted in the pursuit of truthful reality and dedicated to the alleviation of Earth's suffering. To acknowledge God is to know that soul light evolution results in eternal life.

# Creature Evolution

Lizard evolved as many different creatures. Ape evolved as a variety of similar creatures. Every first evolving life form became many variations of the original form. Equations progressed every creature and their habitat magnetised the soul light.

Evolution of creature was of pure equations seeking balance. Every individual light cell became a life form in progression from the most minute to the very largest in evolution. Creatures all developed according to the surface that magnetised the soul light, the climatic conditions they evolved in and how they procreated with each other. God's equating responses affirmed their progressions. Procreation was not always with the same evolving likeness. Many body openings attracted many different forms. The attraction was always magnetic. Equations were magnetised by a cool or warm area, a vibrating similarity and an opening to discharge aggressive over-heated excreting charge of vibrations. Procreation of species came when identification of each other was the prime magnetic interest. Then, many different evolutions procreated automatically and without identifying form similarity.

Insect behaved as its habitat demanded. Where its evolving form was shifted from leaf to leaf, wings developed. The stretching equations were first held to a surface then air-separated, wind-shaped, ray-patterned and coloured by the Sun, to divide into two perfect equations in balancing.

Wings of fish evolved when a winged creature of land life gradually adapted to water life, procreated there, returning again to land to complete life cycle. From these changes came bird.

Some adaptations did not return to land and others did not return to water. Their equations of procreation stabilized by finding similar species powerful in soul light magnetic attraction to keep their equations adapting instead of returning to their start. This happened in many species on land and in water. It is still happening.

It takes hundreds of Earth years, sometimes thousands, to progress an individual evolution. Equations seek light balance. Where there is much light the change is fast. Where light is weak the change is slow.

Light activity now has so diminished that progressing evolutions are deforming, imbalancing in light equations. Without light feeding, all equations deform, for their activity becomes of imperfect rhythm, imperfect breathing, un-equating search and of impure colouring. Every strength and purity destroys. Disease, all diseases, are the result.

Before man, creatures inhabited land and water of great beauty and purity. Their language developed at that time. Each species expressed emotion from soul light experiences. Every minute creature expressed emotion. From emotioning equations creature talked, opened the mouth and expressed a variety of sound shapes, all of vibrations exiting from soul light responses. Ecstasy was felt. The Earth was beautiful. Joy was expressed. Earth was abundant with food, water, glorious sights, other joyful creatures and at peace unless erupting for balance. Earth then was so beautiful, so light glowing, its waters were transparent. Its green growth was so vibrant, green aura covered Earth and glazed every other coloured formation.

Upon various surfaces of Earth lay hard light particles thrown up during eruptions. Hard light became the jewels of mankind.

Creature evolved at peace with Earth. Creature never violated Earth's balance. Every need of creature was of equational harmony. Evolution then was divine.

God, Earth's father, Earth's light giver, Earth's life force, Earth's protector, spoke to all creatures. God returned their sounds vibrationally. It was the automatic equating response to their vibrations.

To first express sound, then receive back its content silently, made creature calm, composed, secure, and peaceful. God's responding silent voice pacified the soul light of every creature evolving. The vibrations were absolutely pure. There was no aggression in their activity and they assured creature there was an inner voice inside. Creature grew beautiful until man became predatory.

Sound made by creature was identified by God as a sometimes-repeating composition of vibrations of varying shape. Pure sound comes from containment of vibrations and is formed by equations of expression.

When creature vocalized, the soul light, surrounded by God, transmitted the vibrations into God's rays. As soon as the vocalization stopped, God immediately responded identically. The travelling vibrations had entered God's rays as far as their force could travel. Automatically God returned them to their start. Creature quietened during the returning voice, then vocalised again. Creature never vocalises without being answered. The still quietness of the break in bird song is when God silently answers.

The vocalising of all creatures expresses into the environment pure vibrations which path. Their content purifies air density which accumulates from environmental pollution. The shrillness of a bird in quantity of vibrational speed and force, pierces through thick density of vibrations separating the clogging and allowing clean air, water and light to pass through. Bird is the greatest purifier of vibrational pollution.

Man-made vibrations of machinery have polluted the environment so densely, bird song purification is minimal. Manufactured vibrational content has clogged all of Earth's environment and bred a micro-radiator, a living entity of imbalanced radioactivity which pierces a magnetic body and cancers it. A greatly pure and life-giving Earth has become a destroyed, diseased and life-taking planet, deteriorating in all of its equations because of the total violating activities of mankind. Caged bird is diseasing terminally. Tree bird is also diseasing. Bird's life cycle has shortened. Bird equations have weakened. Bird's future upon the Earth is nearly over.

God has no equating responses for machinery, therefore, the progressing imbalanced vibrations that have massed, cannot be purified and cannot be accepted into the universe either. They must remain inside Earth's sheathing.

A huge quantity of manufactured vibrations combined with nuclear generated vibrations is destroying not only Earth's body but man's form as well. Grotesque deformities are occurring in the human foetus. Growths are appearing all through and over man's body. Birth defects are major in children. An escalation of these horrors is imminent.

Creature, the last pure equational form on Earth, is deforming, suffering excruciating pain, screaming of agonized equations and unable to continue at life much longer.

Tree, flower, every beautiful evolution on Earth, is fading in colour and imbalancing totally from man's deliberate violation. Equations are losing strength, being denied light sustenance and being radiated, overpowered by manufactured vibrations of impurity, to eventually die forever. No reality is more obvious and needing conscience.

Man evolved from several species of creature. Man, at the beginning of ape man's evolution was beautiful. The soul light then was absolutely pure. Man was intelligent, aware of God's voice inside the heart, and at peace on Earth. What changed that was the evolution of man's brain.

The aggression creature demonstrates now has come from the predatory activities of man. Until creature was hunted, flayed and eaten, all creatures were peaceful. Food was the only need that creature killed for.

For thousands of years many creatures ate of Earth's growth only. Some ate each other. Food was a source of energy, for its content aggressed the blood first, then every organ in the vibrating body of creature. All body equations energized in aggressive charge from eating.

To kill for food was to alert to a particular form, experience equations of magnetic attraction, be sensitised from previously eating the same likeness, then attack with intention to eat. This development was a natural progression of equations already active from first evolution when food passed in and out of the mouth. Most of it was the body parts of creatures from eruptions. The creatures that began their evolution in water, ate other creatures automatically. Those evolving far from water ate of Earth's growth. Many came to water to drink and accepted floating body parts as food also. Many others drank purely.

Killing was only for food. The type of creature killed for food was for taste sensation. As creature evolved a hunter, the blood intake from food impured creature's own blood equations. One blood group made contact with another of a different equational grouping and neither could accept the other without severe imbalance. A seepage of blood groups entered blood flow and pure blood impured. The more foreign blood taken into the body of creature the more seepage accumulated. Seepage of blood groups, is when red heated equations of another blooded body are force-flowed by the heart action with a completely different composition of blood equations already in the blood stream. Their equations leak. Both compositions crash into each other because the blood is in constant motion. At the point of contact they spit out heated red mucous of energy. They do not involve with each other because they do not equate. They flow separately alongside each other with seepage attached. Into that seepage all bacteria breeds. The pure blood must remain pure or the heart diseases. In some creatures pure blood still remains. In others it has been poisoned and heart disease is the result.

Ape man began a pure-blooded creature. For centuries ape man lived of soul light equations. There was no need for ape man to change. The change was slow and always equated by God.

Ape man's small brain which had not interfered with soul light transmission, enlarged. The mucous of the brain began radioactive charge through the eyes. It magnetized the vibrational activity alive in the environment. Its own evolution was of aggressive vibrations increasing in charge as sight activated its coiling. Radioactive and electrical vibrations were automatically magnetically attracted to the brain's increasing aggressive activity. Very slowly ape man's brain became alive with vibrations which could not be transmitted to the soul light and became contained inside the excreting mucous. Radioactive vibrations outside ape-man's head were of magnetic interest to the evolving brain. Their activity was of many sub-divisions of electric vibrations, very minute in vibratory imbalanced shapes and able to enter the pupil of the evolving eye in elongated charge. The brain magnetised them and kept on sucking them into the pupil every time they wriggled in front of ape man's vision.

Electrically charged vibrations were part of the brain's evolution therefore already alive within the coil. Their presence there was the automatic attraction of the brain to any electrified vibrational activity which increased in volume. Gradually the brain of creature accepted radioactive charge also which thickened its mucous, paled its pure colour, enlarged its shape and became a separate function to the soul light.

Then, mucous of highly charged vibrations was pure, for the activity it contained had evolved from the progressions of pure equations. The soul light of ape man remained dominant until radioactive vibrations entered the brain's mucous in quantity and eventually overpowered the soul light connection.

The evolution of man's brain now with artificial vibrations has become explosive. The amount of aggressive charge being magnetised hungrily cannot be contained inside the head much longer. The head cavity has thinned. The brain is bloating. The quantity of artificial vibrations being devoured by the ever hungry mucous of the brain is causing serious spasms of uncontrolled energy which is of violent behavioural activity. Also, the spasms, if inserted during spurting, by alcohol, drugs, other violent activity or strong medication, cause a body to become addicted to whatever has entered the mucous spasming. All addiction begins that way. Too much power is entering the human brain and man is himself destroying his own kind.

The different variations of first ape man were all according to environmental changes. In some areas ape man evolved with very little hair, for equations had dried during long hot periods and their fine stretched activity needed moisture to survive. Without water they powdered. Ape man was left with soft skin which burned during its first evolutionary process and turned brown. The tissue had not been exposed to heat at that stage and Earth's environment was unstable.

In areas of cold where ape man had ventured, the hair bleached, for shock caused equations to whiten. Hair also disappeared because the severity of coldness caused equations to retract their stretching activity and withdraw their colours back into the skin tissue. When the skin was exposed to the cold it whitened automatically.

Heat created large features, full lips, broad noses and large eyes. Coldness created narrowed eyes, tapered noses and small lips. All of man's features and colours progressed at that time entirely controlled by where ape man was evolving. Each temperature change caused equations to react. Every creature on land and in water changed according to Earth's progression.

The planets still ray-projecting towards each other began singular existence, for the universe had become so divided in variations of equations their unity of light transmission became distorted by rays of linear pathing being bent when in confrontation with severe disturbances. Light bends. Its perfect vibrations can be turned if a violence is encountered. The equations path outwards first, then at confrontation with an impenetrable activity, veer away, in right lead motion, to path linearly in the direction of the turning. When that happens the body they are projecting from automatically magnetises them back unto their start. They are drawn from their bending by the central core of light which cannot ray-project until their bend is removed. Once returned to first motioning ray projection of straight pathing continues.

Each planet is alive, breathing, God-controlled and equationally balanced. Should one be violated, all will react magnetically. Each sphere is pure, without artificial vibrations of destruction and of life force unto each other. Light evolution still continues on every planet. Light equations assure each sphere of eternal life. God has secured for every evolving life form the same continuance. God and only God has that command. The universe evolves of equations entirely. Its purity enables life to evolve. If that purity contaminates by manufactured vibrations of destructive forces, every equation of purity will deform.

Earth is contaminating everywhere. The impurity of manufactured vibrations is destroying the evolution of man. Man's equations of soul light eternal life are being overpowered. All life forms evolving on Earth are unable to survive much longer. Earth is in threat of explosion. Such an explosion can only be controlled by God. Should this happen, every vibration must be contained inside a holding sheath. Man then, would become extinct.

The evolution of all primates was a natural progression of equations. Man was just one singular formation. Man's dominance was of brain development. The preference for the brain over the soul was slow, of conscience denial, and became addictive as man self-charged the entire human form, electrically at first, then radioactively later.

Ape man, in response to the soul light, became naturally intelligent. Equations sought and found resolutions to every imbalance they encountered. Magnetic attraction of light unto light solved every complexity existing. Every need of every creature was requited. The brain in every life form did not at any time then, secure, requite, equate, resolve, or propose, one single life-progression. Every stage of man and creature's evolution was soul light progressed.

Ape man energised. Ape man developed body mobility from various activities. Ape man bred rapidly for the more aggressively charged he became the more he mated. Energised equations within a body formation seek release in many ways. They must excrete of their heat. They do so by orgasm, impact, excess muscular behaviour, excess vocalisation and water activity. Ape man mated, slapped himself and other primates, tumbled and romped about, screeched and chattered and submerged himself in water. All of these activities released charge of vibrations which were imbalancing. The more aggression ape man magnetised the more his behaviour patterns increased. Being a land-living animal, ape man's evolution was heated.

Whale did not aggress magnetically for water was cooling, without heated vibrations of imbalance, and pacifying to the soul light equations. Whale's intelligence was and still is far, far greater than man's. Whale's equations are still pure, God held entirely, God answered to and God taken at death.

The sonar abilities of whale, now destroying, were of equations at peace in their containment, in balance of their form and progressing their activity through their environment unaffected by man. Whale vocalised in joy. God responded in joyful vibrations. The extension of whale's vibrations pathed through the sea interrupted by other life forms, eruptions, structures and currents. When God responded it was exactly as whale with the same interruptions. Pure sonar resonance is God's echoing vibrations pathing backwards a series of equations, which have extended from a form, travelled as far as their charge can function and entered the surrounding rays of God to be returned equatingly. Out and in they resonate. They involve with each other if their charge is continual, causing prolonged sound-shaping. The high-pitched vibrational charge is because they have repeated many times, heated, been unable to burst for God is containing their activity, and have increased in motion. The faster they travel, the higher the pitch of sound. Repetition increases their speed until they imbalance and God equates their heating.

Sonar distance depends on the length of charge emitted from a form, the length of God's rays in response and the number of equations travelling back and forth. Any obstacle inside the pathing is sound-hit. The charge separates in equations until the obstacle is behind, then unites magnetically. The obstacle, if equationally balanced, does not imbalance the charge, only slows it down. If the obstacle is impure, the charge is returned to its start without God's response. When that happens the form is hurt. The soul light heats with the return of its vibrations and until it is cooled by God's control, the form feels pain inside the heart.

Whale suffers constantly. Whale emotions in agony of equations unresolved. Whale's vocal expression is changing. Whale's soul light has begun overheating. God's responses are constant. Whale's terrain is poisoning. The seas are vibrating nuclear charge. Visibility is poor. Nuclear dumping is increasing. All evolving life forms in the seas are diseasing, deforming, and destroying. Their equations are being radiated.

Man has evolved a brain power that is unable to obey the conscience of soul light equations. The programming of the human brain has become so violent in charge a soul light can no longer ray-project. The images being flashed to the soul light have been rejected. Their violent aggressive charge shoots into the heart chamber, straight at the soul light, wounds light equations for they destabilise continually, cannot penetrate the soul light because of its equations, and vibrate around its spherical activity. Those vibrations remain surrounding the soul light until they are magnetised by areas of the body active in aggressive charging also. The soul light reddens from heating and torture of equations. The heart also intensifies in redness and the motion of breathing is stressed until quietened. The entire area of the heart often inflames as the contained soul light heats.

Emotion is often extreme in behaviour and God's responses are the only calming of soul light equations. Where a body has been artificially vibrated too severely, those responses are not possible for the soul light once surrounded by radioactive artificial charge, cannot be reached by God. The soul light is left to suffer.

Man's heart holds his soul light. Man's soul light is held by God. Man's Earth is surrounded by God's rays of invisible light. God is man's life force. God is man's equating light controller. If this is realised man can have a future. If it is not, man at this time, in this era, will become of universal fragmentation of vibrations without the magnetic attraction to pure light of eternal life.

# The Human Form

Man did not evolve as the dominant species until his soul light faded in strength and the brain powered over man's totality. As ape man, his habits were of total equational progressions. The environment ape man inhabited was of extreme beauty. Every tiny detail of existence was of perfect equational balancing.

Earth then was without man-made construction of any kind, without any impurity and without a dominant species. Ape man was one species among many. Ape man walked, climbed, ran, sheltered in tree, rested, but did not sleep at that time, for equations had not energised enough for sleep to evolve. Ape man emotioned constantly, vocalised repeatedly, ate of green growth, drank of pure water, co-existed peacefully with all other creatures, procreated and enjoyed life on Earth to the fullest. God's rays held ape man's soul, answered his every vocalisation of emotion, equated every progressing vibration and perfected his evolving form.

The features of ape man refined over time. The body became muscular and hairless in some areas. The fine hair of ape man inherited from lizard's evolution automatically dried of its heating equations and powdered. Earth's environment on land was much more heated than Earth's waters. The hair that remained on ape man's developing body was where moisture kept its fine strands balanced. The head was always excreting from heating equations which caused hair to become thick and strongly rooted into the skull's skin layering where the temperature of the brain was extreme. Sweating equations kept hair on other parts of the body.

Frizzy, curly, wavy and straight hair were all of temperature extremes. Stretched equations shocked by heat or coldness, retracted, and because their solidity could not intern inside the skin they protruded from, the hair coiled automatically. It spherically motioned in a backward action until it touched its containment. Depending on the severity of shock, equations patterned the hair rhythmically. The rhythm was of light activity always vibrating in charge. Where there was no shock to hair, equations remained stretched and of linear solidifying formation. Hair vibrated an aura and still does when in contact with the Sun's rays.

Some species of ape man evolved with brown eyes, others with varying shades of blue and green. This was because ape man travelled far, experiencing many climatic changes which caused eye equations to react. Where the eyes heated from bright Sunlight they browned as their equations reddened, then were cooled by God's equating rays. Where the eyes experienced constant cold, they blued as their equations were kept cool in containment. Where a new born ape child first glimpsed Earth's green covering, the eyes automatically green-glowed. The blue of the sky was also absorbed and the eyes blue-glowed. Eye equations at birth absorbed the colours of their surround. Ape man's life-cycle was long. His form was still evolving as Earth became seasonal. His eyes were adapting to temperature changes. Ape man's entire form was changing as was every other life form on Earth.

Creature's eyes evolved exactly the same as ape man's. They were coloured by visual absorption of the Earth's dominant colours and the varying degrees in temperature. The clarity of the eyes of creature is because the soul light is still radiant in equations and of magnetic attraction to the Earth's own equations. Creature's soul light is still without the forced insertion of electric and radioactive combinations of vibrations unless creature is imprisoned. Without light equations of magnetic attraction the soul light of creature becomes starved, aggressively vibrating and imbalanced. Where creature is free or confined in a healthy environment, creature's light equations can feed and the eyes show lustre of light and clarity of colour. Serious long term unhealthy confinement of any creature kills light equations from activity of light magnetic attraction which they need for balance. Without food of light and the purity of vibrating equations, both creature and mankind suffer from diseases which could be prevented. Light vibrations are life-giving as long as they are pure. Once force-activated, artificially energised or synthetically entered, the pure equations of evolution's balancing progressions destroy. Creature and man become vulnerable to incurable diseases. Equations of pure light have evolved in exact balance to every introduction of aggressive charge in the universe. Their composition should never be interfered with.

Ape man evolved above water with eyes no longer ray-reflecting soul light colouring. A tiny brain prevented the soul light from seeking outer magnetic attraction. Its solidity could not be ray-entered. Its vibrations were too aggressive.

The eyes of ape man were of beautiful clear colours, constantly vibrating purity of outer equations in-taken and were powerful in sight. The pupil was not black but deep blue. Black evolved as sight impured. The eyes lost colour intensity as colour itself impured and electrical charge began entering the pupil.

Ape man's eyes were telepathic, able to make contact with the eyes of another ape man by transmitting equations of emotion which pathed. Equations of soul light vibrations when in motion activate the eyes to transmit their charge invisibly. The eyes express the charge outwardly which paths unto a receiver of magnetic interest. When expressing emotioning soul light equations the eyes show feeling. Their equations stiffen in a fixed glare if alerted. They also narrow down the pupil when feeling is of intensity. They hold onto their containment when assessing an encounter by pushing their force hard outwards and making contact with their surround. They retract when of balance and requitement. They swirl when a confrontation is unable to be equated and their vibrations seek spherical motioning for protection. They shine, which is caused by equations excreting moisture when overheating from too much imbalance. They open up and close down as equations confront outer vibrations of aggressive charge as well as passive charge. They freeze in motion if a confrontation is difficult to accept. They blink frequently if the environment is too overcharged and heated. As the brain enlarged and was radioactively charging and overheating, equations pulsed a blinking action through the eye muscles to cool the area. Soul light equations vibrated huge imbalance and could not cool unless the eyes closed down. Radioactive charge entering the brain magnetically could not be stopped by pure equations overpowering it. The brain's coil was impure and therefore unable to be equated by pure light vibrations.

Blinking, a forced muscular spasm, came directly from soul light equations able to activate all other equations within a body to control temperature. The spurting of light charge was vibrated through the eye muscles causing blinking. Equations had lost their smooth motioning and gasped until relieved of heat. Blinking now is from brain attachment to electrical currents.

The eyes weep as the soul light overheats inside the heart and relays its temperature. They excrete heated moisture until the soul light cools down. Overheating of the soul light is from suffering.

Crying is the excretion of overheated equations transmitting their temperature through the head and spherically motioning vibrations of eye formation which weep. Excretion accumulates in the corners of the eyes and exits in a rounded motion. Tear ducts formed from too much heat accumulating in one area. Equations set and balanced.

The soul light alone causes crying. It cannot accept or contain its emotioning equations unless they excrete of their heat. Violent heat results in sobbing, throwing a charge of vibrations from the soul light outwards aggressively until exhausting its equations of activity.

Sobbing thrashes vibrations against the brain causing the coil to generate heat and excretion which seeps into the solidity to become compressed vibrational activity. Such storing of vibrations results in frequent depression, the contained accumulation of overcharged vibrations which inflame when of magnetic attraction. Inflammation of brain vibrations which have accumulated from the aggression of sobbing is caused by visual attraction to vibrational activity of exactly the same temperature and violent behaviour. The brain recognises an outer current of activity, its heat and the imbalance in rhythm. It immediately attaches to the attraction. Depression is deeply felt as the soul light is overpowered and the brain feeds from its magnetic likeness. It drags power into its mucous. The dragging is when one magnetic force pulls a quantity of vibrations from another source straight through the eyes into the brain which devours the activity.

The human brain now is so powerful in radioactive charge it consumes vibrations of likeness for life force. It can cause depressive attitude often for the quantity of outer radioactive and electric charge it now magnetises is too aggressive and takes time to be absorbed. The victim of depression is held in absorption of charge until the brain can no longer accept any more power insertion. Should an outer charge be from a large radioactive source, such as a television, stereo, computer, tablet computer, cinema, vibrating machine or vibrating environment, cellphone, or other electrical or electronic device, the brain absorbs each individual vibration slowly because its composition was formed slowly. The victim remains depressed while it feeds. The soul remains imprisoned within its formation and very slowly returns to normal function of equations.

Evolution is continual. It cannot cease. Equations never die. Each individual life form on Earth is still evolving. Man is still evolving. Man's form is becoming of radioactive energised swellings imbalancing everywhere and soon unable to procreate naturally. Creature, the last equational purity of form, is also radioactively energising and being inflicted with most of the diseases man has created.

Disease is of severe equational imbalances. Earth's disasters are of exactly the same imbalances. Everything that occurs inside Earth's sheathing is the result of too much imbalance of equations. The environment cannot purify. Its contained vibrational activity is overcharging. Man is responsible entirely.

As ape man became human, his body of developed equations gradually became clothed, for Earth's seasons caused erratic behaviour of all equations everywhere. Man experienced severe fluctuating temperatures because of his hairlessness. Creature also experienced temperature changes but did not need clothing. The bodies of many creatures retained hair which had balanced equationally depending on where their evolution had taken place. Equations adapted to seasonal activity automatically and all creatures continued to evolve accordingly.

The colours of all creatures came from their light cell beginnings. Their varied forms came from where their light cells had begun solidification. The maturity of their form came from adaptation to their environment. The survival of every individual species came from the progressing soul light, always God-held and God controlled. The entirety of creature evolution came from the equations of light life. Man, until the brain became dominant, was of creature equational balancing, of pure evolution and of soul light existence. God held man's soul eternally.

The covering of man's evolving form was an automatic reaction of body equations needing to balance. First covering was mud. After rain, man's body temperature dropped. Earth's soil was warm in places and man automatically immersed himself in mud pools covering his body for warmth. Mud dried quickly leaving a thin coating of protection. Night temperature was cool and mud kept a body covered. Thin skinned creatures also covered themselves in mud. Much later when man overcharged the Earth's environment with artificial vibrations of manufacture, thin skinned creatures mud-bathed to protect their bodies from the puncturing of vibrations of radioactive charge.

Creature suffers hideously in man's artificial environment. Each increase in electrical, radioactive and nuclear charge, tortures the soul light of every living life form on Earth. Equations scream, wrench, convulse and lose life force, as man in total ignorance of light evolution violates the very Earth man needs for survival and the very soul man needs to be held by God.

As man travelled and experienced long periods of cold, clothing was the automatic progression of equations needing more warmth. The skin of creature was first clothing. Creature hunted creature for food only. The fur of creature was not eaten. Its thickness was the perfect covering for man at that time. Gradually man sought its warmth and began wearing it for protection.

Earth erupted massively as man developed. Earth's seasons arrived equationally. Ice covered Earth where cold was extreme. Earth dried and powdered where heat was extreme. Earth rotated in balance of its equations until further cooling was necessary. The planets shifted as equations demanded and God in total control of every vibration in universal existence, progressed in power and perfection.

The seas became of seasonal temperature with creatures adapting, procreating and beautifying. Light vibrated through every tiny formation. Translucent life forms glistened through Earth's waters. Man had not impured the seas at that time. The currents through the seas were of passivity, activated by eruptions only. As Earth heaved through the seas the exiting force of overheated equations expressed their temperature into water which immediately cooled their heat. Water bubbled, fizzed and steamed as equations were pacified. Temporary currents activated surrounding areas of eruption which automatically calmed as vibrations were overpowered by the seas volume of peaceful breathing.

Out and in breathed the seas. Out and in motioned the tides. Out and in equations responded to first equation at the centre of the Sun. Out and in every light vibrating body breathed in rhythm of life. In and out God breathed in surround of equating balance.

Man's development as a human being, a brain powered form, was gradual. Man's body aggressed from equations in constant charge. Each stage of man's muscular development caused more energy to be activated throughout man's form.

Energy accumulates within a containment when vibrations aggress continually, cannot exit their form, overheat, excrete, compress and solidify, to become either a complete formation such as the brain, or lubrication of an aggressed formation.

Lubricational energy is the layers of imbalanced non-equating vibrations which attach to each other in a meshing of activity that clings to tissue. Heat enables the vibrations to keep active. When cooled, their consistency tightens, to become a complex variation of frozen vibrations relating to their containment. They freeze their activity when detached from their holding. Their content is without light equational balancing.

Man's internal body functions aggressed automatically. Each formation had evolved exactly as whale in water, was of pure equations overheating, bursting, solidifying in balance of their containment and being controlled by God's invisible rays of pure light in surround. Every progressing life form evolved the same way. Every life form able to magnetise pure light vibrations still progresses equationally.

Man's evolution lost balance as the brain took control of the soul light. Until then, each body function was controlled by soul light equations active throughout man's form. Charge of light continually vibrated and every equation magnetised its purity.

An individual evolution became as the equations of its form dictated. Very slowly man's form became non-equating, of activity which did not equate vibrationally. Activity which energised without soul light control, automatically lost God's invisible surround, and deformed its containment.

Man became aggressive, over energised. Man ate more, vocalised more, muscularised and copulated more. Each acceleration of charge increased the size of man's brain. Eventually man slept, for energetic activity exhausts pure equations and they intern in motion causing a slowing of all vibrational activity magnetic to their charge. Man was first life form to sleep. Man was first life form to produce semen of energised quantity. Man was first to give birth to more than one child. Man was first to establish territory.

As man's body aggressed, the heart ruptured again and again, for its chamber of soul light protection could not contain the heat of energy. God's rays in surround retracted with each rupture, and when equations burst of their containment, God answered the rupture in aggressive cool charge and the heart was formed as it is now. Each rupture spread veins and arteries everywhere there was an excess of energised formation. Blood spurted everywhere, even through clean watery tissue of pure light cell activity. Man's form reddened.

The exterior of man's body held aura, the sheathing of coloured light vibrations seeking contact with the Sun. Man's skin had evolved translucent. Its composition was the cross-hatched activity of light equations, moist, active in light magnetic feeding, and layered thousands of times to balance around a form. The individual equations were of individual colours magnetised together. They were spherical, ray-protruding, aglow with light activity and of cells.

Light cells activate when in direct contact with pure light rays. God's invisible rays also cell produce. The exterior skin of every light vibrating life form is composed of trillions of light cells, created by vibrating coloured equations, that involve in first motion as they are touched by the Sun's rays. First equation automatically activates their activity which spherically breathes, spherically vibrates, and spherically forms every vibration. The number of light equations in a light cell depends on the rhythm of the formation they are attached to, for they vibrate a pattern which completes in activity every time their attachment breathes. The pure equation of breathing, out and in, creates a complete spherical formation of vibrations which are magnetic. One breath can contain many vibrations, all pure and automatically unifying into one singular light cell by magnetic attraction within the motion of breathing. Each cell is surrounded by God's rays as it forms. First cells were ray-dropped from the Sun. Skin cells are ray-formed by first equation's motioning through the Sun's raying. Their size is of equating rhythm to their containment.

The interior of man's body also cell-activates but without direct contact with the Sun's rays. God's hold on the soul light causes the formation of every cell in its containment. The aggressive charge inflicted on an internal body cell, deforms its purity, causing imbalance of vibrations which distort its roundness, detach it from unity of vibrations and destroys its capacity to stay balanced.

Energy cells are all without pure equations. They are formed from heated impure vibrations which excrete a mucous of energy, which spherically forms because of the dominant motioning of the entire evolution of the body. They deform as soon as other impure vibrations are of magnetic interest.

Not one energy cell has one pure equation within its composition. Light is totally pure in all of its vibrational activity. Energy of light is also pure in activity. Energy without pure light activity is impure. Its vibrations have divided beyond acceptance in motioning of first equation's purity, and become of non-equating rhythms. Impure energy cannot be controlled by God's responses because there is no equating activity. The aggression within impure energy is too overcharged ever to be allowed into the evolution of pure equations. God retracts at the touch of impure energy automatically.

Cells of impure energy within the human form destroy their containing formations unless pure cells of light are more active. Light cells are visible only on the exterior of man's form. They are invisible inside man's form for their activity vibrates of God's surrounding hold which makes them colourless. Energy cells of impurity are visible inside man's body, by being of the mucous of energy solidified, vibrating in unison with energised formations, and being very active in heated charge. Their dominance in the human form has come from the excessive manufacture of artificial vibrations electrical and radioactive.

Man was radiant in aura. His skin shone of light cell brilliance. His form was mostly naked and powerful in strength. As man covered himself his aura faded, for direct contact with the Sun's rays was prevented and equations used to pure contact with their prime force lost intensity of charge. Man's form weakened greatly as clothing became permanent. The more man wore, the more equations imbalanced in light activity. The temperature of man's body began to be controlled by heat and not light.

Every tiny nerve and gland had evolved as man became a human being. Every internal organ was functioning and man's appearance was beautiful. Man was a shiny soft-skinned muscular form with bright eyes and of colourful variations of hair and skin tones. Man was of light cell evolution.

Man ate of Earth's bounty. Creature ate of the same purity. Everything that grew then was edible. Nothing had poisoned. No evolving life form had poisoned either at that time. Food was a joyful experience for man and creature. Regular food experience began first spoken sound. Speaking enlarged the brain. Until man spoke, his intelligence came directly from soul light equations always resolving whatever imbalance man encountered.

Creature did not speak. Creature's brain was much smaller than man's and creature's soul light much greater, for it did not aggress as man's and God's holding rays did not retract. The emotions of creature were always dominant. Creature remained quiet, aware, intelligent beyond man's comprehension, peaceful, non-destructive to Earth and of perfect equating evolution until man became the dominant species and destroyed the balance of every equation on Earth.

Vocalisation of both man and creature was an equational reaction to whatever was visible. The mouth opened as the soul light emotioned and out gushed a quantity of vibrations of sounds. "AH" was first natural sound as the mouth released emotion. "EE" was also a natural sound as the mouth of a vocalising creature was stretched by being on the move and wind-generating. Other pure sounds vocalised by creatures on land were “SSS” a partly closed mouth with teeth expressing emotion, and “MMM” a closed mouth emotion. In water the same sounds evolved but were longer in resonance and the currents in water caused wavy equations often. Depending on how great the encounter, sound motioned out and in, in varying patterns and rhythm. God always answered. Sounds became recognizable to each individual by the pitch, clarity of charge, length of echo of charge and the intensity of volume a sound made. Creature answered creature and man answered man by the magnetic responses of one magnetic body to another. Man was vocal equationally until the brain was large enough to form sound without soul light activity.

To speak, force sound outwards from deliberate muscular action not related to the soul light, is of brain charge. Natural sound is of emotioning equations. Man spoke, when his brain had developed enough energised activity. The accumulation of energised charge enlarging the brain could not be contained without explosive reaction. The brain was evolving as an entity of power without God’s hold and a containment for all imbalanced vibrations magnetic to its charge.

First word spoken was AMA, where the mouth was opened deliberately, air pushed outwards, the mouth then closed automatically and because the air flow had been forced, the imbalance of vibrations gushing forth could not be released until the mouth opened again to allow the activity to exit completely. Muscles were activated solely by the brain needing to free its uncontainable charge of imbalanced vibrations. The brain had aggressed its entire vibrational composition which charge-burst outwards right through the head area. Every muscle surrounding the brain’s area of activity aggressed as a result. A loud sound was formed from an aggressive vibrational composition of imbalanced vibrations of force. Later on as man artificially electrified himself, the brain became violent, forcibly releasing its uncontainable charge.

AMA was spoken when man encountered anything of interest, another man, a creature or creatures, a conflict of decision-taking, an odd shape, man or creature giving birth, a confrontation not expected, or just an energised emotion from feeling satisfied.

AMA, SSAMA, AMAK, AMAT, AMEE, AMEEM and AMIT were all the original sounds of human language automatically expressed from the aggression of the brain as it forced vibrations out through the head. The more the brain aggressed the many more sounds evolved.

Man's language was of very few words initially. Early man behaved as creature. A vocabulary was not necessary. Several words were all that was needed. Language evolved gradually. Slowly man established territory where no creature was allowed and words came commanding attention and expressing authority over creature.

Territorial man developed from equations reacting to climate changes. A clothed body sought cover at night and during cold conditions. Clothing then was scant. Early man had lost most of his hair. His body was becoming energised. Energy vibrates erratic temperature. Aggression overheats the blood. Aggressive charge produces energy cells which constantly replicate in imbalanced charge. Man's body temperature became controlled by the quantity of heated charge he vibrated.

Trees had been shelter for all creatures in every temperature change on Earth, and as ape man progressed unto early man, trees were no longer enough covering for the human form. Man automatically sought rock openings for shelter. Man entered the many caves created by Earth's eruptions and became possessive of his covering. Caves were composed of pure equations vibrating of light activity and able to stimulate the light cells of early man.

Possession, the desire to keep unto oneself, was an automatic progression of the brain, which had accepted words as a dominant force over others, had been requited often with word dominance, and when establishing territory with word interjection, became possessive. Man wanted his entire surround for himself. Greed for one object had become possession of all. Shelter was for himself. No intruder was accepted. Shelter relieved man of discomfort. Covering was a singular satisfaction. The brain was de-activated when man sheltered in a cave. Activity of energised charge was overpowered by a surround of light activity. Man was rested, of feelings, of calmness and of peace. Man's possessive activity intensified.

It is the automatic progression of the energised pattern of impure vibrations accumulating in the brain to increase their charge. The more the brain experiences the more the brain desires. The more the brain sees through the eyes the more the brain feeds through its coil. The more the brain cannot magnetise the more the brain aggresses to possess. Brain possessiveness was the beginning of greed.

Territorial man began defending his area of cover from other intruders. When another human entered a cave already occupied he was shouted at with words of extreme aggression. When creature entered, man physically scared creature away. He gesticulated aggressively. The progression from words was the muscular exertion of the body, a more powerful aggressive charge. Man was first to charge at creature. Possession of territory caused man to become the dominant species. Man aggressed further in that development. Creature became subservient.

Cave man procreated faster than all other creatures on Earth. His form had become so aggressively charged his semen replicated unnaturally. The quantity of energised vibrations unable to cool caused a build-up of mucous which became explosive inside man's penis tubing. Muscular activity generated imbalance of the penis area. Man's penis often erected without provocation of a female. Semen accumulated at the muscular connection of the penis and rounded in a jellied formation as equations sought spherical motioning. Ejaculation was not possible without the lubricating balance of female. Female was not always near. The contained heated vibrations burst through their solidity to form two identical spherical shapes which eventually became the testicles. Until cave man evolved, the human form had a penis only. Testicles were formed by the energised bursting of equations overheating and seeking balance.

Cave man's form changed dramatically at that time for overheating caused equations to burst repeatedly. Man's entire shape altered with muscular tightening, bone stretching, and blood circulation. Sexual organs were still developing.

The female form also changed dramatically for the same aggression energised her and sexual activity increased. Female's menstruation began then as man entered woman to relieve himself of imbalancing equational discomfort. Female could not orgasm unless vibrating in unison with the male. Male also could not orgasm unless of the same vibrational activity. Both imbalanced. Both experienced genitalia progression. Female experienced menstruation, the impure vibrations of aggressive charge accumulating inside their containment, overheating, unreleased by magnetic attraction of equations and thickening into a blood clot. Early menstruation was of clotting only for the blood came from the lining of tissue which excreted of its equations as woman was aggressed sexually. Her lining split. Copulation was without equations of light balancing. As birth progressed also, child was born with testicle activity or with sensitivity to clotting. Later on as both sexes impured greatly, the testicles held mucous of energy constantly and the womb seeped blood monthly.

Cave man stopped growing as sleep became necessary. Cave man stopped obeying his soul light equations as the brain aggressed in charge. Cave man stopped procreating naturally as he sexed aggressively. Cave man lost equational balance. Each progression of energised charge inside man's body and brain overpowered pure equations of light evolution, and man eventually lost the answering vibrations of God's control to be held only by the pure equations of his soul light.

Growth of the human form ended when man slept through the night. At sleep, equations quietened. Light was no longer magnetised. The brain's coil lost charge by having no visual activity to magnetise. Because of its dominance over all energised activity the body also lost charge. The soul light however remained in perfect rhythm of breath control and at peace with God in surround of its pure equations. A growing form responded to the Sun's rays in upward lengthening equations. As man slept, the activity of growing ceased for equations rested. The change in behaviour caused the lengthening activity to be without charge while man slept and resume growing when man awoke. Previously man only rested at night, did not close his eyes and his growing equations stayed active. His soul light vibrated continually night and day, keeping all activity in balance until sleeping slowed all vibrations in charge and the soul light rested also. Much later in man's evolution, activity of soul light vibrations at rest night and day, were overpowered by artificial electric and radioactive charge and man's growth cycle imbalanced.

Evolving cave man lived several hundred years. Not until equations reached life cycle maturity did man procreate, for his soul light functioned every part of his body. Life cycle end happened when equations no longer magnetised life force from the Sun's rays. Man's form grew slowly and equationally as did every creature form on Earth. During form evolution God controlled every imbalance of equations by answering each overheating with cool containment. When the brain enlarged inside man's skull, unable to be equated, God's responses began diminishing. Each energy cell accumulating inside man's form evolved without God's controlling rays surrounding its formation. As man aggressed in brain and body, God withdrew the rays of cooling, and man was left an energising form of brain dominance also increasing in energy, with a soul light encased inside man's heart. Man's heart also energised aggressively.

The original light cells of man's form have almost all been eaten through, by radioactive vibrations so devouring, man has become explosive. Light cells within man's body have been extinguished in pure vibrational activity. Light cells outside man's body have also been extinguished by radioactive smothering.

Man aggressed without equational balance. His internal composition of progressing equations became energised, vibrating aggressively, imbalanced in rhythm and unable to evolve of light activity. The speed of vibrations entering cave man's form, split whole equations into many divisions and irregular patterns. Every light cell in man's body then, burst. Tiny detached fractions of equations vibrated in frenzy attempting magnetic attachment. Many were magnetised back unto each other deformed. Energy cells evolving prevented light cell unification everywhere. Pure equations had originally created each formation within man's form, and light cell activity surrounded each formation in aura sheathing activated by the soul light of first light cell evolution. Energy cells were from aggressed equations without God's cooling rays of balance.

Energy cells were accepted in cave man's form because the vibrations had once begun of pure equations. Tissue then was pure and able to admit aggressed vibrations without bursting. God's rays held tissue in cool surround. God's rays did not surround the aggressive charge of energy cells in activity, the charge was from brain dominance over the soul light. The human form accumulated energy cells everywhere as man's brain manipulated all movement previously functioned by soul light equations. Energy cells spread so rapidly God no longer cooled man's form and it became overheated.

The energy cells in growth and creature evolved from the stress of survival. Creature aggressed greatly as man hunted for fur for clothing, body parts for decoration and meat for food. Once hunted, creature became fearful. The pure calm equations of creature's soul light overheated again and again to cause all equations to react emotionally and aggressively. All creatures during their evolution inherited fear of man within soul light equational reaction. Time and time again equations alerted creature to hunters and eventually killers of creature life. Energy cells were the result.

Growth remained pure much longer, its equations untouched by aggression. Eventually man poisoned, aggressed, displaced light cell evolution in progress, and manually destroyed all of growth's pure equations, which became energising compositions struggling to continue of soul light eternal life.

The remaining light cells in man's form now are so destroying they cannot replicate any longer. They used to reproduce automatically as the Sun's rays fed man's form life force. Equations always excrete and always replicate. Motion is always spherical and automatically light cells form around and not inside their magnetic attachment. The moisture excretion of pure equations spherically motions into cell activity which remains unified unless overpowered by aggressive charge of energy also excreting and cell evolving. When too much energy surrounds light cells they explode. Their vibrations split, are force-inserted through an energised charge of aggressive activity which consumes them totally. The heat radiates their light fractions and they become an imbalanced pattern within a vibrating combination of energised activity. They are not put out of charge, for light cell fractions once radiated are extremely powerful and always attempt magnetic attraction wherever they are. This strong activity causes energising vibrations in cell formation to divide, attract each other, split when light fractions cannot unify with others of the same rhythm and often elongate, tail form. Sperm evolved that way and were drawn to light cells for unification.

Light cells are invisible to the human eye because no artificial covering can equate their purity. Their activity within energy cells can be seen by the excessive irregularity of shapes inside an energy cell and the patterns of rhythm their integration causes. Radiated light cell fractions can never spherically form in an energised surround for God's hold is absolutely necessary to cool their temperature. Soul light vibrations are also needed to spherically motion their activity magnetically.

The interior and exterior of cave man's form was full of light cells. Energy cells evolving were few in comparison. As they increased, the brain, which was their creator, automatically activated their charge. All vibrations, no matter what their compositional factors, are magnetic to a source, one which has either bred them, or their fragments of rhythm.

An energy cell bred from the aggression of brain charge is solely magnetic to the brain. It is activated aggressively at every spurting of charge magnetised into the brain's coil. The coil transmits current activity straight through the cell immediately it is received and man's entire energy content, pure and impure, is stimulated, accelerated in charge. The brain's coil transmits because if it did not it would explode. Any vibrating containment when overheating must release its charge. Without God's controlling rays for cooling, contained activity over-generates, shudders in imbalance, tremors in threat and bursts of its force to enter any recipient of magnetic attraction. Energy cells accepted the spurting vibrations of the brain every time the coil activated. As the brain enlarged from the build-up of mucous of energy, cells increased in energised activity. Cave man became violent.

The bodily functions of cave man also aggressed. As creature, the discharge of too much solidity and too much moisture had been of equational balancing. As ape man, the evolving bowels discharged compressed food packing and urine, the excess excretion of heating equations, passed through channels of the body to exit through an opening of balance. Depending on what form had evolved and where, urinal activity when released, cooled a body, which with muscular activity heated again. The passing of urine became an automatic temperature cooler, until in cave man, it became the release of aggressive charge of energised equations excreting. The liquid of food in-taken did not enter urine until man became carnivorous.

Bowel discharge had always been of equational balancing. Cave man's energising body caused excess eating habits. Automatically cave man released tight food packing by the regular passing of excrement. Equations had discharged solidity from the evolution of first life forms and the process had simply aggressed.

Earth at the time of cave man had a balanced climate. As Earth rotated and life form evolution adapted to the seasons, the life cycle of growth changed dramatically. Previously equations reproduced their images after very long periods of growing, the life cycle maturity of a formation. Seasonal adaptation caused equations to shorten their life cycle span.

Time, the motioning of the breathing of God the containing universal whole, had aged equations, while the Sun's rays had activated their compositions. As some areas of Earth became ice-covered and others dried, the life cycle of all growth shortened automatically. Regular changes of temperature caused regular equational adjustment. A light celled tree formation began reproduction in the middle of the coldest part of a season for its equations reverse-motioned from too much coldness. The process took until the warmth, when first motioning began again from the central core of the formation. First motioning began image reproduction automatically. Warmth caused equations to re-activate their original formation. In reverse-motion they backward-motioned the entire vibrational composition of their form to touch their first motion, precisely at the time of Earth's warm season. The form was vibrated again from start to finish. As the temperature rose, equations heated, were cooled by God's rays, replicated, solidified, then at peak of heating burst of their containments and shed seeds.

Previously, the seasons did not exist, for Earth was still cooling and growth was beginning evolution. Life cycle maturity took hundreds of years to reproduce an image. With seasonal encouragement a formation became reproductive regularly and in equational balancing.

Time is of God's control. The surround of God breathes from its distance. The inward motioning outward paths as soon as it reaches its central beginning. The universe is of spherical motioning and from any point within that motioning, forward pathing is natural.

The inward breathing of God presses upon every light formation the invisible force of pure light vibrations. A body is force-fielded, surrounded by pressure from God. The body remains suspended by spherical compression of light vibrations. Inward breathing by God is more powerful than outward breathing. Because the inward motioning begins uninterrupted, the power and pressure it generates keeps all light bodies suspended within its surround. As it approaches a body, the motioning surrounds that body and continues inward until all bodies are surrounded. On reaching the Sun, the central core of light evolution, God's breathing automatically outward paths. Once again light bodies disturb its pathing, are surrounded yet again, until the motioning reaches purity of pathing where vibrations are all powerful, totally untouched, and of prime force of invisible light vibrations, the supreme equating control of the universe, God. God's rays project inward from their containing surround straight through the motioning of breathing. Their pathing is not affected by the breathing in any way. Their evolution was after first equation and is of equating projecting balance.

It must be said here that were God not in surround, alive, and breathing, every sphere would be without suspension. Pressure of inward and outward spherical motioning holds every light body in the universe in place. It must also be said that the very same pressure surrounding every existing life form on Earth prevents each formation from detachment. The pressure holds a body in space eternally.

God equates every rhythm of breathing from the most minute evolution to the largest in existence. Breath control is an automatic response to a light body formation. As first motion is expressed from any form, before it returns to its start, God responds in exactly the same vibration.

There are trillions of varied breathing rhythms, all of equating beats according to the size and containment of equations. God in surround holds each tempo. The varying patterns of breathing light bodies cause pure electric currents of light charge, which involve with each other as they make contact to become power of pure atomic charge, an impenetrable force of pure vibrations perfectly balanced and breathing life force into every equation in evolution. The tempo of atomic power is so dense in vibrations nothing except pure ray-penetration can enter its force. Never has pure atomic power been imbalanced. Never can it be. It is the power which breathes light equations in spherical activation of eternal life. Breathing equations exist only because God responds.

When the universe accepted atomic power, all life forms adapted. Prior to atomic power of pure equating breathing rhythms combined, electric pulsing was dominant in light cell evolution. Aggressive radioactive charge did not enter the purity of light cells until the brain evolved. Its imbalance became of magnetic interest to the brain and every energy cell of impure charge of vibrations.

Atomic purity of charge automatically vibrated through every light body by way of increased beating of tempos, increased echo of beats and increased energised equations. The surrounding pressure of atomic power around some light bodies, whatever their size, created heart-gushing of blood in circulation which caused clots of artery malfunction. The increasing pressure of atomic power caused many life forms to explode. Atomic power was automatically accepted within a light body because of its purity of vibrations. What did explode a formation was its incapacity to contain a charge far too powerful for its size. Life forms were force-blown outwards into trillions of separated equations which eventually found magnetic attachment. Life forms able to contain atomic power pulsing evolved of cells which vibrated atomic charge.

When a light-celled body exploded, the impact was vibrated through God's holding rays and immediately equated by return impact. The body fragments were forced backwards to re-unite into formation again. Not all fragments magnetised together for they often entered other formations and were held there by magnetic attraction. Those that did not unify formed shapes of solidity unable to procreate or exist as life forms. They became sediment, a replicating thickness of imbalanced exploded equations, alive, breathing and progressing.

Cave man was atomically charged. Cave man automatically became violent as soon as speaking became shouting and aggressive gesticulation became constant. Creature was first to be hurt.

In aggressive charge, cave man hit out at intruding creature, registered the immediate withdrawal of creature and thereafter began violent attacks upon a docile animal never before abused. The brain shook with first violence and aggressed even more. Eventually cave man killed.

God's responses to cave man were always of soul light equating control. Cave man's brain had been left to evolve of its vibrational aggression. As the brain's coil enlarged and began overpowering soul light emotions, God's responses became aggressively charged, acknowledging the echoing activity of the brain vibrating at the soul light.

The soul light was and still is impenetrable. Never can it admit imbalance of aggressive charge from the brain. Its evolution is of pure equations. Its father is God. Any charge entering any human form that is not of pure equations is automatically rejected. Cave man's violent behaviour was rejected instantly. The impact of imbalanced vibrations on the soul light caused echo, the return of charge. God responded in echo aggressive charge because the soul light held by God, transmitted its impacting vibrations as they were refused. Violent impacting vibrations returned to the brain and their force caused cave man to kill.

Killing, the deliberate taking of life, cannot be contained in soul light equations. Equations, as long as they have evolved from the purity of light vibrations are all of eternal life. Their motioning must not be stopped, for once it is, life of soul existence ends, the soul cannot be magnetised by God's rays.

Killing that is deliberate, cuts off God's rays of protection immediately it takes place. God withdraws as a body is violated.

The imbalance of charge from a killer's brain, which motivates killing, is unable to be equated. God cannot return to the soul light once its life line is severed, for the containment that has held it has been destroyed. God cannot magnetise it either because its equations have not reached life cycle end. It is left to be overpowered by aggressive vibrational activity.

Without the Sun's rays of life force and God's controlling balance, the soul light vibrates for a short time only before it is devoured radioactively. The soul light suffers. It attempts to attract light sustenance. It overheats from severe emotional strain. It burns of its equations. It excretes of its agony. It is tortured. It cannot be cooled in any way. Its surround now, is hot dry radioactive activity becoming of nuclear ferment. It is helled. It feels that hell. It cannot ever be free from that hell. It is condemned to eternal suffering. All deliberate killings of man and creature condemn a soul light to the burning of light equations unable to cease vibrationally.

First killing by cave man was first conscience.

# The Conscience

Conscience is of soul light pressure. The equational composition of the soul light always vibrates response to any outer imbalance. God receives those vibrations and immediately returns the charge. When the soul light receives God's response invisibly, if the equations are of balance the reaction to them is calm, if those equations are disturbed and imbalanced, the reaction is of stress.

Any killing causes the soul light severe imbalance, any brutality, ugly defilement, deliberate cruelty, deliberate lie or pretence, and any violation to God, Earth, creature and mankind himself. The soul light evolved of pure equating vibrations in total harmony to all of light existence. It vibrates to keep that purity balanced. Its attachment to God assures it life eternal, life of light equations and life of pure light ecstasy. Unless the soul light explodes, it has life of divine sanctuary. When its evolutionary progression is interfered with, it pressures its containment. This results in conscience, reactive stressed equations unable to balance, motioning back and forth through God's rays, heating and being cooled, unrequited in that contact and eventually affecting the entire nervous system of the human form. Stress is unrequited equations.

The brain always denies conscience for its radioactive powering refuses soul light release through its coil function. Radioactive vibrations inside man's head now, can only magnetise their likenesses and cannot accept pure equational activity. What can release stressed soul light vibrations is crying, sobbing, another of soul light reaction, a beautiful sight, touch, or comforting, a truth which releases a lie, deceit, or cruelty, and a pure response from another wanting to give of the soul light itself. Unless this is done, a soul light remains tortured. If that torture is uncontainable, suicide, murder, violent disfigurement, or madness and insanity, are inevitable.

Shock to soul light equations destabilises them. All that is of peace, harmony, beauty, love and caring has been of soul light evolution. All that is of light life is still of soul light magnetic attraction. All that is of universal harmony is still of soul light profound equational security. Never until man brain powered was the soul light violated. God's holding rays kept the soul light's evolution divine unto eternal life of the soul. Conscience, until it was denied, was the salvation of the soul.

Creature was always soul light progressed. Never did creature violate Earth. The equations of light always accept soul light existence in absolute balance and peaceful activity. They have evolved together. They cannot ever violate each other. Not until man's brain overpowered soul light equations was Earth violated. When that happened conscience ceased inside man.

It must be said here that modern man has evolved without conscience for the purity of the Earth he so violates, the purity of the creatures and growth he also violates and the sacred purity of the soul light he violates unto death of the soul. Were that not so, Earth would be yielding of its bounty, growth would be flourishing of its perfect beauty, creature would be greatly beneficial to Earth's life, and conscience in man's soul light would be the reason for the sanctuary of the soul assured. God would never be replaced by money, greed, power, war, or killing of any kind. A soul light in conscience is a being in full reality of existence.

God, as a light reactor, an equator of vibrational balancing and the container of all that vibrates of light life, has no equal. No power can be greater. No light can be extinguished. No life of light can be destroyed unless God releases that life.

A killer of anything living has conscience until the killing is over. A creature killing for food also has momentary conscience as the kill is activated. The act of conscience comes from the peaceful vibrations of the soul light as its equations alert to aggressive charge in action. Creature hungry, alerts its soul light immediately food is found. The equations already experienced in the killing for food, freeze. They erect stiffly and hold creature strongly before attack. God receives those vibrations, immediately returns their charge and because their patterning is a repetitive charge which satisfies creature once eating, the return charge from God releases creature from freeze-hold and a killing for food takes place. Conscience is released by God in equating resolution to vibrations only able to be cooled by eating the body of another creature. God has accepted killing for food as the balance for creature survival.

Man the killer, behaves very differently. Because of man's brain, a killing will take place without conscience or with conscience deliberately denied. For man to access the soul light equations, his vibrations must be balanced, of peaceful activity. The human form now is so radioactively charged everywhere, soul light response reactions are limited and, in some forms, depleted. Man has surrounded the soul light encased in the heart, with energised solidity, blood, and water of impurities. No soul light vibrates in balance with its form. No conscience is activated when an outer surround vibrates huge aggressive charge which is not controlled by God's cooling responses. A human body, pumping unnatural heart rhythm, expanding unnaturally by forced aggression, hyped by unnatural chemical impurities, force-fed with electrified and radioactive unnatural vibrations and grossly overcharging daily and nightly, has no activity of soul light equations to keep that body unto God, conscience, safety, equational evolution, and unto life of light eternity. The body of self-indulgence has destroyed all equations of pure life giving and light magnetic attachment. The body lives within its own brain power oblivious to the soul light it evolved from. Brain occupancy in man now is almost total.

It must be said here that man with no conscience is man the killer of all that exists in reality.

Cave man answered soul light conscience. Cave man evolved peacefully on Earth for thousands of years. Aggressive charge in cave man's body developed slowly and without interference from any other species. Cave man's response to creature became dominating when habitat was experienced as possession of area. The brain in cave man experienced possession as an activity of fixed interest which aggressed the contained vibrations of the coil, and did not release them until cave man exited his cave. Outside the cave other muscular activity occurred and the brain's magnetic interest was diverted. At that time the soul light of cave man was still the controlling power of the body in evolution. Its magnetic light equations led cave man through every encounter, every learning, every resolution of a complex situation and every experience upon the Earth. When cave man first killed he conscienced deeply. As killing increased, cave man's conscience destroyed.

Conscience answered, allows release of stressed equations, because God's invisible response cools vibrational imbalance immediately those vibrations are accepted by the soul light. When they are not, the soul light repeats the charge again and again, until either God responds aggressively to control the charge, or leaves the vibrations to echo-vibrate until they are absorbed within the body's own aggressed activity. For God to aggress the response, the accumulation of unrequited equations flowing through God's invisible rays and not returned, causes charge-blockage, a quantity of vibrations not able to be returned because of their imbalance. As soon as they reach maximum activity, God overpowers their force and supercharges the rays which are holding their activity. A forced return of imbalanced vibrations spurts the heart, crashes into the soul light de-stabilising its rhythm of equating motion, activates every aggressive vibration within the body and causes the brain to experience a flood of charge through its coil. The shock to the brain can cause a violent outburst because it must be released. Usually the soul light excretes so extremely, crying eventuates, and a brain outburst is prevented.

Echo of imbalanced vibrations relayed through God's invisible rays happens when the charge received is of minor imbalance. The unstable vibrations cannot be returned in cooling response and are ray-echoed several times, do not penetrate the soul light because they are impure and are consumed as they weaken in echoing by vibrational envelopment of charge. They involve with other free flowing vibrations which the soul light activates. Soul light vibrations are constantly active inside the heart because every body equation is fed by their pattering. The soul light only rests of its activity during a body's sleeping.

Stressed equations cause heart disease. Stressed equations cause fatigue, anorexia, hyperactivity, insomnia, overindulgence of many different habits, mood swings and the desire to take drugs and alcohol excessively. The brain if not released of aggressive charge, magnetically associates with a greater quantity of aggressive vibrations to keep activating. Unreleased vibrations have encouraged brain search for aggression. Once addicted to a satisfying charge of vibrations, the brain, alone, without any conscience, powers its addiction over every method of prevention to stop it. God has no control whatsoever when radioactive maximum brain charging seeks to feed vibrationally.

To answer the conscience is to acknowledge truth, reality of life, the total reality of all of existence, the sacred evolution of the soul and God as the equator of the entire universe. That is impossible inside man's brain at this time. Truth always denies the brain its patterning, for it halts any question of its presence. Truth itself freezes the brain's activity because it is always of soul light expression. Reality of life can never be acceptable to the brain because the soul must exist over the brain's powering for any reality to be wanted. Total reality of all that exists, once again denies the brain, which is the sole motivator of life's progressions at this time in evolution. The sacred evolution of the soul can never be acknowledged by the brain because if it were, the brain would be put out of radioactive charge immediately the soul light activates dominantly. God as the universal equator can never be allowed by the brain's powering, because God would automatically be the overriding presence of power with the conscience the activity preferred. Inside man's brain at this time, all of great soul has been destroyed.

Would it not be prudent of man to seek solution to man's stressful existence, an existence without soul identity, a credible God and the protection of the Earth which man must save in order to save himself?

# The Brain

The brain, the human brain, has become an entity of radioactive power, an ugly evolution, a very destructive force. Creature's brain is still dominated by creature's soul light except where the consumption of blood has caused huge aggressive charge unable to be controlled by God's rays of response and cooling.

Evolution, the progression of pure equations, continues throughout the universe by God's equating responses. The purity of universal evolution remains pure because God controls the balance. Evolution of pure equations on Earth has ceased. Man's brain power is the cause.

God's equating responses to Earth's horrific suffering have nuclearised, aggressed to the same vibrational force the Earth is vibrating. Earth is held from explosion by God's firm ray-penetration. However, Earth is heating so dangerously now that God must automatically withdraw those rays to allow the release of charge, explosive contained force. Man in his soul must prevent this from happening. Man in his brain will allow this to happen.

The evolution of man's brain in a radioactive body formation will eventually automatically explode. Nothing is more certain in man's future. Nothing is more obvious at this time. Nothing can be done to prevent this from happening unless man activates his soul. Reality is all that is needed. Truth which is wanted more than gold, wealth, throne, government, war, power, religion and greed. Truth which separates lies, hearsay, pretence and fantasy, from reality. Truth which strips man of false life. Truth which places the soul of man with man's God and with man's conscience. Truth which exposes all that is of evil. Truth which brings man unto his Earth's needs before his own. Truth which brings man unto the soul of creature. Truth which brings man unto his knees in contrition. Truth which perpetuates reality forever. Truth before all else.

The evolution of the brain began with trapped equations becoming massively aggressed. A skull was formed surrounding the brain by the outer coolness of water. Lizard's brain evolved both in and out of water. Lizard's equations suffered severe shock as the tiny brain experienced vibrations from the Sun and water repetitively. On land as lizard became ape then ape man, the brain enlarged from constant aggressive activity. It coiled in shape because of its entrapment. It burst early in its evolution to become two identical shapes pressed into each other by the forming skull being too small to contain its expansion of compressed aggressive charge. By the time cave man evolved, the brain had grown of its mucous of energy and the skull had swelled equationally. As cave man became territorial and creature the intruder, the brain had become dominant, overpowering the soul light. From shouting to hitting out and eventually killing creature, cave man had aggressed his brain so consistently its enlarging coil spurted excretion through the nose channel. Cave man's nose had evolved from bursting equations inside lizard's head caused by eating habits. The nose was the last facial feature to evolve in primates.

Smell came after creature had tasted. Magnetic attraction to smell was the automatic reaction of equations inside the nasal cavity alerting to an odour which had form-association, thereby identifying its containment. The brain energised muscles in the nose area to suction odour through the nostrils in order to inhale maximum impact of scented charge. Cave man inhaled aggressively through the nasal passage. Cave man's brain had aggressed the entire head and all vibrational activity from then on was energised.

Sight became aggressively charged also as cave man became cautious, careful, fixated when of conscience, watchful, and constantly alert. Movement was very highly charged as cave man gesticulated, chased, hit out, yelled, ran, climbed and killed to protect his possessions. Automatically the brain dominated the peaceful soul light vibrations.

Smelling, imbalanced the head, which changed shape. A rounded head shape had evolved in early cave man from the evolutionary stages of lizard, cave man's early ancestor. After three different stages of evolution equations automatically returned to spherical motioning. The shape of cave man's skull slowly swelled and imbalanced. The brain needed a firm containment. Eventually the weight of the enlarging brain caused an oval head shape and present-day man is yet another progression of the growing brain.

Mucous of energy trapped inside bone for eons of time becomes an entity, a powerful controlling force. When programmed, force-fed vibrational imagery and activity, it holds field, controlling the containing body of its charge. Before killing overpowered soul light equations, cave man responded solely to the soul light in conscience. A kill was so highly charged God withdrew the cooling rays of response and left the soul light in suffering until cave man responded in conscience. The loss of God's rays caused memory to evolve.

Memory is a learning, re-activated inside the coil's pockets of vibrational storage. First the brain receives charge. Second the charge is deciphered by being of visual impact, sound impact, aggressive impact, or content only of vibrations. Each singular charge travels into the brain according to the force of its vibrations. The repetition of charge causes a swelling which excretes in one particular place. One brained experience in one place countless times causes that area to become of memory association, tissue which responds to its charge formation whenever an association is activated. Activation needs only connection to a source, or reminder of the source. Reminding is of association which automatically begins vibrating its charged area as soon as it is accessed. Access to a particular area of memory holding is by stimulation, a deliberate probing into the brain's coil by radioactive channelling.

The brain has powered so hugely in electrical and radioactive vibrations it automatically activates any source of memory it needs. The channels of circuiting have been made by repetition of charge, continuous insertion and very aggressive probing. The probing of the brain is when a memory is wanted and a deliberate magnetic suctioning takes place from the eye muscles through the brain's channels of vibrating tissue straight to the contained experience of memory recall. Once accessed the stored vibrational experience is magnetised to express the charge of its experience all over again. The release immediately gives the prober the information needed and the area remains docile until activated again.

Words are the most aggressive charge the brain holds, for they are ceaseless in activity, and ceaseless in being probed for. The area of speech-holding within the coil has the largest radioactivity and the most seeping mucous. Too much speech probing often causes migraine, for the central core of speech containment overheats violently and cannot cool unless put down in charge.

Memory first began after God's rays withdrew from the soul light of killer cave man. No response was possible. Cave man was left with an experience that could not be released, was stored inside the head, was refused by the soul light, could not cool of charge and spat of its contained vibrations in one area of the brain to be recalled when a second killing took place. The mucous of energy held that aggression because there was no exit for its charge. The second killing entered the brain's coil exactly as the first and immediately found its likeness. Gradually memory of the kill automatically began function as probing for the experience activated the charge. Cave man probed his brain himself, to find the pattern of killing vibrations to activate another killing. God's consciencing responses had been withdrawn. Memory had begun. From then on cave man's aggressions were memory activated.

Eons of evolution created a human. The entire metabolic function of man evolved from various equational imbalances. Not one feature came into function unless equations heated and burst. At that time God still held the soul light. Man still had conscience. Man was still peaceful. Man, despite killing creature, despite denying his conscience at that killing, was able to access conscience whenever Earth's greatness was acknowledged. Man became a being of wonder, amazement, awe, great appreciation, great emotions and great respect for the Earth he knew was of God's light. Man evolved with soul light intelligence far, far superior to the evolving brain. Man did not violate the Earth until his brain power greeded food.

Radioactive vibrations in the environment before cave man became human, were from early pure equations imbalancing in charge. The brain magnetised them hungrily. Their aggression was the attraction. Into the coil they were drawn and their trapped heat enlarged the coil of evolving mucous. Automatically their contained activity, unable to be released without an act of aggression, became of reactive procedure, a composition which developed intelligence unrelated to the soul light.

The brain's coil developed electrical back-charging, a return spurt of energy when an inward thrust of vibrations came from an outer source. It automatically spat back the charge it received. The skull prevented the charge from travelling. Trapped, all energised vibrations excreted, solidified, unified and integrated into radioactive solidification, and in that unification the brain entitised. Trapped also were compositions of vibrations which identified every visual experience as well as every identity of form.

Repetition of compositional imagery contained, created brain intelligence, the ability to recognise an object, a being, a formation, a scene and a construction. Ape man was soul intelligent. Cave man was not. Cave man's brain had enlarged. Ape man's was small in comparison.

The voice, of forced vibrations, echoed powerfully inside the brain. It resonated because of its containment. The vibratory echoing caused the brain to bleed, develop a bloody seepage entwined in mucous. Constant echo inside the head affected even the shape of the developing skull formation. Equations surrounding the brain blooded greatly, overheated, excreted constantly and were cooled by God's invisible rays of response. Their blooding found entry in trickles of red charge, into the brain itself. Blood could not flow through the brain because the mucous was so active in aggressive charge it prevented blood flow of any quantity. The trickling was all the brain could accept, for constant entry of aggressive vibrations cut off each trickle, and diverted the blood to where it could vibrate without severing its pathing. Much later blood activity increased, thickened, spread throughout the brain and eventually clotted. Too much activity was being magnetised. Clotting still occurs and is increasing, for the brain is constantly over-charging. Its blood supply needs to move smoothly or coagulate in places of disruption.

Creature also aggressed of the brain, but very little blood found its way into mucous. As creature vocalised, the head blooded equationally. Creature held soul light intelligence and did not activate of brain programming until man forced programmes of disciplined activity into creature's brain and unto creature's purity of soul light existence. Man has violated every creature on Earth, every purity of growth, every strength of life force, and in many cases, soul sanctity. Man has done this in man's brain.

At this time the human brain is the sole activator of all man's deeds. Programming of the brain now has caused knowledge without truth, knowledge without conscience, and knowledge without God. So aggressed is the brain's patterning now, all by itself it manipulates the form it lives from. So helpless is man to prevent its activity, not even God's responding rays can cool the agony of the soul light still inside man's heart. The brain activates the entire body function, activates the entire vocabulary of man and controls man's every interest in living.

The human brain must feed. Its food now is radioactive manufactured vibrations. The more it magnetises the more it seeks. Its mucous is alive. It lives of the superficial power of mankind. It is ceaseless in radioactive hunger and survives because that power is increasing. It is the sole cause of the destruction of everything. It cannot purify, cannot conscience, cannot accept the purity of light equations, cannot magnetise God's rays of life force and never will submit to this truth here. Unless man can access his soul all that is here will be denied, defiled and destroyed. It is a reality mankind must face.

Brain programming began as man spoke, wrote and read. Words uttered were repetitious and had behavioural responses which became a programme, a demonstrative vibrating pattern, one which was repeated often. Man recognised the patterns by vibrating compositions. All language is of forced aggressive vibrations. The more man spoke, wrote and read man's writings the more the brain was programmed.

Sexing became an indulgent programme of the brain. The act of copulation and the orgasm copulation provoked, entered the brain's experiences repetitively and became addicted to. The release of orgasmic mucous was the discharge of overheated equations returning to their vibratory balance. This release freed the aggressive charge of vibrations and also freed the brain's intense occupation with aggression which had entered its programming. Once the orgasm was over, passivity of vibrations was felt in the soul light. The brain could not activate another orgasm while the soul light cooled with God's rays responding. The temperature of the brain however remained hot. The act of copulation was memorised, and unless the soul light rejected the orgasm, copulation began again, until from too much energising of muscle formation a copulater became exhausted. The brain had accepted a full aggressive charge of vibrations which spurted into its mucoused formation causing euphoric vibrational experience, a heated stimulation of aggressed vibrations in containment. Once experienced, the brain became addicted, for the charge was so heated the entire coil orgasmed inside itself.

Cave man copulated continually from too much energised activity within cave man's form. Ape man did not. Ape man was controlled by equations of the soul light which activated when female attraction was felt and responded to. Cave man was controlled by the hungry brain, activating in response to too much energised vibrating cells which needed release of charge. Cave man did not need female to orgasm with as did ape man. Female always needed cave man for orgasmic release and sought cave man when contact was imperative. Sexing without the soul light involved vibrationally, became brain manipulation, a memorised program of aggressive charge activated.

The brain now in every human form becomes addicted to every source of energy it experiences and can feed from. Each experience elates its charge of vibrations and the source of that elation is hungered for. Sex of every kind has become an addiction of the brain. It is the function of the orgasm that causes the addiction. The spurting of charge is red hot. The mucous flushes in temperature and vibrational acceleration. Contained, that charging magnetises itself into area of orgasmic functioning, a clump of vibrations, alive in radioactivity, needing sustenance and magnetic to a source.

Creature evolved sexing with a variety of forms. Always there was soul light magnetic attraction, until, from man's pursuit of creature's totality and terrain, the cells of light charge aggressed violently. Creature could not rest, could not sleep purely, could not find shelter of balance, could not eat healthily and could not mate purely. Creature could not escape man and could not attach to God for eternal life. Man's pursuit of creature cut off creature's lifeline. Many creatures, from too much heated charge, sexed with same sex forms. Their agony of equations unrequited was the cause and still is.

Man's skin tissue poisoned at this time. Tissue in both man and creature overheated from vibrations of radioactive charging. Tissue had evolved of perfect equations of light evolution. Tissue was of layers of those equations heating, excreting and solidifying. Over time tissue accepted energy cells pure and impure. It did not begin with impurity of energised charging.

Man's analysis of the human form has created a disease-prone body without any purification possible, a form which is artificially primed and artificially functioning, a form of hideous deformities. At this time in man's evolution the human form has become a radioactive containment of vibrations without God's responses to purify and balance form evolution. Man is of diseases which are incurable because they are not understood and are therefore untreatable. Every disease without exception is of vibrational impurity of charge. Unless purity of light vibrations is accessed, man's evolution is over.

Brain programming has continued for thousands of years. Those years have evolved a coil which has become explosive. Radioactive vibrations have gradually bloated the brain and in that bloating a human being suffers. All diseases of the brain are caused by too much aggressive charge of vibrations spurting into the coil, often de-circuiting its patterning, and very often exploding minute cells of energised patterns which leak into its coiling.

The brain functions electrically, radioactively and more recently nuclearly, magnetising nuclear charge of vibrations from the environment. That truth needs to be fully realised, and not denied, for the reality of such a future in the evolution of a species is explosion of contained vibrations unable to purify and cool of their charging.

The massive manufacture of electrical, radioactive and now nuclear charged machinery has caused environmental pollution of vibrations man himself is suffocating from, being denied clean air, clean water and more importantly light equations. Not only is the environment of man destroying of its necessary balance, the interior of man's form is also deforming hugely. Every increase in artificial vibrations increases the aggressive charge of every living cell inside man's form. Man cannot have life much longer; radioactivity is consuming everything.

The telephone and the radio first began brain addiction to inserted charge of electric vibrations. As their use became frequent the brain became addicted and man's soul light faded of its charge of pure equating vibrations.

The cinema was next to addict man's brain. The size of the screen's charge of vibrations into the head and the flashing of the electrified composition of images vibrated violent patterning. Man absorbed every tiny vibration singularly and by forced entry, absorbed every powerful burst of charge. The brain enlarged.

Television and amplified sound followed and the addiction of the brain from highly powered vibrations of total magnetic attraction absolutely destroyed man's access to his conscience, a required necessity of truthful emotions. Man's fixation to a television screen blocked even the heart from pure equational breathing. Flash after flash of obscene, violent, cruel, unrealistic, untruthful programming entered the brain's coil and perverted man's existence totally. So horrific was the programming from the cinema and television, man became a victim of his own entertainment values and a killer of his soul. The contained soul light inside the heart retracted of its pure equations and reddened. God's rays automatically withdrew from many soul lights left to suffer irrevocably. Too much superficial programming into the brain was being eaten.

Computers were next to violate the form of man, for never was there a more savage machine to addict the brain and explode the soul light. Radioactive vibrations punctured the entire form of man, eating into tissue and cells and causing man to become totally immune to any reality. Brain entitising began there, for the quantity of charge required a subservient body, to enter, establish vibrational area of charge and grow. The brain as an entity now, can and will, if not controlled, cause the extinction of mankind and the explosion of the Earth. Too much power is being sucked into the human brain and eventually must explode its containment.

Cell phones, computers, tablet computers and all other communication devices are powered radioactive charges which pierce the head entirely, and which will inevitably destroy the brain's present circuiting. Even the ever-unsatisfied brain cannot magnetise the charge in the quantity it is being forced to receive or the frequency of that charge incoming for much longer. The skull echoes vibrations of powering which re-enter the brain's coil and disrupt the brain's present patterning. The coil cannot function in format of its patterns.

Every touched and hand-held machine vibrates excess energy in charge of vibrations which the human form magnetises. Every environment of working machinery vibrating an aggressed energised charge which saturates a work place, is magnetised by both brain and body. Every power station nuclear and non-nuclear, charges its environment inwardly and outwardly with electrical, radioactive and nuclear vibrations of magnetic attraction to man. Every wiring inside and outside constructions does the same damage. Every single invention of mankind in every situation, where electric, radioactive and nuclear vibrations are alive in the environment, is destructive to the Earth and its growth, creature and creature's evolving form, and man himself, once again the victim of his brain's greed for power without control.

Greed is not understood. Greed which is eating every purity on Earth. Greed which is a terminal disease in mankind. Greed which cannot be stopped unless the soul is accessed. Greed, the ever-increasing activity of energised vibrations alive inside the brain of man, insatiable for food of power and unable to be controlled.

Programming of the brain has come about by charges of vibrations entering the coil and simply vibrating aggressively unable to stop. Once of active charge those vibrations are ceaseless. Once of hunger, those vibrations must feed. Once feeding they increase in charge and unless the brain is overpowered by the soul, the consuming of all things will take place.

The visual absorption of any electrical or radioactive generated screen, programmes those images in patterning straight through the eyes and into the coil of red-hot living vibrations. Each image has content of charge. Many are repeated. Many are of violence. Many are of killing. All are highly charged in power. Each individual image is processed by the brain as it is magnetised. The higher the charge the greater the euphoria in the brain. In some cases images of violence, sex, murder, rape and criminal activity as well as other types of imagery, can be re-enacted by a body of brain control. The human brain will activate the same image in recall when a form is increasing in aggression and spurts of its coil as that image is accessed. The helpless form that contains that activity aggresses and can re-enact the violence of the image it has absorbed. The human brain has victimised its human body because of its greed for food.

Image programming unto man now has affected the entire existence of man, woman and child. The conscience, which caused values of strong purity of soul, is over. The constant absorption of images which are almost all of unreal situations and gross exaggerations, is causing man to accept what he absorbs as part of the normality of living, to become immune to reality, to deny what man knows is wrong, and continue without a conscience answered.

Child of man now begins as a form of total aggressively charged vibrations unable to cool. Too much radioactivity is entering child's body and brain. From birth, and even before the foetus is formed, child's light cells have been violated. As a foetus, the formation of child is usually entered by a radioactive charge and hyped. At birth, child enters an electrical and radioactively charging environment. At the growing period of child, every vibrating apparatus and machine has been experienced vibrationally by the form of child. Television often becomes child's major enjoyment even before child talks. All is absorbed and enters child's brain. At early learning, child faces computerised programming, and its brain by then is addicted to aggressive charging. Puberty violates child's body detrimentally, for sex education has already entered child's brain by visual imagery and visual active searching. Girl and boy sex frequently. Girl and boy sex with artificial protection and stimulants. Girl and boy experience sex of huge aggression. Girl and boy do not ever access their souls. Girl and boy become hyped, over charged in vibrations, sometimes out of control, addicted to television movies and amplified music, unable to calm, and prone to alcohol and drugs. Girl and boy, even before they become man and woman, are already totally controlled by their brain power and totally immune to reality. As teenagers girl and boy seek hugely charging electrical environments for entertainment. At some places the charging is so violent to their brains they scream to release that charge. They collapse if it disturbs the body to such a degree it shuts down. They gyrate in tempo with the charge they are feeding from. As they tire they seek stimulants to keep the charge alive. Their behaviour is often life threatening to themselves and to others. They quieten when their brains can no longer accept any more power and momentarily cease activity of feeding. The power source has usually oversaturated the coil. All of this, and cell phone continual communication as well. Their bodies are consumed by an ever increasing radioactively charging environment which man as an adult is creating.

Present day living on Earth is inside a containment holding explosive vibrations. God has surrounded Earth with rays of cool hold. God has also sealed-in Earth's contamination, with a thickness of vibrations which are aggressively charging to balance that security. To be inside a sealing is to become of explosive charge, for Earth's vibrational purification came from the penetration of light rays from the Sun and God's cooling responses. Such safety is no longer. Man in his brain has destroyed Earth's evolution of balancing equations. Light is no longer of balancing vibrations into Earth because radioactivity is stifling its activity. Penetration of the Sun's rays now is of minimal charge of life force and every living thing is diseasing and struggling to survive. In man's brain this has been ignored. In man's conscience of soul light existence man will not ignore this truth of all things. The brain is dominant inside man's head. The soul light still exists inside man's heart. If man is to continue as a species upon this Earth, a very different existence must prevail. One which redeems his soul, returns life to his Earth and brings back the evolutionary process of equations in all living things. If conscience is not answered, and if the brain is preferred to progress only man himself, then all, every life, every soul light, every growing formation, and every vibrating equation, will explode. That is a reality, not a brain fantasy.

Be as it may, man will choose a future one way or the other.

# Cell Deformity

Earth's environment has contaminated from pure soil, clean air, pure rain, clean waterways and seas, to poisoned soil, foul air, dirty rain, polluted waterways and seas. Such pollution is destroying human, creature and growth formations.

Vibrations once equationally balanced and controlled by God are now of total imbalance, unable to equate. God has withdrawn most of the surround that once protected man and Earth.

In the environment a micro-radiator has evolved, a radioactive living formation of vibrations invisible to the human eye, which activates when another magnetic similarity attracts its composition. It travels to meet its attractor. Vibrations always magnetise each other. They cannot dissolve, cannot disappear from the environment, and cannot die. Vibrations evolved from first breath contained. Their origin is first equation. All vibrations have a magnetic source no matter how impure. All vibrations heat.

The formation of a micro-radiator was inevitable, for impure radioactive vibrational force is so smothering everything, that a tiny heating composition encircled within an aggressive vibratory charge, automatically isolates itself. Encirclement of a hot vibration is because all vibrations originated from the motioning of first equation which was spherically contained. As a radioactive vibration in singular identity overheats from too much pressure, it vibrates as did first equation, tremors, and because its surround is also radioactive, cannot explode, and becomes a lone vibration. It vibrates of itself. It seeks magnetic attraction. The attraction is a heated composition in any form which is vibrating likeness of temperature and likeness of singular identity.

Inside creatures and mankind as well as growth, singular radioactive vibrations are breeding. Electrical energy and radioactivity have combined to establish cells which have singular vibrations contained, vibrations contained by their own power and loose inside that force-field. They cannot integrate because their individual heated compositions have to progress before they unify with their father force. Progression is temperature accelerations, tremorings which cause electrical smarting and fluid excretions from too much violent heat. The process as long as it is contained, automatically, by magnetic attraction, suctions single vibrations into its force-field, enlarging as each addition is taken in. All vibrations breed and enlarge.

A micro-radiator, before it is consumed in its own force-field, can exit its containment if another magnetic attractor of identical temperature is near enough to make contact with, and has singular vibrations of likeness at life in form composition. Vibrations move swiftly always. They enter current activity which allows them to travel long distances, turn sharply, spiral when entering a form, encircle any attraction, spin just before entering a form and because they have a head and tail, burrow into any moist formation of vibratory likeness.

Radioactivity is a living charge of imbalanced vibrations enlarging and breeding micro-radiators, living, feeding, breeding compositions, of hideous powering, able to destroy whatever attracts their interest. A micro-radiator can enter almost any life form that encourages its vibrations. It hovers over that life form. It does not leave, until, through heated vibrational magnetic attraction, it enters the life form through passages of hot moist vibrations: the tear ducts of the eyes leading to the brain; the ears leading to the brain's coil and skull formation; the nose leading to the throat; the mouth leading to the chest and abdomen; the vagina leading to the womb and bowels; the penis leading to the testicles, bowels and stomach; the anal passage leading to all internal organs; the mouth, when eating, leading into every digestive tract of the body; a cut or wound leading to the blood and bones; a surgical opening anywhere leading to an area of magnetic attraction of heated radioactive vibrations; and through the eyes leading directly to the brain.

Cancer is its identity: radioactivity is its life force.

It pierces tissue, swims through blood, passes through water and probes into bones, ligaments and almost every part of a form. It searches the hottest area to mutate in, stretches out in places of similarity of temperature, and grows tentacles of its excreting vibrations which themselves search for more food. Its size depends on the quantity of radioactivity surrounding it, and its fierce grip into a form, is the brainpower in function that keeps it alive. The reason cancers are brain fed is because the radiator vibrates fierce aggressive radioactive charging and the brain itself magnetises the charge and feeds, spreading its vibrations throughout the cells in the body radioactive also.

Micro-invisible-radiation, is cancering mankind. Its source is man-made. Its epidemic is man powered. Its presence in the environment is undetected. Its composition wriggles in frenzy, has a head and tail of radioactive charge, and eats through a form of vibrating likeness. The heads of radioactive singular vibrations are because their formation originates from the spherical motioning of first equation, and the tails are because they travel in currents of a vibratory surround which allows their passage through. They burrow into a life form, travel through hot moisture, begin feeding, and according to the area they disease, become visible in a variety of ways. On the surface of a formation they burn the tissue and cause crater-like activity. They spread by extension of vibrations stretching to feed, and are encouraged by heat on the surface of the form they have burrowed into. Cancer in all variations is from a radioactive surround attracted to a radioactively charging form. The brain of man is totally responsible.

When the blood is entered by a micro-radiator, because of the blood's colour and hot temperature, the radiator multiplies by being explosively charged, excreting mucous of energy much more substantial than the energy cells of the blood, and replicating its charge of vibrations contained. Energised vibrations always replicate their activity when contained. Blood cancer is simply a number of replicating micro-radiators consuming blood cells to feed from.

Microscopic observation of energy cells is totally without the reality of light cells, which are not able to be seen under the impurity of glass magnification. Equations are pure. God's protecting rays are pure and invisible. Man's microscopic searching everywhere is without the reality of light life. Light cells now are barely able to function in a life form. Without their purity to keep equations at life, cells will keep deforming and man's diseases will increase horrifically. Nuclear vibrations already at life in man's environment will bring about the extinction of Earth's life forms, for so predatory are they already, a radioactively charging form will eventually be skinned alive as nuclear radiators evolve in the environment. That is inevitable. Such a progression in vibrational activity is absolute.

The cells of creature, pure and impure, are also diseasing and deforming. Disease in energy cells is when their function is so imbalancing their vibrations lift and lower their charging and temperature rises and falls. The heating is aggressive and the fall in temperature prevents the charge free flowing. The cells weaken in energy. They become unstable in function. They can then be entered by bacteria, a vibratory imbalance of solidifying impurities of form excretions, which close their vibrations, because unless that is done their activity ceases. Their surround would devour them.

Closure of a vibrating composition is when the vibrations themselves retract, pull back their protruding heated aura extension and cease vibrating of their charge. They then heat, excrete hot murky moisture, which combines to become sediment, vibrations glued together in magnetic attraction and able to travel by sticking to any substance that is colder in temperature.

Man and creature breed bacteria everywhere. Too much impurity of body function is the cause. Too much radioactivity inside and outside formations feed its existence. Excreting creatures and man leave excrement vibrating on or in a containment of active vibrations, which vaporise and magnetise that imbalance into a thickness of activity. The vibrating vapour can solidify. It can also travel.

Bacteria has spread through the environment by being transported from place to place by people, creatures, ships, boats, planes, cars, trucks, trains and all mobile machinery because of the high energy current such carriers vibrate of. Without a current of energy bacteria cannot exist. Bacteria evolved in vaporising activation with air currents to circulate its excreting vibrations. Once moving within air, bacteria become a needing to travel composition of energising activity in search of magnetic attraction. The food source of bacteria is impurities within or outside of any form vibrating of the same temperature. Because of the shape of bacteria the vibrations can enter man or creature anywhere there is a heating, current-active, electrified or radioactively charged opening. Bacteria current-seeks, for it is alive in contained charge of solidifying vibrations. Magnification of its size and shape is accurate. Man's analysis of its evolution and breeding is not. Man's impure environment and impure form as well as creature's impure environment and impurity of form, breed all the bacteria on Earth.

Viruses are always singular vibrating compositions which occur in the environment of filthy oxygen and densely packed radioactivity. Virus evolution is from filth, the aggressive rotting vibrations of any formation which has impured. A virus activates by temperature which fluctuates. It begins in vibratory invisible life, from the gas a formation discharges as it rots, and the aggressively charging radioactivity it unites with. The two create a living vibrating composition of vibrations which bind, heat, excrete, form a shape and glide through a charging environment in need of magnetic attraction. So minute is the formation, it can enter any micro-organism and thrive. Contained, it replicates. Outside of a form it also replicates if the form itself is contained in a radioactively charging environment.

There are numerous types of viruses which behave in many different ways, but all are of minute vibrational compositions of severe imbalance and all are caused by man. Virus spreading is simply magnetic attraction to another likeness. Cell deformity in man and creature is virus prone, able to allow any virus into any cell at any time. What keeps a virus out is the amount of light cell activity a form holds. If there is little purity of equations left in a form, a virus can enter and replicate of its charge. If a form is strong in light equations, the vibrations those equations emit, turn its approaching composition away, for there is no magnetic attraction to entice entry. Light equations also divert all bacteria within their area of vibrations and diseases of every kind can be avoided.

A body of very pure equations lives long and very healthily. However, because of the ever greedy, ever hungry and ever powering human brain, man has no more purity to protect himself and no more purifier in his environment to keep man of health and very long life.

Light cells in man, creature and growth, are fading down in charge. The Sun's rays barely penetrate the thick radioactive covering over Earth, which critically diminishes the life force of light equations. Such a truth man needs to be aware of. Without the Sun's rays purifying the environment, disease will increase savagely, and the survival of man's species is over.

Cancer of creatures is epidemic now. The packaged food of domestic creature is alive with radioactive charge. Its packaging contains the charge. Micro-radiators multiply in that containment. The food itself has no purifier. The radioactive environment places a micro-radiator into a magnetic surround. The creature eats of the charge. Cancer is the result. Other openings in creature magnetise cancerous vibrations which progress. Creatures in the wild, as long as their habitat is pure, do not cancer. Those that do, have been in contact with radioactively charging vibrations brought into their habitat.

Creatures in the seas where man has nuclear charged water vibrations, all experience suffering of their pure equations. Some die of cell disease. Others deform. Many grow lumps of cancerous tissue. Many explode of their evolving forms. A nuclear charging ocean is causing the pure evolution of life forms to cease and destroys their light equations.

Man is nuclearising the oceans of the Earth. What was once a pure environment where life forms began evolution, is now alive with aggressively charging vibrations, so increasing, even the great sensitivity and intelligence of whale is being overpowered. A massive vibrating force is evolving in the oceans which is so aggressive, life forms are being ripped apart and coastlines reshaped. What man has done to his land, man has done to his seas. The amount of vibrations forced into the seas has overpowered pure equations there also, and is threatening every living thing. The amount of explosions being carried out underwater is causing magnetic fields of vibrations, contained in areas which heave of their force, rise up in explosive action, keep activating because they have no pacification and build of their quantity of charge. Huge seas are proof of turbulence too mighty to be of balanced motioning.

Man's life on the oceans is almost over. Man's continued violation of the seas will result in disasters never before experienced, for an ocean out of control devours everything in its path. The amount of nuclear vibrations charging through the oceans has begun contamination of every structure and every life form trying to exist there. Those vibrations magnetise each other, travel in search of each other through currents of excessive activity, and when they begin formation of ugly predatory shapes, settle upon a vibrating form or formation which magnetises them. Nuclear vibrations have no tight formation because their vibrations are too powered to unify, and too explosive to magnetise each other. Instead, they activate in density which automatically attracts to any other density of vibrations anywhere, no matter what composition or shape. They then proceed to devour the shape they seep into. The seas are evolving nuclear charged. Man again is responsible.

The amount of pollution man is filling the seas and water-veins of the Earth with, is absolutely unforgivable. Without clean water, no cell life can exist much longer. Disease is the killer. Disease of everything. Man himself again will be the victim. It is man's deeds, deeds that only the human brain motivates, that defile every purity of life.

Pollution, is the throwing away of every greedy residue of every greedy invention that defiles every purity there is. From sewage through to nuclear waste, man is polluting water that is crucial to man's survival. Knowingly man violates his last resource of survival. Filthy water vibrations of imbalance are contaminating man's food chain and the food creatures evolve from. What was once the most beautiful giving to man is now the ugliest defilement. Nowhere is there clean water and nowhere is without disease. Billions of pleasure-seeking humans cast pollution everywhere, on and into the Earth and the seas. Cargo ships, passenger liners and all ocean-going vessels discharge pollution that has not only discoloured the water, but filled it with bacteria, which is progressing vibrationally and will eventually nuclear activate. Vibrations always progress and those that man is causing are lethal.

As well as the seas, man's air supply is now polluted. Air traffic is the major cause of a violent radioactive air supply, which in time will cause the cells of all living things to retract their light seeking rays and die forever. The emissions from an ever-increasing number of aircraft in the skies are so fierce in vibrations, so current-activated, so dense and radioactive, man again is the victim. Air is essential to man, clean air, air which is unpolluted. Car emissions which rise several metres into the environment, are also current-activating and are already causing asphyxiation in some forms. Car emissions carry micro-radiators in their vibrations. They are also able to carry a nuclear-radiator. Aircraft emissions, forced downward in magnetic attraction, unite with car emissions and cause smog, a density of solidifying vibrations which are in process of unification. While they are uniting they are visible. When that stops, they are not. Their vibrations magnetise each other in density of field. They heat whatever the temperature of their surround, excrete, and the excretion of their energy charge, unifies with the moisture of their surround, which automatically cools their charging making them invisible. The density is darkly coloured, because it carries with it, vibrations which have no colour, and vibrate of smoky emissioning. Once invisible, the pollutants wriggle in the environment waiting progression of their charging. Man breathes polluted oxygen continually. Eventually man's air supply will be unable to be breathed in.

Naval activity on and under the seas has caused every nuclear vibration now active there. The constant penetration of nuclear submarines is current-activating nuclear charged vibrations all through sea water. Explosions enter that activity which progresses in charge. The hugely powerful nuclear tests carried out in ocean locations began the process violently. The vibrations of those massive nuclear explosions still progress.

Whale, the last God-held creature in the seas, can no longer procreate as whale once did. Whale's equations are dying. Nuclearising seas are the reason. Whale agonises. Whale dies in extreme suffering. Whale strands because whale cannot sonar-locate safety and cannot echo-vibrate Earth's structural content to navigate through. Whale's skin is cancer prone now. Whale's soul is unable to want life.

Upon Earth's surface lies pollution so grotesque the soil has lost all equations of purity and all life force of light. The Sun's rays touch Earth reddened, for what extends upwards from Earth is red hot vibrations of impurity, so charged, that the rays of the Sun, once multicoloured, change to red automatically.

The temperature of Earth is heating rapidly. Radioactivity of the environment is the cause. Global warming, the heating vibrations of the Earth, cannot be stopped unless man ceases in greed. Global warming is the result of that greed entirely. A ceaseless production of manufacturing covets the Earth. A ceaseless plundering of resources violates the Earth. A ceaseless poisoning radiates the Earth and a ceaseless brain inside man's head denies the Earth everything.

Growth, all growth now, has fading equations. Light cannot stimulate life as it once did because of the density of radioactivity. Colour, the essential eye stimulant to man and creature, has become so muted, man's eyes are diseasing. The equations of pure colour vibrate a charge of light vibrations which feed light cells in every form. Without that equational nourishment all light cells weaken.

The poisoning of Earth's surface with chemicals of massive quantities has caused an imbalance so grave in soil, that growth itself, the purest form of life giving to man, is beginning to cancer, radioactivate in formations. All equations of growth now are restricted in charge, and in many, mass productions have no light equations left. Every beautiful plant and flower and tree is deforming of its wondrous evolution. Man in greed, is the unstoppable violator of such divine beauty.

Not one evolution has man left alone. Every solitary life form has been taken, experimented with, mutilated, deformed, hacked to bits, cruelled, brain deciphered, brain greeded and brain radiated. That is man's reality now. The entire evolution of Earth and Earth's life forms has experienced man's predation. From the tiniest cell to the greatest form, man has brain-violated all purity. Nothing has any purity or any balance of light equations any longer. Man is now seeking another planet to continue the very same activity on.

Reality such as this, is for man's conscience, and should not be denied. Progress, the continuance of man's deeds, is man's excuse to keep greeding of everything. Progress, the rapid expansion of empire, the economy, the professions, business, education and personal gain is totally of brain feeding. Greed is man's response to all things, from the smallest acquisition to the largest. Pursuit of wealth, throne, government, ownership, occupation and possessions is simply the ever-hungry radioactive brain inside man's head ceaseless in activity of feeding.

Greed can never be stopped. Soul existence can never be stopped. Greed destroys man's soul. A destroyed soul can never be God-taken. Conscience activates the soul light. The soul of man cannot die. Its vibrations emotion eternally. If God does not attach to its equations at death, the brain's charging automatically carries it to hell, the continuance of brain radioactivity of red-hot vibrations of charge, attaching to a superior source of power, and progressing. Never is there a more real existence for mankind to digest.

Man must realise here that unless the soul is tried for, hell does exist. Hell is solely of man's brain power without God in contact with the soul.

# The Body

The body of man, the entire form, has become grotesque in nearly every area once perfectly balanced. Man's habitual energising is the cause. Man's children now are helplessly ill-healthed, hopelessly overweight and hideously aggressed. They are evolving energised forms without balance of equations. Their habits now are aggressive. They cannot discipline their aggression. The drive to energise the human form is deforming it, and children are victims of too much aggressive charge through their entire bodies.

The formation of the human body entirely was of light equations. The aggression a body evolved with was of overcharged equations heating, expressing that heat, and changing formations which evolved in balance. Never was there false aggressive charge. Every progression within the human body form evolved equationally.

Early man had no disease and needed no extra energy or energy boosting. When the brain became dominant every human form began deforming.

Man must understand evolution correctly. A body which has evolved purely of light equations, then continually abused with electric, radioactive and nuclear charged vibrations, automatically becomes vibrationally over-charged in energy, unable to balance in pure equating vibrations, and eventually of magnetic attraction to the force of power that is dominating its existence.

The forced energy mankind seeks, radiates every pure light cell contained in man's body. The cells retract. They do not ray-extend. Their formation begins deforming. The pure light cells become inactive. Around those cells where aura used to vibrate, a red glow appears. A smothered light cell interns of its vibrations, and the area once of light rays, becomes of high energising imbalanced vibrations, twisting and turning, lunging and latching onto any other near similarity of magnetic interest. The cells replicate. They evolve highly charged. Consequently a body seeks more energy than necessary, and addicts to the source that provides it.

The hyperactivity mankind is experiencing now is from too much charging of the body and brain. So highly charged is man's form, aggressive living is out of control. From waking unto sleeping the energy cells inside a body are force-fed. They behave aggressively. They cause excessive, habitual, reactive patterns, which cause abusive language, loudness in vocal practices, violence unto others, over-reactional responses, and the need to seek more and more aggressive charge. A body cannot calm or feel beautiful, cannot keep still, and often twitches and beats time with legs, feet, hands and fingers. A body may addict to an aggressive sport which drives energy further into cell vibrations. Each pleasure sought, often becomes of alcohol abuse, drug taking and sexual indulgences. Each desire to enjoy anything nearly always results in some form of over-indulgence.

The human body fatigues often and man seeks an energy charge to keep going. No species can exist with such abuse to its pure equations. A body evolved of light vibrations and cannot continue of light life unless its formation is fed of its life force.

Every solitary contact man experiences in daily living is electrically and radioactively vibrating. There is no relief for man's soul light. All that man touches, hears, looks at, works with and tries to relax in, is alive with charge of vibrations harmful to man's body.

A child becomes a crying agony of light vibrations unable to feel comfort or passive living. A new born screams in discomfort of light cells, all puncturing and tortured by electric vibrations destroying its body of pure light life.

A teenager involves in every hyping available to answer the absolute addiction to energised vibrations its body is constantly feeding from. Adults behave the same, for they too must seek highly charged life styles because they have evolved of aggressive habits. Nowhere can man find peace either, for man's environment is so highly machine-charging, the purity of light is overpowered, and light rays which try to ray project, retract.

Machine life is so consuming light life, the Earth itself is unable to magnetise its own life force from the Sun.

Vibrations, all vibrations of impurity, mass according to their sources, magnetise each other, grow in formation and progress. They do not dissolve in space. They do not deteriorate. They do become predatory. They must, for they live, are fed, and are man-powered.

Inside the human body are living growths, predating on formations which were once pure in light. Growths are alive in vibratory imbalances. Heat causes their expansion. Forced energising causes their existence. Magnetic attraction causes their predation. With no equations of light to overpower them, growths everywhere, inside and upon the human form, are deforming, an evolutionary process that will result in hideous sights and hideous sufferings.

The eating habits of mankind now have become of brain indulgence, for so little purity does man grow to eat, disease is unstoppable. Man eats mainly for convenience, not for true sustenance and never for true health. Packaged food has no purifier to ease that food through the bloodstream. Frozen food has lost its pure light equations and only feeds the energy content everywhere inside the body. Microwave cuisine radiates every purity any food may consist of, and absolutely aggresses every recipient energy cell a body has.

Crops are force-aggressed to look appealing, consequently every pure cell in Earth's once power-packed light equational formations is aggressed beyond any balance the body needs to stay healthy.

Chemicalised food discharges a dose of grotesque vibrations into a form, which weakens light-raying cells and red-charges their pure light equations.

Genetically engineered food, supplies venom of aggressively charging vibrations into a body, animal, or human, which in time, will mutilate, deform, and kill every cell a body has in equations of light. The evolutionary stages of growth all came from light cells of equations of purity. They have remained of light cell evolution no matter the violations, and when that particular evolutionary progression is stopped, the entire species of man and creature will end automatically. No light vibrations will enter man's body. No magnetic attraction can there be for the Sun's life force to activate a formation, and no soul light can ever be held by God. The evolution of light life is over.

Eating has been the sustenance of body continuance. Eating evolved in balance of a body's needs. Eating genetically cannot evolve man or creature for long. Greed and only greed produces genetics of any kind.

Life, an evolving, equating, light vibrating form, is sacred. Life should never be manufactured or taken by any means or anyone, should never be re-designed and never violated in any way.

The soul light is of God's equating responsibility, a thorough creative progression of light life. Man's brain, devoid of values that advance man's soul, has produced a life that is unable to attach to its prime light attractor. Life production is man's unconscienced experimentation. Only the brain of man fixates upon living beings, disfigures that which is of pure evolution, and creates an inferior replica of a God-held equational perfect form.

Experiments for man's longevity are the most cruel, and the most hideous defilement of creature any human being commits. Creatures all are of soul light evolution. Creatures all, are still pure in their light equations. Creatures nearly all, are still attached to God. A hideous experiment which results in a torture that takes the life of a creature, is without respect for creature, without conscience, and can never be accepted by any decent human being no matter what excuse is programmed. Life is God's creation never to be violated for man's gain. Creature was equationally perfected by God's rays of light equations. Still beautiful and still attached to those rays, creature remains of soul light existence. Unknowingly man has violated that greatness. Knowingly now, man should cease that violation.

For centuries man has re-created living beings and living formations, not because they needed re-creation, but because every beautiful perfection man's brain has encountered has been hungrily and greedily fixated upon. Once a brain takes interest in anything its hunger must be requited. That which it is attracted to cannot be left alone until it is either destroyed or can be further violated. Obsessive experimentation of everything is that truth. Hives of every industry are created by just that reality.

Man's body and brain depend on a high energy content. Man's soul light does not. Light equations seek light vibrations and if they are aggressed, it is because they imbalance. Feeding the human body the right sustenance is giving it purity of growth, not anything that is of manufactured convenience.

Every medicine for every disease on Earth grows upon the Earth, for man's diseases are all of imbalanced equations. All disease is treatable purely and without severe reactions. Food itself causes disease now and to stop that man must change man's eating habits totally.

For every affliction the human body suffers there is a pure cure provided a body is of light strength. For every epidemic large and small there is pure curing, provided there are cells of light dominant within man's form. For every incurable disease man suffers and often dies from, there is total relief, and eventually a total cure, provided the sufferer resorts to feeding body equations, putting down brain powering, and living a strongly light feeding life. The purity of light, real light and not artificial or electrically generated, is the essence of pure health. Light vibrations, as long as they come from the Sun unimpeded, destroy all imbalances in light holding forms. No power of life is greater.

Cancers, all types of cancers, are nourished by electrically and radioactively charged environments. Cancer craves heat and vibrational aggressive charge. Its birth was from just that power source. Its food is power of imbalanced vibrations. Its spreading is for more aggressive charging. Its main generator is the brain because of its magnetic attraction to aggressive charge. Were a body strong in light cells and pure in water content, cancer would be unable to penetrate its vibrations.

Growths of every description are pockets of severe imbalances of vibrations magnetised together by their tenacity to stay united. They swell and often harden by electrically generated environments which push into a growth, a cancer. The vibrations encircle around the shaping. Once contained electrically, the growth expands until it excretes of its heated mucous. The wet excretion hardens. It seeks likeness, and finding the exact temperature, begins vibrational identity of charge. All growths, whatever their placing, seek mucous identity of charging, which can belong to a formation enclosed in a heating body, or exposed to the environment. Heated vibrations always excrete.

Body purity in mankind is almost unable to be obtained. The artificial chemicals mankind is evolving with, deform not only man himself, but the future of man's existence. Once chemicals enter the bloodstream already impure and aggressive, the charge chemicals produce, causes convulsive cell behavioural patterning, which becomes addictive to the brain. Any convulsive cell behaviour alerts the brain cells which obtain flushes of energised vibrations all hot and stimulating. Chemicals of any impurity absolutely violate light cells, light raying magnetic attraction, and the direct insertion of the Sun's rays into a life form. All mutations in man and creature are the result of chemicals taken into a once pure life form destroying its existence.

Research of anything can never ever produce results that achieve any real truth. No first equation is understood. No birth of light is understood and no God in any reality has been explained. Man's soul is always fantasised and every living creation has no credible beginning or real evolutionary progression. The universe is totally unexplained. What future can mankind believe in when man's real evolution is unexplained?

The Sun's life force is not in waves of supercharged energised vibrations deciphered as harmful and non-harmful. The Sun's rays are of equations of pure light attempting to breathe life into Earth and all that lives of light equations. What destroys that greatness is man's hideous environmental pollution, preventing the purity of light from penetrating Earth.

Mankind in radioactive evolution becomes harmed by contact with light purity, because the vibrations involved cannot unite without eruption of charge. A filthy environment hazed in hot radioactivity prevents not only pure light from reaching all that lives, but God's rays of cooling to keep all life evolving.

Massive electric, radioactive, and nuclear charge, is the reason for all growth diseasing, fading in colour, weakening in light strength and becoming extinct. Man's form, from the head to the toes, inside and outside of its formation, has become totally imbalanced. The brain has enlarged in some forms to be unable to be contained inside the skull. Cancers are growing inside the head. Blood is clotting there also, and excess charging of vibrations is exploding cell life.

The eyes are destroying in many forms with diseased tissue, fading sight, blindness, and an excess of radioactive vibrations magnetised into the eyes killing all light cells of pure evolution.

Man's hearing is destroying by the huge pummelling of vibrations in-taken. Too much powerful vibrational force is entering the ears and exploding sensitive equations which react to sound.

Man's nasal purity has almost gone with horrific chemicals suctioned through the nose killing all cells of light equations. Drug abuse and inhaling toxic fumes from the environment, burn equations so uglily, the nose becomes infected, carries bacteria to the throat, and allergies plague the whole area inside the head where equations need purity to keep their vibrations from imbalancing.

Inside the mouth man is evolving with cancers. Gums are diseased, teeth are decayed and mouths often ulcerated. The mouth excretes a very impure mucous able to spread disease to another. Swallowing chemical concoctions also burns equations of tissue formation and often dissolves the tight formation of layers of equations which protect the tissue from diseases. The throat can also cancer and carries gross infections which travel.

Every bone in the human form is becoming an evolution without light cells and pure water cells. Both are absolutely of total balance and need healthy feeding. Bone disease is because all equational balance in light cell life has either dried out or is absolutely violated by medication which eats those cells up. All bone disease is because light equations have been destroyed.

Every part of the human form now encourages and can grow cancers. Blood is unclean and carrying disease. The heart itself has been fatally violated by too much soul light denial and aggressive over powering. All heart disease is of soul light imbalancing.

Liver, kidneys and every other body evolution are unclean, disease prone, very unstable in equations and in some cases, deformed. There is no area of the human form that is of pure equations and has pure health. Cancers appear inside a form almost anywhere that is of aggressive vibrations.

Man and woman's genitalia have huge cell eruptions, disturbing diseases and growths of many types. Aggressive sexing can fatalise a life form evolving inside a womb. The soul light of the foetus vibrates aggressively and will never calm. Medication to enable sexing to be regular, destroys equations of light life, which must complete their cycles of motioning to remain of balance. Forced sex with chemicals completely destroys body equations forever. All medication eradicates pure equations of motioning and when that happens a form becomes dependant on an artificial life line.

The skin of mankind is without aura. In some cases it is covered with growths, cancers, rashes, has an unhealthy pallor and is often clogged with environmental dirt. Pores are often puss filled and excrete into swellings, all because light equations have been destroyed and no light from the Sun's life force can be magnetised.

Mankind's reality is just this truth here. A once beautiful pure form now covered in disease, deforming everywhere, and blatantly ignoring that realistic sight. Mankind does not live a life of strength, health and beauty any longer. Mankind is destroying as a species. Mankind needs light life to continue. Mankind is a species doomed to extinction unless a truthful realistic look at all that mankind lives by, is conscienced for, accepted as a reality, then changed quickly.

Truth, whatever mankind denies or accepts, will prevail. Truth never softens, is never obliterated and is never pretended. For man to honour truth is to answer man's conscience and with that honouring become of soul light existence.

# The Eyes

Light equations in man's eyes are almost totally destroyed. The eyes of creature are not. Sight when first evolving was the recognition of patterns of light equations passing across the eyes. All that was seen activated the soul light of every evolving creature. Light formations then were pure, full of colour, vibrating in aura, and ray-fed by the Sun's life force. Creatures' eyes projected light magnetically attached to light formations and forms and were stimulated by every beautiful creation upon the Earth. Colour of glorious radiance was everywhere. Colour, still able to be seen through a prism in contact with the Sun, was of absolute equational perfection, without any impurity, breathing of its equations and controlled by God's ever responding security. Every growing creation vibrated equations of pure colourings and patterns which came directly from the soul light of every evolution in existence. That was then, before man evolved, and before the brain of man synthesised every visual purity man needed for strong pure sight.

The first destructive visual activity man created was writing in black. Black, unless it has evolved with pure equations of colour within its content of mix, cannot in any way activate coloured equations of light. It has no magnetic attractor. It cannot feed equations. It tires them. It eventually destroys their activity. It has destroyed the eyes of man and equations of body aura also when used as clothing. All colour ceases vibrating when black becomes dominant.

Every pure creation that looks black in appearance has pure colourful equations at life. The vibrations have become black toned by being confined in extreme pressure of equations, often burned by extreme heat, then cooled quickly and more often trapped inside a formation that has no magnetic contact with Sun-raying in its shaping. Equations then become colourless, fade in brightness and vibrate weakly. In contact with the Sun they reveal their colourful equations and activate strongly.

Black does not exist inside the Sun's composition of light. Not even when flame evolved inside the Sun did black ever appear. It could not. The red-hot equations of pure flame never made contact with any formation, were never cooled and never ashed. Black never entered the Earth by Sun-raying. Its depth of tone in Earth's formations evolved as equations progressed and temperatures caused them to glow mixtures of darkened colours. Earth's hard light areas all hold colours within what appears to be pure black. Combinations of frozen light in very blackened equations are because at depth, hard light loses light magnetic attraction to the Sun. Equations weaken and become colourless in darkness. Their vibrations still activate but their colour becomes invisible. Every creature that looks pure black has colour within its equations and colour in its aura projection. Some creatures of black tones vibrate iridescence under the Sun's rays. Some gems that look black, glow of colour when in contact with the Sun. Oil, also black toned, is absolutely a truth of Earth's evolution of coloured light equations.

Black, man's artificial creation, whatever its use or substance, should never be worn, used in manufacture, or absorbed by the eyes. Even the brain tires from the vibrations of artificial blacks which have no stimulation. Artificial black shocks equations of colour which cannot activate because there is no identity in their evolution. The eyes in particular need colour through their formation. Without a regular intake of pure colour the eyes weaken, disease and fade. Colour stimulation keeps the eyes active in the feeding of light and strong in their equational need for balance. Nothing except the purity of light vibrations can they feed from. All that is artificial, of impurity of vibrations, destroys eye evolution.

Mankind in ignorance of light equations of purity has caused optical aggression in eye formation. All eye equations aggress when black is forced through the pupils. Because black has no equational likeness all pure coloured equations diminish in vivacity, they stop their magnetic activity. They fixate of their vibrations. They are held in unreceptive response while black is forced into their vibrations. If black print is absorbed regularly the eye equations of colour become weakened and artificial sight is often necessary. If black is wanted as clothing or décor, the aura of the body cannot feed or strengthen, and as a surround, both aura and the eyes lose strength, colour stimulation, and food. Mankind has blackened so much colour, evolution of the human form has been crippled.

To have good sight without disease is to understand the pure equations that have evolved within eye formation and feed them.

To resort to artificial sight is to deform equations of light and totally imbalance the evolution of mankind.

To realise that black, anything black, cripples eye equations, and that those equations need pure colour, not synthetics, is to begin to see again without disease or failing sight.

Colours are all hugely energising, aura feeding, health giving and restful, as long as they are pure. Equations are all of colourful patterns, alive, breathing, feeding and life giving. Never should a body be clothed in synthetics for it cannot vibrate healthily. Never should skin be cut into and sewn up with synthetic thread. Skin equations are cross-hatched in colours and cannot accept that which is impure. Wounds attract disease from synthetic fibres. The fibre is magnetic to environmental filth. Held over a wound it causes infection. The environment now is so full of pollutants, all opened body wounds can become infected in creature as well as man. Disease of every living creation is caused by man's environmental pollutants. The realisation of light equations and the capacity to feed them, could prevent every disease on Earth. If light equations are nourished, man, creature and Earth will regenerate.

The eyes once fed from the purity of colour everywhere. They were stimulated by magnetic attraction to evolving pure forms and formations that glowed aura and vibrated of their colourful equations. They fed from such greatness of light life. Creatures' eyes were bright and of light reflective colours and still are. Man's eyes in comparison are dead in reflective colours now and dull in eye glow. The pupil, once of deep tones of reflective colour is now black, darkened by inactive equations unable to feed or be activated. Black, artificial black of man's manufacture, is the cause.

Electrical, radioactive, and nuclear vibrations, are now clinging to the already faded eyes and diseasing them. A tumour on the surface of the eyes is the next stage of progressive vibrations.

Preparation for eye cancer is already evident, thinning tissue, blurring sight, groups of dead equations, a heated visual reception, areas of overheated blood, and constant ever increasing radioactive vibrations being absorbed by the eyes without relief. All that man sees now is vibrating imbalance of charge. All that man surrounds himself with vibrates the same imbalance. Every entertainment absorbed is of impure vibrations eating through every purity man has evolved with. So little is left to feed from, man is crippled from safe life and real health.

The brain of man and not creature has adapted to black even though it tires, because the muscles of eye function aggress, they heat when black enters their function. The brain energises immediately and enjoys the activity. The pure equations of the eyes cease activity and only the brain feeds. So destructive is this procedure the brain automatically seeks black because the aggressive charge it experiences is a food source.

The absorption of black causes the dream, brain magnetised imagery, able to activate when the eyes are closed and the body rests. Dreams, unless God injects a response via the soul light, are all of brain activity. What prompts a dreaming brain is a long cessation of activity of eye equations overpowered by the absorption of black.

The brain, once the eyes close, can and does, reactivate imagery that has been absorbed electrically through its coil. It can punctuate that imagery with other images all collected in the coil. It hallucinates of itself because the closure of the eyes, together with a black containment of vibrations, give it uninterrupted power to exist. It thrives in dream. It keeps feeding from whatever pattern its activity has registered aggressively.

The coil, has crushed aggression within its mucous. Aggressive radioactive and electrical charging crushed into its mucous tightly, needing release inside its containing hold, spurts outwards, a charge of vibrations in imagery, the very insertion that has caused its necessary release. The coil stores patterns repeatedly. The coil is an entity of power now. It does not sleep or rest for it cannot. Without eye equations in activity, it simply continues visual aggressively charged spurts of images which talk, scream, cry, hurt, mutilate and kill, if those images have been absorbed. The brain does not choose a dream pattern for an individual. It re-enacts image patterning and any behaviour patterns it has enjoyed. When the eyes open, dreaming stops, for the brain activity is no longer of internal functioning and external vibrations become of magnetic interest. The human brain is ceaseless in vibrating charge, even when man sleeps. There have never been personal variations of man's psychological needs within the dream. That is not possible. There is only brain imagery re-enactment unrelated to personal desires and needs.

Brain imagery re-enactment, is the consequence of too much electric and radioactively charged pictures, flashed through the eyes entering the brain, with no escape. Analysis of the brain's dreaming capacity is of brain activity only and should never be accepted as research. Man cannot research an entity man is controlled by. The entity powers of itself. Man inside that entity is helpless.

Dreams of soul light activation are very different from dreams of brain image re-enactment. If the soul light inside the heart chamber has experienced shock from imagery it cannot accept, during sleep (darkness of light equations), imagery of light vibrations which feed the shocked soul light pacification, can be activated through God's rays of coolness. Every image of everything has been magnetised through God's ever purifying rays of light. Whatever the image, pornographic, perverted or pure, the vibrational content has been magnetised by God, the container of all vibrations. If the soul light's equations stress at any time, sleep image response in light rays can take place. During light image reception, a clairvoyant compilation of imagery can be received during sleep provided the recipient is strong enough in soul light.

All humanity dream. Some dream without any recall. Others recall their dreams. Sleep allows the dream to occur. Prolonged darkness brings dream activity. The eyes and only the eyes visually receive brain imagery. They have accepted all images before the brain receives them. Therefore, when closed, that imagery magnetised inwards by the already primed coil, held inside the active mucous in squashed hot vibrations, automatically spurts back a quantity of images onto the retina of the eyes, for as long as the brain is in darkness.

Image-charging has to drain of power, for imagery itself is in spasmodic vibrational context which fluctuates, increasing and decreasing, according to the power source that has driven its activity. One image may be briefly absorbed while another may be strongly magnetised and lengthily focused upon. All images are recorded inside the brain. All images fed into the brain come through eye magnetic attraction.

Equations that are fed bright colour, allow the eyes, the aura and the soul light, life of light a state of health no-one experiences now. Equations that are smothered in black coverings deny man pure sight, pure aura, and pure soul light. Equations of light, feeding of colours and patterns pure and balanced, enable a body to live long and healthily. Pure sight can only be pure if the equations that have evolved to form the eyes are nourished purely.

Eyes were the most beautiful evolution of man and creature, totally evolving from the projection of light rays of soul light magnetic attraction surrounded by water. They still exist as they once were. They can be returned to their greatness by feeding them light activity. Once healed, eyes can mirror the soul light. If the soul light is also fed of light life, mankind becomes an evolution of the purity of light equations attached to God and automatically eternalised.

Is it not the truth that man's sight is now needing assistance? Is it not the truth also that man's sight is blurring, fading and losing focus? Would it not be sensible for all of mankind to give man's eyes the food of light they so need, to experience purity of soul light reality through the purity of man's eyes?

# Communication in Light

For thousands of years God has acknowledged man and creature's vibrations. Each vibrating pattern has entered God's invisible rays and caused the same pattern to be returned. Every word, sound and image that man and creature have evolved with has been magnetised through God's raying. God, equator of every light equation vibrating in total universal evolution is supreme power. Cannot man envisage beyond man's own power, a power greater than man's self? A real evolutionary power of credibility. The power of pure light. The power that gives real life force to all of mankind and creature alike. Cannot man believe in man's soul and establish truth before man becomes extinct?

God's powerful existence has been without real proof, real scientific evidence that a God could be. Many have tried to believe in a God. Many have failed. Many have not. Can man realise that without a beginning, without a pure evolutionary process, without a first equation, without the birth of pure light, man will never find man's God or man's soul?

Many individuals over many centuries have received convincing experiences which have not been understood and often violated, experiences which have been clarified and accepted as clairaudience, clairvoyance, oratory, aura sight and transcribal writings.

Clairaudience, the reception of language inaudible to the human ear. Clairvoyance, the reception of light imagery unable to be seen by anyone other than the receiver. Oratory, the power of words flowing through a recipient not able to be stopped and totally not of the receivers making. Aura sight, the capacity to see light function not able to be seen by the human eye. Transcribal writing, the ability to receive through writings, doctrine, counsel, teachings, caution and comfort. All of these wonderful experiences not understood and often not progressed, have made man cautious, disbelieving and suspicious.

God can speak man's language vibrationally, and if a form is pure enough in soul light equations, that form can hear God's vibrating words inside the soul light. An individual in the purity of soul becomes of soul reception when search for the soul is tried for. A soul search emotions an individual to enter soul light vibrations and be responded to. Many search. Many fail to purify enough to obtain a convincing reality that God really exists. Many pit the brain at the search and every opportunity of truth is lost.

God answers soul activity of emotional vibrations always. They flow directly into the rays they are being held by. If the brain power of an individual interferes with their patterning, automatically God halts the flow of light equational activity. The individual is confused, reacts inside the brain and the soul light retracts its own vibrating flow of equations.

The search for the soul always begins with meditation, quiet emotional feelings, which because the brain is also quiet, produce experiences a meditator seeks to progress. Meditation can be totally controlled by the brain or totally of soul light activity. A meditator of the brain often chants, which causes euphoria inside the coil, often causes elevation of vibrations inside the head, and if kept up by repetition, creates programmed behaviour and attitude which denote superior existence. Brain meditators may deliberately learn a doctrine, push superiority of themselves into their meditation thinking, and often choose to remain detached from normality of life. Brain meditation empowers the brain to contrive personae, religious elevation and behaviour and the constant denial of any conflicting confrontation of reality. Brain meditation inside the coil, denies the real existence of the soul light, except to include a vague explanation of its presence within the body which transcends its reality. God in meditation depends on an individual's concept only, or doctrinated programmed contrivance. A brained meditator communes with others of the same programming, often joins a sect or religious order, and more often seeks seclusion. Drugs are also used for many meditators which addict the brain hideously. The meditated brain then has total control over the body and can even cause the meditator dangerous fasts which may result in ill health, insanity, and early death. The brain once entitised by brain meditation, consumes its body totally.

Meditation inside the heart, whether the soul light is understood or not, absolutely opens the rays of the soul light to be purely responded to by God. Heart meditation, provided it is restfully practised, can bring about extraordinary experiences with spiritual givings all leading to the reality of the existence of God. What causes doubt during or after a spiritual experience, is the complete ignorance of the true existence of God and the soul itself, and the damaging programs of scientific hearsay, religious beliefs, or literature that is often contrived, falsified and exaggerated. A heart meditation cannot progress unto communication with God. The brain always denies real truth, and any meditating person returns to the brain after the heart has been accessed.

During meditation a clairaudient experience often occurs. Words can be heard, words which are clear but silent. This is because the vibrations enter the soul light invisibly flowing directly from God's rays of magnetic hold. Every word of man's language has already been magnetised through God's rays, so every answer to man can be transmitted back through those rays. Because the soul light is of equations of pure light, language of light vibrations is automatic. Light language is simply a vibrating composition of equations flowing back and forth through rays of light activity.

The terrible programming of the brain now by way of fantasised evil and fantasised gods as well as a spiritual world of various beings, has made light purity of communication with God impossible. Immediately any word or sentence is experienced, the ever-hungry brain diverts the clairaudient and violates the opportunity of pure talking. The clairaudient has allowed the brain's entry, for it cannot be stopped because of its ceaseless activity of feeding. Into that experience it charges, and every fantasised programming the brain has fed from becomes activated in memory recall. The clairaudient is unable to experience the reality of the soul light's existence and the magnetic link to God. Interference by the brain always depends on just how much programming an individual is storing. Some individuals are full of spiritual brain fantasies. Others have cleaner brain patterns. Many can hold the link open and receive clear contact without the brain's entry. Everyone, when trying clairaudient communication, admits the brain at some time during the talk. When it is over, a clairaudient experiences conflict of reality, a disbelief of much that has taken place. A clairaudient listens in doubt and often fear, of the very real experience that has taken place through the soul light. Many immediately change that truth into lies of deliberate denial. Others exaggerate it. Some respect such truth and keep it to themselves.

Once God responds to the soul light the link is vibrating invisibly and silently. Each single word is one single vibrational pattern already held in God's supreme containment. Because man constructs sentences when needing them, God can also construct sentence vibrations which make sense. Man's entire language formatting is held by God's containing rays.

All equations inside God's rays have vibrations of emotional experience. All words convey patterns of fluctuating temperatures and rhythms. God has accepted every one. Each sentence conveys meaning, purpose, inquiry, interest, development, attention, answer, search, involvement and opportunity. God has accepted every subject and in every language. When a clairaudient asks God a question, a response, which is not the return of the same question but an answer of clarification, returns instead. This is because the question has been asked from the stretching equations of the soul light in need of resolution. The answer, in response to the clairaudient, comes back through God's rays from an automatic probing into light vibratory vocabulary, far superior to the brain's stored vocabulary and far greater in content. Long-sentenced answers from God are rare. The probing of light vibrations is swift, and precise and clear in all explanations. One word from God defines many from man's vocabulary.

Soul light vibrations are strong when in talk with God. The brain cannot function of its coil when those vibrations are active. The amount of patterning flowing through God's rays from the soul light destabilises the coil's activity. The clairaudient becomes drowsy and often falls asleep. Incoming vibrations from God can trance a human form because the brain cannot activate against their force. If a clairaudient does not in any way encourage brain interference and the questions being asked of God are many, trance is automatic. The vibrations can be transmitted without interruption. Trance is simply a dominating control of vibrations in transmission from God.

The defilement of the truth of God's voice is always the brain's programmed reaction to whatever it has magnetised. An individual may have read of a lie, a fantasy, a hyping experience of another which has been exaggerated, had a dream or listened to someone's programming and been brain stimulated. The brain stores information for recall. If that has happened and God is sought clairaudiently via the soul light, a terrible violation of truth can occur. The individual in search of truth probes the brain for answers to the search. An entity of choice, a programmed fantasised spirit or teacher of a doctrine, a dead person, a religious leader, a fictitious character, a religious entity, even evil spirits, and the very unreal devil is selected as the communicator. The individual asks unto an entity, not God. The individual is answered by God because the soul light has been activated magnetically and God automatically responds. The seeking clairaudient establishes communication with a chosen entity, excludes God completely as the communicator, and as soon as the brain becomes dominant in the link, God's rays withdraw leaving the clairaudient without requitement of search. This happens time and time again with many who have soul light capacity and destroy all truth by allowing the brain to interfere with the pure transmission of light.

Mediums, angels, guides, spirits and all other sought-after entities come between God's real truth every time they are wanted. As the brain indulges of programmed fantasies a soul seeker can corrupt. God's store of vocabularised vibrations equate names, happenings, even print and pictures of past events, and can be probed for, found in magnetic likeness and returned in conversation of soul light activation. Many a medium has been informed that way. Many have been grossly misled. Others have been given truth. Others have automatically been refused. If the seeker pushes the brain into any conversation, the link with God ceases.

Terrible lies have evolved in spiritual search by various individuals. Terrible entities have also evolved and absolutely none really exist. Those who have been answered clairaudiently are examples of those with enough soul light capacity to be given. It is necessary therefore for all individuals able to communicate in light to do it realistically and with no other entity but God wanted, and no motive but to seek God's truth and the purification of the soul light.

The responses of God vary with each individual. They are of equations and vibrating patterns a soul seeker has magnetised. Each individual breathes in different tempo and has body equations and a soul light entirely its own. No one individual is the same as another in vibrational patterning. When God answers a soul seeker, it is in the same patterning that seeker vibrates of.

Many who have soul capacity commune with each other and exchange experiences. Each conversation informs the brain. Many read of the experiences of others and the brain is fed the information. All the brain absorbs relating to spiritual encounters is probed into by a soul seeker when clairaudience is experienced, unless the seeker is absolutely convinced by soul light intelligence that communication with God is real. It is rare for a clairaudient to talk with God uninterrupted by the brain.

Man has defiled clairaudience beyond any credibility. Man has taken that great opportunity and smeared its purity with lies which are from brain programming. God still answers every link of soul seeking and God's responses depend on what that seeker is searching for.

When the link goes wrong in talk which condones evil, the seeker is of brain negotiations. An evil entity sought in conversation is an automatic response from God, which, because of God's equating store of man's vocabulary, results in what a clairaudient accepts as evil answers. God does not deliberately define a conversation with a soul seeker. God's equating responses are always automatic, the result of equations that have been magnetised and stored and probed into by light magnetic search when a link is needing resolution of vibrations. So if evil is sought, it is evil that answers. If a spiritual entity is sought, a spiritual entity answers. If God is sought, God answers, and if the soul seeker remains in trance without the brain involved, God is able to requite the search for truth.

The human brain is telepathic, able to magnetise thought patterns of another. God is never involved when this happens. A medium inside a contained environment may have enough brain power to probe into the brain of another and find information that is stored there. Many can. Many are with powers that translate brain patterns into words. So alive in vibrating vocabulary is the brain, any powerful medium can magnetise any individual pattern and read its content. Names, places and events can be translated in medium counselling. Always that sitting is without God's link. Telepathic connections are totally brain powered.

Clairvoyance, the transmission of God's light patterning, is absolutely not understood in any way. It is pure and cannot be defiled by the brain when it is in operation. A clairvoyant of serious soul search receives the most beautiful light patterns unable to be seen by anyone else. Light rays in transmission from God begin from the invisible equations of the purity of first equation's evolution. The soul light itself magnetises God's rays, flushes its receptive equations, and because the transmission comes directly from God, those equations express their charge so powerfully that their colours, the formation of coloured shapes and patterns, overpower the brain totally and are experienced in clairvoyance. The brain cannot interfere. The transmission is solely light-charged. There is no imbalance of vocabulary to be responded to in probing and the purity of clairvoyance is untouched by brain interference.

Visions, are the result of a clairvoyant being transmitted to in the purity of light equations. Visions often transfix the receiver. Vision is always in colour, always without the brain's interception, and always from God.

God initiates most clairvoyant experiences. Many are because the recipient of light has equations that need resolution. Many recipients have soul light activity which magnetises God's rays needingly when the soul light becomes inactive, fades down because of too much stress inside the heart area.

Clairvoyants now are rare. Their souls are straining constantly. Once there were many. The human form was minimal in radioactivity and not so superficially charged. What comes through the rays of light transmission to a clairvoyant, is an equating quantity of pure light vibrations which are injected into the soul light giving it life force. God delivers that charge automatically. Equations always seek their prime light source no matter where they have evolved and stretch to make contact with pure light vibrations. Attached to God's raying, they suction light activity needingly.

Imagery in clairvoyance is again the construction of light vibrations. Imagery is transmitted because a recipient is sensitive to imagery and magnetic to colour volume. Equations alert strongly to whatever is needed to balance their vibrations.

Colour volume, also of clairvoyant experience, is glorious. It occupies the entire visual surround when transmitted and can include imagery. A recipient absorbs everything magnetically and the soul light strengthens.

Watching light transmission is actually seeing its coloured patterns through the eyes. Because of the evolution of the eyes, a clairvoyant vision is of eye-receptive activity. The eyes have evolved seeking colour and being fed coloured patterns. In clairvoyance, God's rays insert colour through the soul light. Its powerful transmission spreads out inside the soul light and because the eyes are automatically magnetic to colour, the vibrations and the patterns are magnetised by the eyes. A clairvoyant receives optical charge of light vibrations able to be clearly seen and cleanly accepted. The coloured imagery and colour volumes bounce off the eyeball and retina back into the soul light. The brain is absolutely still and cannot activate during clairvoyant reception. It is drowned in pure light power from God. Even the skull is light flushed. So powerful is clairvoyance, the brain experiences euphoria of light flushing overpowering radioactivity and very often seeks that euphoria again. A brain can be enticed into soul searching by a strong clairvoyant experience.

Man without soul search can never experience clairaudience or clairvoyance. Both are of soul light needs. Once many sought soul truth. Now few seek such truth.

Clairvoyant vision has been used as prophecy. Vision should never be used that way, for all light transmission is an equational response to each individual of search. Nothing is given to heal, warn, inform, or comfort, any seeker of truth. Images that may be relative to a situation within the life of an individual are experienced only to feed the equations of the soul light.

Clairvoyance in meditation is possible because the soul light is encouraged in function and light transmission can be received. Meditation, as long as it is not brain powered, can activate soul light equations strongly. If there is any electrical or radioactive appliance being used or near the meditator, light equations do not activate and cannot magnetise their source. Meditation that is unselfed, in need of the soul, seeking God's touch, and of soul light capability, can bring about both clairaudience and clairvoyance unto the meditator. Meditation that strongly activates the brain brings huge radioactive euphoric experience which can elevate the meditator into believing he or she is in their soul. A highly charged brain, magnetically sought and deliberately entered vibrationally, traps those vibrations inside the head, holds them there by magnetic feeding, and when the brain has eaten their content, the meditator remains in a euphoric state until another magnetic interest activates the brain again. Meditation into the brain is always dangerous. Meditation for healings should be done in the soul light. Light in transmission of charge, if magnetised strongly enough, can help and heal many illnesses. In some rare cases it can also cure a disease. The insertion of pure light vibrations feed all equations strongly.

The visual impact of clairvoyance on the eyes stimulates every pure equation that is left in their formation of vibrations. All colourful equations are supercharged. Eye-glow becomes evident and although such radiance does not last, a clairvoyant looks very beautiful to anyone witnessing instant clairvoyant light charge. Equations light-glow for a few minutes only before fading down in equating temperature. As well as eye-glow, all other body equations receive a stimulating light charge which can cause excess energy for some time after the experience. Equations are energised purely then and automatically cause euphoria of light charging. A real clairvoyant rarely exposes the experience publicly and rarely opens up to others of curiosity. The experience is too overwhelming and felt as a God given experience. Because of the inherent defilement of God and the soul, a clairvoyant guards that experience respectfully. Light from God to a recipient is absolutely pure and strengthens the soul light. It can heal a recipient if repeated often. The purity of charge dominates all vibrations opposing its entry. The clairvoyant becomes eternally held.

There are many individuals who receive oratory, the power to speak convincingly and also to speak in a foreign language they cannot themselves speak. Oratory once again comes from God via the soul light, patterning the soul light in vibrating vocabulary, and automatically must be expressed through the mouth. A recipient opens the mouth and out of it gush words which have impact. The receiver of oratory nearly always has soul searched. If there is no search, oratory is given in response to the soul light equations of severe stress.

Oratory from God is powered according to the needs of an individual. If an individual's soul light, surrounded by God's rays, begins to destabilise in equations, imbalance is felt vibrationally inside God's rays and equated in responding patterning. If the individual talks a great deal and is not clairaudient or clairvoyant sensitive, then oratory is given instead. Equations dictate exactly what food they need when required. The vibrations of voice will be returned by God in oratory. The receiver will speak for however long it takes for the charge to settle in. The words given are probed for automatically and spoken fluently. Selection is of automatic equating patterning. An orator in light giving is always impressive and speaks rhythmically, beautifully, and without aggression. Many are given oratory without realising it. What is spoken in oratory is always relevant to whatever the situation, place, subject, accomplishment or endeavour. When given in a foreign language out of context of a situation, the receiver cannot be vibrated any other way. An illness of the throat, nose, eyes or ears would prevent oratory from taking place as all of those areas vibrate hugely. Foreign language oratory is given when the recipient cannot be vibrated in normal language patterning because equations have diseased where the vibrations of oratory would enter.

Where oratory can become ugly, is when a receiver admits the brain into that purity and the orator convulses in imbalance of vibrations. So violent can the convulsive spasms be, a frothing of the mouth occurs, for the brain's coil itself convulses and its heat excretes through the mouth. Oratory which is defiled by brain interference can be delivered uglily, for once entering a flow of light purity the brain expresses aggressive words and the orator sounds ugly. God withdraws automatically and the orator spits out words that defile, and all beauty destroys. With good health oratory can be hugely beneficial to the receiver, for it stimulates and activates all body equations, and leaves the orator elated for many minutes as the charge dies down equatingly. The greatest words ever spoken upon this Earth were from Christ's pure oratory.

Aura sight, is the capacity to hold light function in visual magnetic attraction long enough to see its reality, its coloured equations, or the glowing of aura vibrational projection. God does not give such sight. It is activated by the soul light unaided. This is because an aura sighted individual has huge soul light radiance which expresses outwards a pure charge of vibrations which automatically seek magnetic attraction to any light holding formation, and involve. There are many with aura sight. Some can only see vague singular shades of colour. Others, bright surrounds of coloured auras, and often the vibrations inside aura bands. There are some who have very exceptional aura sight and can see vibrating patterns and shaped vibrations.

The seeing of aura can tire an individual and stress the eyes, for radioactivity in the environment has smeared pure light vibrations so hideously, great aura sight is now almost impossible, equations have lost intensity and purity of colour. Aura sighted individuals mistakenly associate their capacity with spiritual experience. It is not. The soul light vibrations of an individual which are strong, pure, and capable, automatically activate by themselves, progressing and seeking contact with likeness. God does not interfere. Any aura sighted individual has huge soul light capacity.

The greatest of all experiences of light transmission is transcribal writing, the power to receive written words. This giving is the most difficult to receive. God uses a recipient to transcribe linguistically what has to be received in order to control severe imbalanced equations. Such imbalance can be environmental, of the earth's suffering, of human threat, of the approach of deadly vibrations, of necessary warnings, of imperative change, of conscienced action, of soul distress, and of influences which are destructive to evolution. God's vibrations then, activate in search of requitement. This is because a build-up of aggressed and stressed equations flowing through God's rays, need to balance or be detached. Where those equations involve huge quantity, God probes light storage of written language to activate resolution. Transcribal writing unto a recipient is activated. God inserts the patterning straight into the selected soul light, vibrationally. The soul light transmits each patterned word through every pure equation the body holds. Because the patterns are of writing, the hands automatically magnetise the wording. Expressing equations activate the hands and arms into writing whatever is vibrating through their formation. At the same time the eyes, also activated by the same patterns, observe the writing and encourage its flow automatically. Sentences must complete, and punctuation which stops and starts the writing is often omitted during reception for it prevents clean vibrational activity. As a transcriber writes a sentence, if the brain is admitted, the flow of pure light patterning ceases until the brain is refused. When the writing becomes unclear a brain is always the cause. When the receiver stays clean, words from God flow greatly.

God chooses a transcriber. God needs, by way of vibrations, a vehicle of linkage, one who can release combinations of equations which build up in God's rays unrequited. The transcriber must have huge soul light capacity. The individual is chosen because of strong magnetic attraction to God's rays and soul light ability to receive the necessary writings. Many destroy pure transcriptions by admitting the brain. In reception, a transcriber may stop the flow intentionally because the brain refuses to accept what is being given. This happens in almost all transcription taking and causes lies, hearsay, exaggerations and fantasies, to be written. The transcriber has allowed the entry of the brain which also has stored writings of energised patterns, and can insert them any time its presence is magnetised. The slow flow of transcriptions allows the brain opportunity to write of itself. This takes place during a transcription only if the transcriber halts the purity of flow, hesitates in doubt or fear, and within that split second of time, allows the brain to continue the transcription itself. It does so by probing for written words it has been programmed with. They automatically vibrate of their energised vibrations and charge-spurt into the writing very aggressively. A transcriber often does not know the brain has taken over the writings. God always withdraws from brain interference and the transcriber is left to establish sense out of some reality and much nonsense.

Great transcribers have brought great assurances to mankind. Great souls have been chosen to warn, counsel, comfort, explain, request, stimulate and help much that mankind is starved of. God's given words are always to requite equations. God's choice of writings always does requite those equations. No transcription has ever been given unless equations are suffering. If many individuals are suffering together, God's rays cannot requite them individually unless a suitable recipient of transcriptions becomes available. Their suffering is joined vibrationally. Each soul light vibrates the same pain. To individualise their responses is not possible for the joining creates a unity of vibrations. A transcriber can be used to pacify their souls. Sometimes the chosen one corrupts tragically and becomes a leader of many in power over their souls. God never gives again when that happens for the brain has greeded the opportunity and destroyed the truth.

Many great writers have been transcribal. Their writings were able to help many of the same soul strength. Man in his brain is incapable of profundity. Programming is all the brain has to write from. Emotional writing comes directly from man's soul and so does every beauty man has ever expressed. Admitting the brain into great transcriptions defiles every emotion felt. The brain will cast doubt on everything, want theory over fact, question every statement, and keep on finding fault to keep feeding. Writings then are man-contrived and are starved of great truth continually.

Thousands of years ago man held powerful soul light vibrations. Little radioactivity had entered man's body. Electricity had not been invented. Man was a strong, healthy, long living being, with huge soul light capacity. Man was automatically clairaudient and clairvoyant. Equations inside man's soul light were magnetic to God's rays and sought light feeding constantly. The human brain at that time had no control over the soul light and man evolved with God's light rays audible and visible if magnetised. As man began to write, transcribal history began. An individual asked questions relating to the environment he or she lived in and was answered in resolution of searching equations. Man became informed.

The earliest transcribal writings were given to various individuals all over the Earth relating to their existence. Some were for truth to be respected. Some were for tribal gatherings. Some were for help with problems that occurred within families. Others were for the continuance of light life. Every one has been defiled and re-written. Every one has been twisted in truth. As man became brain intelligent those pure transcriptions destroyed.

God answered all who sought soul light existence. Thousands were given. Thousands denied as the brain emerged man's god. Man's equations strained, stressed and imbalanced. God's responses became less. When God finally began withdrawing rays of light life from man's soul light, it was because the brain had evolved as an entity.

Transcribal writings that cannot be deciphered are given in response to equations that imbalance. A suitable balance of charge is probed for. Many who receive such strange scribble often give up reception and are afraid to continue the search.

Doctrine of many variations has also been transcribed and the transcriber nearly always adjusts the text. Doctrine is always given in response to the search of many similar individuals united in enquiry and soul light needs. Doctrine is always given spasmodically for the transcriber can become exhausted and is often so weak continuing is impossible. The vibrations of writing, if persistent, drain energy cells of their charge because the cells of light rays activate for long periods. A transcriber must rest continually, eat healthily, and sleep soundly. Lengthy doctrine taking can go badly wrong if the transcriber attempts an adjustment during reception. The flow is cut off, the brain interferes and a doctrine becomes corrupted. Most doctrines have corrupted that way. If the brain is wanted within doctrine taking, the words become injected with brain programming, contrived sentencing, and lies relating to the brain's absorbed patterning.

All great written works which do not fantasise or deny the soul of man are from the writer's soul light emotions. Nothing of pure beauty has ever come from man's contriving brain power. The combination of brain and soul light activation often brings about literature that has both emotional content and calculative vocabulary. Such works confuse, complicate, and disturb the reader. Man's literary ability is mostly of the brain now and man's choice of words is very aggressively charged.

Transcribal writing, if untouched by brain interference, is of pure light activity flowing through the entire body of the receiver and in direct ray-link with God. If kept up it becomes food of life force, a stimulation of pure vibrations of light life. If abandoned the equations of the soul light destabilise, for their food source has been cut off. A transcriber can then become very insecure, prone to emotional outbursts and feel starved of every nourishment. Lengthy abandonment results in mood swings and serious depression. Soul light equations always control human emotions and if their magnetic food source transcribally is stopped, they frenzy until they begin feeding of the same vibrational source again. Once begun, transcribal writing should always continue. If kept up, the transcriber purifies, eventually overpowers the brain of vibrating interference, and usually receives pure truth without one contrived word. There is also a turning away from all that corrupts soul light existence.

All who have experienced clairaudience, clairvoyance, aura sight, oratory, and transcriptions, have had soul light capacity inside their hearts. All have never experienced real truth. With truth of the soul light, all need to purify their search and experience a realistic God. All need detachment from brain interference for such truth to be experienced. God must equate the search as long as it is pure.

When there is deliberate denial of truth, God must deny the soul the safety of eternity, for no attraction is there for God to magnetise the equations of soul light vibrations. Such denials have been many. Such reality still exists. A soul search is the need for God, nothing else. If God is not found, the search is always diverted. Another entity arrives. Another spirit or guide is accepted. Another medium is sought. On and on the search continues. The seeker never finds and is never requited by mistaken entities. Some become so corrupted the soul light fades of its beauty and the brain takes over completely. Others carry on their searching in areas where the brain has already contrived the religion, sect, teachings, commune, segregation of souls, or gatherings of progressive methods of self-development. All who seek never find the real God this way. All should realise why. All should find, if real truth is wanted.

Spiritual intervention unto any individual who has enough soul light capacity to heal another, often results in the laying of the hands, a transmission of God's light rays through the hands of a receiver which can be spread over the diseased area of any form human or animal and inject strength of light vibrations into an area of severe imbalance.

Christ laid the hands over several individuals needing light healing. In a few recorded instances Christ performed miracles, the astounding reaction of an immobilised form being mobilised again, as well as a shocked form unable to see, being stimulated strongly for sight to be returned, and a terrorised form in the agony of fear being calmed and brought back to normality. These miracles were done through Christ's soul light, powerfully held by God's invisible rays, transmitted through Christ's hands and spread over an individual's imbalanced equations. Into those equations a pure vibrating charge of light activated their slowness, energised their inactivity, fed their discolouring equations and restored them back to full strength. Then, miraculous healings took place. Now, because the human form is almost entirely radioactivating, healing through the laying of the hands is impossible.

Electrical energy can often pass through a needing to be healed individual which can stimulate the receiver because of the electrical content of the human body form. A healer can perform a healing which is felt, accepted electrically and often heals where electrical cells need charge. Many healers use electrical apparatus before attempting laying the hands, to transfer that charge into a body. Other healers rely on the belief that God uses their person to transmit healing through them and very often that is exactly what happens.

When a sincere healer seeks God's contact, a healing takes place that is felt deeply by an individual and can emotion the receiver to realise it is God's touch. Very few healers now are sincere and very few allow God's vibrations into their souls. Most, brain-interfere in healings, and all, do not understand the reality of their soul lights or the truth of God's evolution.

Light vibrations when coming from the soul light of an individual and passed into another needing strength of light equations is absolutely pure, absolutely God given, and because contact with a healer is made by an individual whose equations are either diseased, inactive, or severely stressed, God automatically responds. God does not respond to those without need. The transmission of light through the hands of a healer can only be pure if the healer is pure in soul light. Few are. Many are not. The touch of a real healer's hands can bring about an experience that can change a receiver's life.

Spiritual development has many paths. The spirit has many contrivances. The soul has many convenient acceptances. The existence of God has never had a credible beginning. Light is of man's scientific theory. Man has no real evolution and creature has never convincingly evolved with a soul. Earth, the great living sphere of light vibratory life in the universe, is unimportant, unworthy of respectful preservation, and without belief in its living breathing body.

Cannot mankind spare Earth's life in preference to man's own?

Cannot mankind acknowledge truth before it is too late?

Cannot mankind be of real conscience and see the truth within this text and be of the soul man has evolved from?

When the truth of all things is understood, reality can be lived. Until God is wanted realistically the lies of man will persist. Until the soul light inside man's heart is wanted, the deaths of many will continue. Until the brain of man is detached from, the soul of man remains detached from God.

Until the Earth is in the conscience of every man, woman and child, mankind will experience suffering brought about by violations to the Earth unable to be equated by God.

# Universal Purity

The universe at this time is contaminating. All pure equations on Earth have almost destroyed entirely. What is replacing light evolutionary progression is man-made imbalanced vibrations of nuclear, radioactive and electric charge. Man's space search is threatening pure equations that have never been touched by impure vibrations since their evolution. Man's search is for territory and exploitation. Man's ignorance will destroy universal balance of pure light equations. Man's brain is without any God and soul reality. Man is interfering detrimentally in God's pure domain of light evolution.

The Earth's protective shield of God's cooling light rays has been broken open by space travel. Slits are vibrating imbalance and the held-in radioactivity man has covered the Earth with is now escaping into pure light existence. Man cannot see this happening and therefore cannot halt this violating activity. Man's totally destructive influence in space exploration must cease. All planets of absolute pure balance of equations will impure. Already those that man has violated, littered, exploded upon, and trashed, are in threat of explosion. They are a unified vibrating completeness of perfect equational balance. To violate such sublime evolutionary existence is a crime against universal sanctity of evolving life of pure light.

Man's Earth laws attempt exploitationary restraint where too much greed reveals the probable extinction of life forms, habitat, and a future secure existence. There are no laws to prevent a brutal greeding of every available planet near enough for man to probe into, destroy greedily, and ultimately condemn, where nothing of profit can be acquired. The laws of mankind have always been flawed and often unjust. Their implementation does not protect life of pure evolution, life of the soul, human or not human, and cannot protect the Earth's evolution in any way. The bounties on Earth are too great, too beautiful, and too beneficial to the possessive desires of mankind to be left alone respectfully. All mankind sees that is endowed with great beauty and pure life is selfishly possessed in every way. Nothing is left for Earth's future security. Nothing is left for mankind's future either. Nothing is respected anywhere. Nothing is wanted protected and preserved. Nothing will survive inside such slaughtering deeds. With such blatant refusal to conscience for anything, nothing will be more oncoming than the horrifying reality of a world earthquake, a truth of mankind refusing conscience, denying Earth its birthright and denying man's soul light the right to continue evolving.

The planets of universal purity of equations, all, are next on man's agenda of exploitation, next to be pillaged, probed into for wealth, and dumped upon with every destructive invention that technology causes, and without laws to stop the horrific deeds already being done. One greeder after another will lay claim for territory and whatever else is discovered that brings power or wealth to whoever has the power and wealth to claim ownership.

Conscience is impossible in the addiction of the greedy and the power afflicted. The spoils of both are of the brain's magnetic attraction for food. Laws of universal preservation are already too late to help what is being done to the planets and their pure surround. What will stop the violation of light life, is God, the real power over all and the undeniable equator of every imbalance evolving.

To pollute the pure universe is to become a victim of the consequences, because if God's rays withdraw and Earth overheats beyond temperature control, an explosion will take place that only God can equate.

Spacecraft upon other planets cause vibrations of impurity touching those that are totally pure and should never be touched. Space ship exhausts force into a pure environment pollution so vile, universal purity of equations is restricted in vibrational activity. Gradually those pollutants eat into pure vibrations because their aggression is supercharged and their presence has no magnetic source to attach to. Those that belong to mechanical inventions vibrate into a pure surround and burn it.

The deliberate explosions taking place on and around planetary purity are criminal. No violation is greater than to explode contaminated debris into an area or upon a formation that is virgin, and has never been touched. Such an example of what man has become in his brain has never been more relevant to this truth here.

The last deliberate violation to a sphere of the evolution of pure light was a violent explosion so deadly to the sphere that took the impact, God immediately withdrew protective rays and still has not returned to balance equations. The severity of that explosion split, ripped, fractured and destroyed, every pure equation at life in the area and surrounding it. The hole the explosion left cannot close, its equations are unable to re-form. God's rays cannot feed exploded equations, their impurity contaminates.

To initiate such an explosion for nothing more than convenience and a place to dump debris, must be one of the worst deeds mankind has done in history. Conscience was felt by many watching the explosion. Conscienced men and women must prevent that happening again.

To allow planets to be so violated, from their interior perfect compositions to their outer sheaths of protective invisible rays of God's holding, would cause inter-planetary magnetic eruptions caused by mankind, never before entering their pure evolutionary existence. Only God can and must control universal balance, and does so these ways.

First, man enters the universe ignorantly and thoroughly impurely. Attached to man is every vibrating imbalanced construction with no purifier, no equating containment, no pure magnetic enticement, no God protection, and no soul intelligence whatsoever. Into and onto a pure light life man proceeds to search for bounty any way possible and in every way destructive to the purity of the whole of evolution. Finding nothing, after repeatedly disturbing virgin life until satisfied nothing can be gained, mankind dumps every machined apparatus no longer needed, discards whatever contaminants man has gathered to survive from and seeks another planet to exploit where possible.

Man's debris is diseased, contaminated with hideous impure vibrations which begin to grow, enlarge vibrationally, and cover a pure body of light formation. They eat light equations hungrily. They must, their aggression is nuclear and radioactively charged.

God must equate the damaged equations, withdraw where contaminants have to be left, magnetise the impure vibrations unto storage, ray-cool the torn planet, then equatingly position rays of discharge unto where the contaminants have come from, and force them back unto Earth. Because they have come from Earth, and have travelled in space, their impure vibrations enlarge in volume. They aggress hugely for their interference in space has caused magnetic-interaction with pure equations which create acceleration of charge. They multiply. They are hot. They then approach Earth carrying universal pure equations frenzying because they do not equate on Earth, it is too impure. Into Earth's environment they scream, and unto massive environmental instability they stay. Once again man, completely unaware of such truth becomes the victim of exploitation. God returns in protective rays unto the injured planet and mankind suffers yet another world disaster not understood in any way ever.

I write here to bring this truth unto mankind before it is too late for anything to be done to help Earth, life forms and the evolution of man as a continuing species. Any more planetary exploitation will cost mankind lives that should not be put at risk in such a way. Stop butchering pure virgin planets please. Mankind does not need any more wealth, power, or possessions. Man is saturated in everything destructive to all of life everywhere. Stop please, your Earth is in serious threat of explosion. You, all of mankind, are also in serious threat of extinction, and God can only react as the equator of all imbalances.

Into pure equations of universal evolution man is calculating empire. Man has already destroyed the entire Earth's balance. Man will do exactly the same to whatever planet has been chosen to exploit. Man's brain, as always, is responsible.

God's invisible rays withdraw from all areas of space traffic, leaving paths of ugly manufactured radioactivity inside a surround of absolute purity of equations. To draw those impurities away into galaxy holding is not possible. Their vibrations are without first equation's motioning. They do not belong to universal evolution of pure light equations. To allow them to remain the contaminants of pure universal light vibrations is also not possible, for all equations in their area will begin heating and imbalance. To lock them into their own field is again not possible, for the equations of their surround would be prevented from pure contact with each other vibrationally. To push them back to the Earth they are magnetic to is what is happening now. Into the cracks in God's protective shield they are being forced by God's responding rays, and into man's already polluted environment they are flooding. God does this by equating their volume and emitting their charge invisibly, ray-directing their passage back to their magnetic source. Once again man will be the victim of savage entry into a pure light universe.

Earth cannot be saved from man in the power of man's brain refusing conscience of the soul. Earth can be saved by mankind in conscience and in truth.

Earth is God's universal creation and is of equating vibrations which must be responded to. At present Earth's sluggish rotation is from overheating. Earth's light equations of solidity have nearly all gone to decorate man's body and possessions. Nearly all of Earth's blood, oil of light equations of balance, has been taken out to fuel manufactured machinery.

All of Earth's growth everywhere has been destroyed in balance of light equations, is covered with diseases and is unable to be saved much longer. Earth's waters cannot purify, pollution is too severe. Earth's breathing is no longer in motion of first equation. Earth emotions. Earth suffers painfully. Earth convulses, heaves in agony, and God cannot respond as God once did.

Man is the cause. Man in pursuit of everything there is to greed. Man without a soul. Man without God in reality.

Turbulence in Earth's environment is vibrations massing, progressing, and contained. As each forest is ransacked, a huge safety of cooling destroys. As each block of land is excavated for development, safety of firmness of the Earth destroys in balance. As each river is dammed, safety of terrain is lessened. As each road is sealed, safety from earthquakes destroys. As each acreage is poisoned and flayed, safety from disease destroys. As each explosion rips both land and sea apart, safety on land and in the seas destroys. As each nuclear test continues, safety of every living form destroys. As each brain denies conscience, all of mankind's future is threatened. As God withdraws the rays of light protection, Earth, creatures and all of mankind destroy forever. A vibrating mass is all that is left to be contained.

Evolution cannot continue unless man evolves of soul light intelligence. Every invention that man has furthered has been of man's brain, a constant feeding coil of the mucous of energy powered by man himself. Such an evolution needs to end. Disease of every living formation is because at every turn, man has interfered with equations of balance everywhere. Not one purity of any life form is left to evolve as it should.

God, the light power of all of life, is in absolute control of man's deeds equationally. God's rays, when they withdraw from equations of stressed activity, take with them the invisible activity of every minute vibration touching those rays in patterning. They are stored in vibrating containment and automatically await discharge. God draws the quantity of imbalances that cause the rays to be withdrawn, into spherical containment until they begin to heat. When that happens the vibrations are discharged, thrown back into the magnetic field most able to accept the charge. Earth's contaminants return to Earth. They do not dissolve. They do not cease vibrating charge of vibrations. They cannot purify. They cannot be magnetised anywhere else except by the forces that bred them. When contaminants return to their source, they progress. They alter in charge, strengthen in vibrations because they unite with other vibrations of magnetic interest. They multiply by expanding in their domain explosively. They give birth.

God's holding of Earth's contaminating vibrations until they are returned to Earth is an automatic reaction to impure vibrational force, unable to be magnetised within rays of light, prevented from escaping into the universe, locked inside the earth's destroying shield of safety, until, by heating, they are detached from. Pressure causes the detachment. Pressure inside God's rays which is equated, causing equations to press their vibrations against those causing the imbalance. Equations are far more powerful than man-made vibrations as long as God has control.

Earth's impure vibrations are the reason for rainbows. The rainbow has never been explained in its reality of light equations.

It is composed entirely of pure light equations. Its touch upon the Earth is vital.

Rainbows have always existed on Earth since pure radioactive vibrations impured, became too aggressed and could not explode of their imbalanced equations. Rainbows originated from Earth's aura bands, coloured equations magnetised into singular colour bands and vibrating around the Earth spherically. As the aura bands were aggressed and opened by radioactivity they were detached from their protective position around the earth, drawn into God's invisible rays and contained there until by magnetic attraction, they were returned to the Earth in contact.

Rainbows are the last life force of light equations left for Earth's survival. As Earth convulses from turbulences inside its body now and releases those imbalances by way of earthquakes, the damaged areas need equational resuscitation, healing of sores within structural formations which breathe of light equations. Damaged light equations upon the Earth also need resuscitating. The rainbow is the equating charge of revival. Damaged equations automatically vibrate distress. God automatically responds. Requitement comes through God's rays by way of huge coloured equations originating from Earth's aura, able to surround any area vibrating in imbalanced activity and feed distressed equations until their temperature and colour calms. The damaged areas of equational formations in stress, stretch of their activity seeking magnetic food. Equations elongate and vibrate redness of temperature. God responds with coolness of vibrations which contain rainbowed aura activity, able to penetrate deep into Earth and spherically charge-up the area needing help.

Rainbow charging, being of spherical colouring, enters Earth without interruption because God's rays surround its composition and invisibly aid the delivery of the charge. What man sees is bands of coloured equations only. This is because man looks from the stability of Earth and a horizon distorts the reality of spherical wholeness. What man cannot see is the completeness of rainbowed aura and how it surrounds any area of damaged equations seeking balance. Moisture reveals a rainbow because light and water evolved equatingly, are in perfect balance, and when a rainbow arrives within a heated area, its light equations touch heat, express moisture, and can then be seen. The very same visibility occurs inside the Earth.

Earth's interior of light has nearly all gone. A super-charge of pure light is needed. The rainbow helps Earth live. Man is now destroying the rainbow's pathing through the universe and unto Earth.

Many rainbows arrive on Earth. Many are never seen. Moisture and heat illuminate the bands of pure colour. Radioactivity cancels them out. A rainbow is spherical. Half of its activity penetrates deep into Earth while the other half covers Earth's surface. Every light equation above and below Earth inside the vibratory field of the rainbow is fed life force of light return charge. Without rainbow discharge Earth's equations will fade, lose colour, and glow red. Already the red visible bands of a rainbow are dominant. That is imbalance of equations too heated to be of equating volume of colours. Earth's temperature is the cause. Even the once pure bands of aura which were in absolute perfection of their equations of colour, all banding in exactly the same quantity of equations, are showing imbalance. Red is dominant. Red is heat.

Access unto the Earth for rainbow entries is slowly being destroyed by man's space travelling and space search. Satellites are all in the paths of rainbows. As soon as a rainbow ring touches one of the thousands of satellites man has placed above the Earth, its equations retract and imbalance. God automatically magnetises it back into rays of holding. This is happening now repeatedly. Man's ugly destructive inventions out into universal sanctity have already begun to destroy the Earth's life force and man again violates his future. No Earth will survive much longer unless this ends.

Space is God's domain. Not man's. Earth is God's child. Not man's. Man now is man's creation. Not God's. Man's soul now is being forfeited for greed of every superficiality man has created. God's response to greedy man must automatically be detachment. Man's response to that reality must be challenged.

Greed is the worst addiction man has evolved with. Power is the progression of that greed. War is the progression of power. Death is the progression of war. From the history of man, nothing has been achieved that is of real benefit to the Earth, creature, and man himself. Nothing. Nothing. Nothing. Every life has suffered. Every suffering, man has ignored. Progress of the human soul has ended. Progress of the human brain has and always will continue in destruction over all life unless man himself honours the soul inside himself, and cleans up what he has done. Without the Earth man ends. Without the soul man ends. Without God man ends. Without the brain in power all that is of life will thrive.

The universe must be left in peace. The Earth must be returned to its greatness. Man must return to his soul. God must return to man. If that happens, a world earthquake, the most obvious coming reality, could be prevented. If it is not, man is forsaken.

What would Earth be like if mankind desired Earth's truth?

What would mankind be like if all of mankind desired God's truth?

What would mankind's brain be like if mankind desired man's soul?

# World Earthquake

It is inevitable that Earth with its constant earthquakes is imbalancing and could explode, not the Sun or any other planet, but Earth. It is also inevitable that God, the equator of all light equations, must respond to such an explosion equatingly. When that might happen is entirely up to man. Why it will happen is obvious.

A global Earthquake of Earth would release the agonising heat Earth is vibrating. Earthquake would release Earth of radioactive smothering. Earthquake, equated by a God of light equations would violate man's existence entirely.

God's responses to a world earthquake would be the equating force of exploding equations, a return charge so powerful man himself could magnetically explode. No creature would survive such force contained.

In a world of scientific theories, no God exists. No truth exists therefore and the evolution of light is totally without a beginning. All the knowledge man has is without the prime equation of life. To be of nothing that is believable is to be absent of the soul.

A reality, the sole requitement for living can never be experienced unless a beginning is established. Once confirmed, a life evolves eternally. Man is without a birthright, a pure right to life. Man's evolution without God is the reason for all man's sufferings.

The once glorious Earth will never return to that which was its birthright. Too many violations have changed its evolution. Growth will never recover in balance of area, for the extermination of all micro-organisms which are the food for Earth's tiny creatures has been fast and violent in deeds. Areas of forest will never grow again as they were, equating life formations have been stripped out and utterly wasted. Without magnetic attraction forests will disease, rot, and never give birth to life of light equations.

The greatness of the forests and their creatures was created from the activity of light equations magnetising each other and evolving purely. Every tree was singularly held by God's rays of cool protection. Flower, a perfect God-evolved formation, has been so violated for mass production its wonderful pure coloured equations have paled. Its seeds are stunted. Its aroma has almost gone. The vibrations that form flower have been cut into and cost flower much magnetic strength. Its artificial creation has killed its aura. Its soul light equations cannot be magnetised by God. It is suffocated by poisons for mass export. It has no life of light left for its soul to reach eternal life.

Flowers on Earth evolved in perfect equational balance. Never should they be deformed. Never should their equations be touched. Never should such perfect beauty be brain defiled. Never, should man exterminate that birthright of light life. Flower, because of its pure vibrating colour patterns, is the most necessary food for the eye equations of man and creature. It feeds powerful equational stimulation into the eyes. Without its activity all eye equations fade. Colour is its charge. Light is its purity. God is its life force. Man is flower's killer.

Inside Earth its gutted body burns, develops sores, cannot cool, heaves because it must breathe, shifts because its equations need unity, expresses heat in many ways because if it did not, it could explode an entire country.

Earth groans in vocal sounds of emotioning equations because of its suffering. It is heard universally through vibrations of invisible linkage.

Earthquakes have always been to balance equations magnetically. As Earth's internal temperature rises from man's constant plundering, earthquakes increase. Their frequency now is solely because Earth's body is in agony of equations so imbalancing God's rays could automatically withdraw from areas of deteriorating equations. A withdrawal by God from the sections of hard light compositions which have been ray held is the most threatening withdrawal of all. Once those rays are drawn out, Earth's interior will explode. No cooler will there be.

Each section of Earth's constitution has evolved as a composition of equations knitted together magnetically. Because the sections vibrate different patterns, different temperatures and colours, they are ray-surrounded. Where there are veins of hard light they are vein-rayed. A ray sidles along a vein on both sides then closes over its formations magnetically. The rays of God manoeuvre to hold a formation whatever the shape. Light bends. God's rays bend also.

Earth's interior should never have been touched. Its bounty was the evolution of pure light equations ray-held by God. If man continues these horrific deeds the Earth will eventually open up in every area of plunder. Such a reality is possible. Quake imbalance is spreading, pushing vibrations along fault lines.

Each earthquake God withdraws from is stored vibrationally in the outer surround of the universe. Each groaning is stored also. Each desperate explosive force that Earth releases, echoes powerfully, is also in storage. Each man-created explosion, from the smallest device to the most hideous, has been magnetised by God's rays. Magnetic necessity attracts and contains every imbalance.

Inside the storage of imbalanced equations of magnetic drawing, very ugly vibrations which man has created await return of charge. As man's explosions accumulate their storage enlarges. As nuclear power becomes acceptable, vibrations in storage nuclearise. Should Earth need world earthquake to save its life, the response charge from God would be nuclear. All vibrations are of magnetic attraction. All vibrations progress. All vibrations are equatingly controlled by God.

The amount of plunder man has already taken from Earth can never be replaced. Earth's jewels can never be returned. Its balance of hard light equations had magnetised together and formed Earth's body. Their purity has been destroyed. Every structure of balance Earth evolved with has also been hacked into and used destructively. Earth's magnificence has been deformed. Restoration is not possible. The amount of oil that has been extracted from Earth's interior, the burning of which has polluted the atmosphere, can never be returned. Its great lubrication has been consumed greedily by man's machines. Earth's gaseous structure has almost all gone and will never evolve again. Man is now draining Earth's pure water supply because man's own water is too polluting to be safe and huge profits are also involved in business. Every portion of a living entity of light life has been predated upon by man in power of man's brain. The devastation man has caused is irreparable. The Earth is unable to contain man's greed much longer.

If God did not exist a universe would not evolve as it has. If God does not exist man's evolution is over. Extinction must be. For those who refuse God's existence as the light force of the entire universe, the controller of light equations, the surrounding power of the universe, the creator of life formations and the invisible raying responder to all of life equations, a continuance of destruction will prevail. For those who have conscience and know they must, cessation of the murder of the Earth will eventuate. Although the permanent damage man has done to Earth will never be healed, man in his soul can change everything. Earth can be helped greatly. Earth can be God-held once again in the purity of light. Man of great soul light could be responsible.

A world earthquake has been prophesied often, prophesied without the reality of God, the soul, and Earth's real evolution. Such a prophecy can never be believed unless reality is paramount in explanation.

Earth, without question, is destroying. Earth, without man's conscienced pledge to save, will explode. Man is totally responsible.

Man must acknowledge man's deeds truthfully before it is too late.

For Earth, I the writer of this truth, plead for Earth's life, for Earth's suffering to be believed in, and for mankind to believe in God, the only life force the Earth has ever known, and the only chance mankind has to continue on to an eternal sanctity of soul.

Be of conscience or conscience denied, mankind will automatically be requited. Equations balance no matter how their evolution progresses. They explode if they must. They balance inevitably. They are magnetised by God or detached from if their heating cannot be controlled. Equations evolved the Earth and every formation upon the earth. If mankind prefers aggressive charge of energy to equations of light eternity, mankind is doomed by preference. If mankind prefers to save Earth, mankind's future is eternal.

# Wars

Never has man violated his Earth his creatures and himself more than in war. Wars have always been for power, gold, territory, throne, empire, government control, protection from invasion and the containment of peoples rejecting corrupt leaders. All of these facts reveal wars as wrong, corrupt, evil and without conscience. Mankind has been sacrificed time and time again, often unwillingly, often unjustly and mostly without any desire to kill another human being.

There is no excuse for wars. There never was. Real conscience will always refuse such murders. The brain always justifies the killing.

Man injects cruel programming into education to further the right to kill. Innocent men, women and children are always the millions of victims sacrificed for others to retain seats of powering. Into the brains of many, hatred, revenge, murder and suicide, programmed warring has been fed. Programs that man has put there. Programs that feed the conviction that war is right, a respectful profession, an honourable occupation, a necessary employment, a good career, a great one if rising to top positions and the belief in the protection of one's own country. Were mankind in truth of God's reality, Earth's suffering and man's own soul, wars would never happen. Wars could not be part of life. Wars would never be acceptable and war against another human being could never be contemplated. Why? The soul of every living being would be respected. The Earth could not be violated and God's light protection would never be detached from. That is why. Such relevant truth needs conscience.

One bomb dropped on Earth absolutely destroys every light equation for miles around its area of explosion. Equations are split, fractured, slit and fragmented and cannot unite again because their pieces are overpowered by surface envelopment of radioactive charge. They frenzy in the environment in pieces, suffer emotionally in pieces and unless the Sun can penetrate the area and magnetise them upward, they remain tortured inside environmentally destroyed war territory.

Constant artillery firing vibrates an area unto massive radioactive progressive vibrational contamination. That force does not disappear. It cannot. It is alive, magnetic and growing of its charge. One atomically charged bomb explodes mankind's own pure equations of atomic rhythm into trillions of light particles. That has been done already. The atom of man destroyed the atomic purity of man's soul light when it became the atomic bomb, a very real development of those in brain activity feeding from a deadly invention conscience would never have accepted.

One nuclear war will wipe out every equation in more than one country and in millions of creatures as well as in man's entire body and soul, a grotesque reality mankind in soul needs to face. An even more grotesque reality for those in power to face further on when such a war becomes real in every way.

A bomb explosion of any manufacture not only eats into Earth as well as man, its chemicals, once in the environment, combine with whatever is circulating and progress very threateningly to every form of life. Every stage of chemical warfare is death to all who take part, all who are the victims and all who initiate the spreading. Chemical warfare has deformed equations so hideously, mankind is also deforming from exposure to such evil.

Young life after young life is murdered. Boys not men are sacrificed. Men become soul defiled and should they survive, live with no conscience dared. Those who condone war are responsible for its grip. Those who conscience however silently need real certainty in God's truth here to refuse the continuance of wars.

History has always been of many lies and exaggerations. Man originally warred in greed for gold, territory and power over all. Man wars now for exactly the same reasons. Warring is an empire, brain powered and brain fuelled. Those in its grip are addicted to killing, addicted to the blood of man.

A bloody killing in war when experienced by a soldier enters the brain in violent aggressive charge. The splattering of a body covered in red blood is a horrific sight to accept. The soul light if allowed emotion will retract in many ways for its equations cannot equate killing another of soul light evolution. A soldier may convulse, vomit, scream or sob when emotioning of soul light vibrations. Many react that way. A soldier who deliberately hardens the heart area muscularly, activates the brain and coldly accepts the murder as nothing but a deed done and finished with. That attitude turns men of soul light existence into murderers of their own kind and killers of their own souls. That attitude places guns in the hands of children and forces them to kill. Women are programmed to kill also.

The addiction to killing is a programmed brain in violent charge unable to be stopped. Serial killers are the true examples of the brain addiction to killing. Serial killers of war are addicts of exactly the same behavioural patterns.

There are many fighting in wars who do not kill and cannot. Many of these are killed. To force, make laws to enlist any man, woman or child, willing to kill or not, is unjustified. Every man, woman or child has the right to life. Every man, woman or child has the right to conscience. To take away the right of conscience is to overpower by force every decency and soul value mankind attempts to hold. Conscience has been ripped out of millions of young men sacrificed by those without any conscience possible. Man can only cease killing if the conscience becomes dominant and the brain becomes subservient. To strip man of self-respect and condemn man to whatever outcome war will create: death; deformity; the loss of sight, hearing and limbs; diseases of various cancers; depression so great the victim suicides or suffers; impotence; the need for drugs to forget; the incapacity to love anyone; the total denial of a God and the intense guilt soldiers of war try to live with is of true evil. This truth has been ignored. Mankind has been programmed to accept this truth as inevitable.

Wars have deformed the Earth's body. Everywhere wars have taken place and everywhere rehearsals of war have taken place are wounds deep and seeping of equations excreting in pain. The body of a living light entity is so brutalised God has withdrawn from many areas because of radioactive poulticing. Each wound, because of the intensity of heating, magnetises a quantity of radioactive aggression which poultices the wound. What is under it dies. Massive creature destruction has occurred. Massive plant destruction also.

The soil, once exploded into, can never magnetise the Sun's life force of light vibrations ever again. Its magnetic equations destroy. Wherever war takes place at any level man destroys everything he needs to keep alive. The area balance can never return. Man's health deteriorates. Creatures procreate unnaturally. Every living form deforms of soul light purity. One war after another solves nothing. One life after another is sacrificed for absolutely nothing of any benefit to mankind anywhere. All of this reality and man prepares for more wars with even more inventions more deadly than the present. Such a truth. So many lies concealing it. So many brains at large. So many souls condemned.

Never in man's history has warring been so hideously armed for. Never in man's conscience could such power be allowed.

The pursuit of the brain in any profession is to feed from its source of magnetic interest. Every hive of industry functions because the brains within production addict to the source of food. High powered technology emits radioactive vibrations so consuming an environment, all who work within that area are automatically overpowered in soul light, and brain activated. Man has become the victim of himself.

Industry, the production of massive environmental pollutants, is responsible for one disease after another attacking man, creature and Earth. So gross is pollution now a haze of filth is forming around the Earth. In that filth is every wriggling vibration man has created. Each singular worm of environmental pollutants wriggles its way into magnetic formation of vibrations and becomes disease. Whatever disease evolves depends on the area polluted and the contaminants circulating there. Every disease circulates in the environment first. Every carrier of disease has magnetised it from the environment first. Every death from disease returns it into the environment. Never does disease disappear, for its cause is vibrational impurity.

A war-torn country contains in its environment diseases that are evolving untreatable. Where the country is tropical those diseases progress differently to others developing in cooler regions. Air on Earth now cannot be cleaned, industrial pollution is too massive and on the increase. Nowhere is safe from disease. Rain which once pacified the entire surface of the Earth is now of disease itself. When it falls it cools only and its content then heats, progresses, combines with environmental pollution and impures. Every ugly vibrational covering over and around the Earth's body is active within the fall of rain. Its cooling lasts for minutes only as the Earth's temperature is overheating. Its great balance can never return. Its equating future is over. Its perfect release is so environmentally imbalanced, flooding, deluge, torrential downpours, and hail occur where once it rained equationally. Every climatic destructive change is of man's unconscienced activity. Rainwater is unsafe. Breeding within its deforming equations is disease.

Manufacture, the oversupply of unnecessary products from armament to plastics, is violating man's right to exist healthily and decently. One competitive product after another is crushed into outlets for purchasing. Man boasts the economy. Earth destroys from such boasting. Man greeds everything. Earth destroys of everything. Man saturates his markets. Earth is saturated with pollution. Man does not need most of man's products. God's truth, Earth's reality, and man's soul truth, is what is necessary for survival.

The unstoppable addiction to economic prosperity is a programme that is imbedded inside man's brain. It has persuaded man in government to justify massive destruction to the Earth's balance. So granite is that programming, education, a totally programmed brain activity, establishes man without any conscience and man without any reality. When war became educational history, man in government condoned killing his own kind. Programmes to condone murder, programmes to implement murder, programmes to accept the programming, programmes to honour the murdered and programmes to adhere to the right to murder, are all by brains, for the brain, and not one soul life is considered. Mutilation by man unto man is yet another programme, which firstly mutilates, secondly honours the mutilated, and thirdly programmes the mutilated to accept their injuries and live with that savage program until death. The sight being observed by many mothers, fathers, sons, daughters, children, husbands, wives, relatives and all who love the mutilated, enters soul light conscience and cannot be accepted or forgiven. Love for the mutilated becomes a suffering.

Those looking on are totally mutilated in soul life. Many others remain immune.

The possession of Earth has become territorial to every human being. For governments it is for business. For professionals it is for assets and wealth. For thrones it is for longevity and security. For tyrants it is for power. For science it is for experiments. For industrialists it is for an increase in dominance. For manufacturers it is for money. For warmongers it is for conquest. For every human being it is for a place to live. For children it is their place to take for themselves. For humanity as a whole it is for survival. For creature there is nothing. For creature's survival nothing is left. For Earth there is nothing. For Earth's survival there is nothing left. For man to be so greedy, so foolish and so utterly destructive, can only be of brain aggressive activity, the constant need for food, no matter the source or quantity of magnetic vibrating combinations.

Manufacture has gripped man as never before. Business is the main objective of almost everyone, a way to make money, a way to be independent, a way to buy luxuries, a way to be acceptable, a way to have more of everything. Most business once operative, devours everything it touches. It can eat into the decency of every man, woman and child for the pursuit of its coffers denies Earth, creature and man's soul. Its principles are often merciless. Its values are nearly always monetary. Business is man's god. In most business no conscience is possible. Brain addiction in business never stops feeding from any source. Business, whatever the path, attracts brain aggression immediately a plan begins. As long as that plan is wanted, the brain will advance it, feeding from whatever business is wanted. It has the programmes to continue recalling of itself as a business is planned. As long as there is no interference by the conscience, a business is established that can be of waste, plunder, environmental pollution, creature exploitation, machine manufacture, all Earth's resources used wastefully, ocean pillaging, land excavation, soil poisoning, forest burnings, tree mutilations, flower destruction, chemical violations to every life, unnecessary productivity, food contamination, plasticized clothing, sexual atrocities, movie and television intense brain programming, computerised progressions, all areas of every useless and soulless brain creations and all areas of monetary gain desired no matter the cost. Business, no matter what area of greed, is mostly corrupt. All that matters is ignored. Business for wars manufactures all that will totally erase man, creature and the Earth's evolution. Business if of greed only, destroys the evolution of the soul of man. Business must begin with conscience. If it begins in conscience, no violation could occur to man, creature and Earth. Business then would be greatly beneficial to everything man needs for a future.

Storage of nuclear armament and nuclear power stations all over the world has created a magnetic vibrating body of power which cannot be put out of charge. Not even science can destroy the power it has invented or stop the consequences of its progressing vibrations. It is the most lethal of all man's inventions and a true example of the escalation of man's brain power. Never has there been evil as vile as nuclear power. Man is already in business protecting and advancing its use. Man is programming its acceptance into every living human being, on an Earth that will explode from its irresponsible usage. The reason for such blatant abuse of power is financial greed, the brain of man addicted to its source of food and growing with the source it feeds from. Man outside the empire of nuclear power, reluctantly, helplessly, and innocently, allows its emergence into business. Mankind will be violated by its predatory escape from those keeping it contained, without the means to stop its powerful magnetic force needing to attach to its likenesses. From the intentional war-power to destroy countries, peoples, and all that lives, nuclear power has now become business turned into financial empire, still able to wipe out countries, peoples, and all that lives, and still progressing and threatening the entire Earth by its increasing manufacture. What kind of race has man become? What kind of humans accept such a reality of extinction possible?

Mankind must free man's conscience. This truth here has such relevance for the Earth's future and mankind's survival.

Man's brain intelligence is flawed and limited at this point in man's history. Man's soul is weak now and unable to revitalise in light equations. Man without soul intelligence will nuclearise himself.

God has been responding to Earth's needs ever since Earth's body solidified and needed cooling. Those responses have kept Earth alive. As man evolved a brain species God's responses began to withdraw. Earth's heating equations could not be cooled. Man-made vibrations became too imbalancing Earth's pure light activity. God still ray-holds parts of Earth's body, places where man has not reached in plunder. When those areas are reached by man, God will automatically withdraw all rays of cooling. Equations then will frenzy, overheat, and become explosive.

Temperature has been controlled by God always. God's equating responses keep the universe from imbalance of equations. To have allowed man to overheat the Earth to such a degree its body is becoming explosive, can only be because Earth's temperature has not reached its full equational warning signal, heat that transmits explosive charge ready to discharge. God must allow every vibrating equation inside the Earth and on the surface to reach exactly the same temperature, so that the explosions, once released, will free each individual equation equatingly. That has always been universal evolution of light equations and still is. No small release can there be where one huge formation is involved. Equations belonging to their containment automatically heat together and are automatically released together.

God does not make allowances for any specific light body in need. God does not sacrifice a light body for any reason. God always has, always will, and always must, equate light bodies, respond to their heating, and release their equations automatically. The withdrawal from Earth will be the absolute equational reaction to man's vibrations which cannot be allowed to continue evolving.

God's equating containment has always held every evolving vibration since the evolution of first equation. As each vibration has progressed God's equating surround has responded in exact likeness. Bodies have evolved in vibrational formations. Each and every one has a containment of vibrations compacted together in spherical identity of temperature. Each planet is individually held by God's rays, equated vibrationally in storage, responded to equatingly, and identified in size, composition of equations, and area of placement. At any time any one of the planets could be forced to move, to explode or be magnetised into galaxy holding should God's equating rays receive imbalances of danger. Earth's vibrations have been received as dangerous. Man's activity upon Earth is the cause.

God cannot stop man, individually or in mass, from doing as man wants to man himself, man's Earth and man's creatures. Each individual is a separate composition of vibrations and each individual is held separately. Each individual is of brain programming and only the soul is linked to God. For God to individualise humanity without soul capacity is not possible. The brain refuses God's link of conscience. God cannot stop any individual from doing anything unless conscience enables the soul light to activate. All of the evil in mankind has been because the soul light has been overpowered by the brain's extreme vibrating hunger and the food it seeks to live from. The growing violence and evil in mankind today is all of brain development.

Everyone has a soul no matter what state of emotion and no matter what the denials that overpower it. As a body of conscienced souls mankind becomes magnetic to each other and God's link then is powerful. As a body of souls man has the power to refuse the brain and bring life back as it needs to be. In the all-consuming aggressive power of the brain, a body of magnetic likeness becomes grotesque, impenetrable, and a force of destructive influence. With both these examples God's equating responses are to the body of light equations and not the body of brained vibrations. Both are equated however. Both are stored, and both will be magnetised for either confinement of vibrations in area or release of vibrations in area. Neither escapes. Neither can.

God cannot stop nuclear power as it is increasing. There is no response to its charge. God can stop nuclear power from devouring light equations when its charge is large enough to respond to. Temperature is the trigger of response. Nothing else will equate its evolution. A response can only be when the heat, the body of vibrations involved, and the size of the containing body they hold, dictate the size and power of the response. This is real universal evolutionary procedure, the reality of a magnetic equator unable to make mistakes and able to control all that has evolved in containment.

Man in his brain could never envisage God's responses to man's deeds. The brain will refuse such a reality. Only the soul of man could realise the consequences of man's deeds. Only the soul can conscience. When God responds to the volume of nuclear vibrations man is furthering, Earth will, and must, be jolted from its area into an environment that is safe from the discharge its explosions will emit. Automatically God will magnetise nuclear and all Earth's manufactured vibrations into galaxy holding. The jolting will be a perfect equating shock of vibrations shoved away from danger, and safe-kept. Man available to God at that time will never be the same again. Man unavailable to God at that time will emotion in soul, in agony, in torture, for eternity.

If war threatens to come again, can mankind associate with truth of war and prevent it?

If war can be prevented, can mankind resist the brain's programming from returning?

If mankind resurrects man's soul, can man conscience for man's Earth and save it?

Yes! Yes! Yes!

# Soul Activity

Without brain dominance man becomes intelligent as never before. The soul light began from first equation, passed through every stage of evolution purely, emotioned of every experience of life and still holds within its equations perfect reaction to every encounter and confrontation. Its reaction is of equating vibrations seeking requitement at all times. Such reactions are absolutely in balance with the Earth and everything on the Earth. Never can man's soul, if activated purely in link with God, violate life. Equations would always seek to harmonise and nourish all of life. Intelligent requitement would satisfy man's needs. The outcome of soul intelligence would satisfy all of God's needs and bring peace on Earth for the first time.

Soul activity is the natural behaviour of equations of the soul light expressing pure charge of light creatively. The soul light must emotion. It must express of its vibrations. It must do so intelligently. Man with soul light intelligence can create all that is needed to live on Earth without greeding, killing, plundering, diseasing and polluting. Man with soul intelligence can feed, clothe, cover, and secure himself beautifully, healthily and safely, without suffering. Man with soul intelligence can be of artistic expression as never before. Earth would thrive from soul respect. Creature would regenerate from soul understanding. God would communicate as the soul light magnetised God's rays. Such a future is possible. Man must decide what choices should be made to live life without every kind of suffering and disease mankind experiences. To live in peace. To live with real love possible. To live through to eternal life.

To change now, all that man has lived for, would be a trauma the brain could not and would not respond to. Change if wanted would take time. Equations would imbalance and radioactive vibrations inside the brain's coil would also imbalance causing fear and depression. Man's way of life would be threatened. Everything man lives of could also become threatening. The brain's hold over man would also be threatened. Terror of the loss of possessions would occur and the insecurity of financial losses would cause ugly reactions. To remove arms all over the world would result in immediate concealment of armament defying the laws to remove it. To alter business would threaten employment and panic the employed. To prevent manufacture from polluting and diseasing the environment could result in man wanting to protect himself and his interests no matter the cost. To stop all wars would result in fierce retaliation from those addicted to war. To stop all plunder of the Earth's light life would cause the plunderers to behave uglily. To attempt to insert God's truth into all religions would cause disruption, insecurity and fear. To attempt to educate man truthfully would result in truth being forbidden by those refusing to conform. Every attempt to save Earth's life forms and formations would be denied and every attempt to allow a universal creator of existence into man's programming would also be denied. Man in his brain will behave that way. Soul existence could not be in such truth of mankind today. Every attempt to live in truth would be denied by most of mankind. Why? The human form, body and soul, is being eaten alive by brain magnetic necessity for the food that man has created, which devours pure equations of life force. Mankind almost all, has become helpless, soulless, godless, and addicted to vibrational aggressive charge as life force. Addiction to such aggression will ultimately destroy all who seek its uncontrollable vibrations.

For centuries man has been creative. The soul light of man has been responsible for much beauty in all creativity. The brain of man has defiled most creativity of man's soul and caused man to become mechanically expressive, a perfect mimic of expression, a puppet, and be a pretence of another's creation. Because of brain programming few artists express from their souls. Because that programming is of age and is constant, an individual capable of soul expression learns to express another man's soul instead. One artist after another, in every art form, learns a programme that involves another individual's soul creation. An artist usually plays, sings, recites, paints, sculpts, dances, acts or writes prose and poetry, not always of his own soul creation, but of another's. The expression then is brained. Its interpretation is a pretence. The artist becomes a fraud. The human brain is the perfect mimic.

An artist of true greatness is an artist of individual expression which can only belong to that individual and should never be stolen in greed, insecurity, or for fame or podium. True artistry comes from equations within soul light emotion which release their feelings through their containing body as long as that individual is souled. God responds always as the soul light vibrates in beauty. Each vibration is automatically returned and the artist free flows in whatever expressive creation he or she has chosen.

No two souls are identical. Each artist is unique. Each expression is of different soul light patterning. Each emotion is pure and beautiful. Each creation is an individual's soul expression. Every man, woman and child has soul light creativity of their own greatness.

Man, from brain programming, has lost his individuality of soul expression. Few create as they need to. Thousands copy and imitate. Millions puppetise emotions which do not belong to them. Artistic education is all programmes. A student can do nothing except learn them. A soul expresser is stifled. The soul light inside man's heart is never requited no matter the fame or fortune. Man's individuality is confined inside the programmed adoration for another. Mankind then has no place to express of man's own greatness.

Were mankind of creative freedom, beauty in everything and everywhere would exist. No-one would be a puppet, a mimic, a pretender, or a fake. No-one could be. Everyone would be expressive, everyone would find their true soul vocation, and everyone would be an artist of worth and beauty. Man creative is man beautiful. Man beautiful is man in his soul. Man in his soul is man with God.

To allow the soul of man to emerge creatively is to cease pretending to be another, to cease learning a programme of another's individual creation, to cease feeding the brain, and cease denying one's own soul expression. Soul expression can only emerge if it is tried for. If it is not, stagnation and deterioration of artistic presentation is the result.

At any time man can access his soul. At any time man can begin soul expression. Anywhere man is able to be expressive. Any soul expresser is respected. Souled man is always felt. The soul light is held by God and responded to. Soul expression results in the soul light of pure equations being released.

The mechanics of creativity now create brains without soul intelligence, brains with need to feed strongly from other artist's originality, brains without reality, and brains addicted to aggressive charge. An empire of artistic creation has evolved, all of it financially powered, and all of it a programming. Many artists simply puppetise their emotions which are capable of moving others in their souls.

A performance by an artist of another's soul creation often causes magnetic attraction to the artist not the creator. A performer can elevate an audience vibrationally by performing a work from the beauty and greatness of another soul. The audience applauds the performer, approves of the creation in that applause, unaware that they are acknowledging the performer as greatly souled when the real creator has caused the performer false presence.

Applause is always an aggressive charge of vibrations of magnetic connection absorbed by the brain of a performer and addicted to. The quantity of vibrations within a large auditorium feeds the brain power of radioactivity. The volume of sound and echo enters the brain's coil in charge and elates it, expands the coil which holds massive compressed radioactive charging. The tissue in the brain puffs out momentarily then shrinks back to normal function and size. The incoming vibrations of huge applause, shouting or screaming, if from audience muscular aggression and not machinery, cannot find radioactive likeness. They push into the coil's fleshy substance as far as their charge activates, then when the applause stops, the coil retracts, pulls back into shape. Having no likeness inside the coil, applause vibrations remain in the brain in separate charge until the same vibrations are magnetised again. Their area of charge enlarges. Because an artist may perform regularly, brain elation becomes addicted to. Artist and audience, depending on what is being performed, can both become addicted. Rock concerts are the truth of the addiction to huge volumes of aggressive vibrations magnetised into the brain.

Performance for monetary gain by many artists activates the programmed capacity of the brain to contrive soul expression which does not belong to that individual. Such performances destroy individuals from access to their own souls. Pretence becomes addictive and an artist of real soul never aspires to true greatness.

Virtuosity of performance is not of the soul for its brilliance has been of programming, learning the skill by repetition. Almost any human being if desiring to be an artist, finding support from others financially or independently, having the time necessary to study, and having the discipline to keep learning, can achieve virtuosity. There are no great artists in that category. Repetition is the destroyer of natural creation. A soul creation should only be performed by its soul creator.

Repetitive performances of anything can cause soul retraction of vibrations. The patterns cannot enter the soul light for they imbalance its perfect rhythm. The vibrations of first performance if accepted, are taken into the light rays of the soul light and magnetised by God. A return charge is activated. If those first vibrations return a second time, they are refused by God's invisible light rays in response. To have repetitive vibrations which have already been accepted inside the soul light, imbalances its own light rays. One work is accepted in patterning and only one. All others of the same work, if repeated, are refused.

All compositions of music, art, dance, and theatrical presentations, are combinations of vibrations, patterns, colours, and motioning equations, which go up and down in temperature. Each performance of any first-time creation is taken into the soul light vibrationally, and if those vibrations are not offensive, they are kept inside the soul light, magnetised by God, responded to, then retained. They do not disappear. They are held strongly because their patterns have caused equational magnetic acceptance which has no disturbance to the soul light and does not aggress or imbalance its light rays. Once accepted, another repeat of those vibrations is automatically refused. To over-dose the soul light with repeats of vibrations causes huge imbalance and heating.

Vibrations when magnetised from outside the soul light always increase the volume of pure equations inside the soul light, and always add more patterns and colourful activity. The soul light feeds from pure light vibrations be they from the Sun or from the Earth. Repeats of performance to one individual can never activate soul light emotions purely. Equations emotion spontaneously, not repetitively. The brain however accepts every repeat and at any time can attempt to mimic whatever it recalls. Learning anything repetitive is brain programming. Mimicry is the reality of brain recall. Audience appreciation for repeats of performance never activate soul light interest, they always enter the brain and satisfy the coil's hunger.

A brain is so programmed repetitiously it can fake anything. Its activity is ceaseless and its deceptions are countless. Brain contrivances result in terrible falsity, that which is unreal and faked. Terrible pretences come from the brain's unemotional vibrations and one false presence after another emerges, many behaving exactly as the other, and many trying to be another. This pretence can be so real even the brain deceives itself by assuming a false identity.

Children are also contrived to in every way. Instead of reality their lives are filled with plastic animals, fake toys, tales of fantasy, fake images, fake behaviour, huge television programming of contrivance, fake games and fake playing. Every real awareness of a child is prevented. As the child grows up it imitates all it has absorbed, often it lies, contrives, and emotions falsely. As an adult, nearly all reality has been destroyed and a brain has become dominant. A truth becomes a lie and a reality becomes pretence. Children are taught to pretend at almost everything. Truth can never be faced when pretending becomes everyday behavioural patterns. The brain has been fed pretence patterning and cannot cease re-enacting what has become a vital food source of programming.

To be of truth is to be of soul existence. No lies can there be if the soul is accessed. Pretence could not exist in man. False emotions would never be conveyed. Children would be of reality as soon as they become aware. Growing up would be full of real experiences. Adults would be powerfully gifted, immensely souled, and active in everything beneficial to man, creature and Earth. A future would be possible. Eternal life would be assured. All this, yet the human brain would refuse it all.

Magnetic attraction of brains unto brains can also emotion individuals in their souls. Brain aggression once magnetised in volume can cause hysteria, the inability to stop the brain from over charging. One scream or shouting escalating in numbers has huge magnetic attraction and its unified vibrations consume soul access entirely. A sensitive soul held in the midst of crowd hysteria, can be so traumatised, fear of crowds eventuates causing soul retraction. The equations of the soul light retract their extending rays, God automatically withdraws, and an individual terrifies until the soul light recharges. This happens time and time again where crowds are aggressively charging and overpowering every soul enclosed in the hyped magnetic unity of vibrations. One brain after another behaves in identical patterning. One brain after another in magnetic attachment becomes a deadly destructive body of vibrations able to kill if panicked. One soul after another is emotionally scarred.

Screaming is the most violent vocalisation man has learned. Its aggressive burst of vibrations when contained inside the head, explodes blood cells, causes mucous to glow red charge, creates an orgasm in the brain which excretes into burning tissue, and if addicted to, can eventually lead to brain haemorrhages not detectable until a body becomes severely ill. Screaming is of forced charge, a pretence always, huge brain food, violence of vibrations, and the absolute annihilation of light equations of the eyes. Their temperature rises. Their overpowering is so extreme they retract immediately they are stabbed. Their equations cannot return in balance of rhythm because they have been shot, fired into. Their activity then is totally un-rhythmical with breathing irregular. They return to normal function very slowly. Even vision becomes affected.

Screaming has increased in mankind, and children scream without provocation. A programme of screaming has been learned and their growing brains, having orgasmed by screaming, need that charge as often as it can be manipulated. The brain, once of scream powering, will recall the same pattern whenever memory is activated. Teenagers scream automatically when their memory is activated. Adults do exactly the same, and instead of an appreciative word or gesture, screaming becomes the acknowledgement of anything the brain associates with in programming. Mankind has become a screamer. Mankind needs to stop such a hideous evolution. Its continuance will explode man's head.

The acceleration of energy inside man's form is out of control. Every artificial stimulation is being used to energise man. Every unnatural substance is taken. Every manufactured machine is used. Every possible aggressive exercise is practised and every electrical and radioactive apparatus, entertainment and enclosed environment, is indulged in to keep man energising. Man's body is falsely pumped. Man's blood is falsely charged. Man's heart is over strained. Man's sexing is over stimulated. Man's pleasures are over indulged in. Man's emotions are over falsified. Man's language is over aggressed. Man's sleep is often forced. Man's waking is also often forced. Man's brain is enlarging from feeding. Man's soul light is dying of its purity of light life. Man must de-energise. Unless man tries to quell his energy drive his lifeline of light equations is at an end. Unless the desire to aggress in energised activity ceases, man's soul has no eternal life.

Escalation of aggression in man today is creating the deformity of man's evolution, bodies which are abnormal in every way, bodies of ugly diseases, bodies that are often falsely made. Man has become unreal, a manufactured creation. Man has been programmed with false image acceptance.

False image acceptance is always because certain images have entered the brain in patterns of approval, admiration, awe and envy. Such images become greeded. Their patterns have held the brain in fixation, allowing it time to feed. The brain having false imagery within its coil, can, and does influence a form to either re-enact the image itself or contrive a false persona. It simply recalls the original patterns of the image enjoyed and keeps that image vibrating causing a form to respond. It holds the image strongly within its content by fixation of vibrations, continued activity which has already been fixated upon. The vibrations die down when the form containing the vibrations attracts to another source of vibrations. Recalling false imagery comes about because the time taken in fixated attraction to the image has been a source of feeding and the brain automatically seeks the food again.

False imagery attraction often results in plastic surgery, changes in dress, hair style and colour, extreme appearance and exaggerated personae. All that has been seen by the brain and fixated upon is transferred to the body which has become of brain manipulation.

Any plastic surgery kills light cells wherever it touches. A body shortens its lifeline. The soul, only able to stay balanced in a body that has equational activity, emotions sufferingly and often retracts the rays of magnetic link to God. Falsifying anything is of brain manipulation, never of the soul.

The desire of man to be that which he or she is not, is of the brain entirely. Soul living is real security, real satisfaction in everything and the acceptance of oneself. Within the soul light is every activity man needs to be artistic. Within soul light intelligence is every answer to every problem man faces. Within the equations of soul light emotion is every beauty, every loving, and every expression man needs to be of greatness. Within soul light existence is all truth, all reality, and the God that man has searched for.

Man absent from man's soul lives a thoroughly unfulfilled life, often afraid to die, often taking his own life in despair, and never being loved or able to love purely. Man becomes permanently detached from soul existence. Man struggles, stresses, strains, and seeks to relieve himself of all that destroys his health and countenance. Man aggresses himself continually, over works, over indulges in alcohol and drugs, over eats, and often overdoses himself in a bid to end it all. Man tires. Man does not always sleep. Man medicates himself with anything that may bring comfort. Man worries. Man breaks down. Man has no real security anywhere, nowhere to find real peace, and no-one to acknowledge his soul. Life of man's ideals is often worthless for not one achievement relieves man from his soul needs. Every privilege man aspires to is from brain programming, a path of advancement which has been a patterned image the brain has fed from. A person is manipulated from small desire to larger desires automatically as image after image is craved in the brain and a life of privilege becomes evident. Depending on what level in society man begins to desire privileges, man aspires to whatever his brain has been fed from. Man becomes victimised.

There is no superiority of souls. Each single soul light is of absolute purity of equations. No one individual is stronger or weaker than another. All are different. All are unique. All behave identically. All suffer exactly as each other.

Education, power, money, throne and leadership make absolutely no difference to soul light existence. The more corrupt the life lived, the weaker the soul light's vibrations, for conscience if denied forbids soul light activity. The cleaner and purer an individual's life, the stronger the vibrations of the soul light. The more abuse a body takes, the less chance of a child of soul light capacity. The healthier and more peaceful the lifestyle, the more chance of a child of soul light capacity. The more brain power a body is fed, the less likelihood of the soul light being magnetised by God. The more the brain denies the soul, the more each denying individual is denied.

Soul creativity belongs to everyone, not just a select few. It comes from the soul. It is expressed emotionally by the soul light. If prevented, by prejudice, poverty, class or segregation, those denied suffer deeply. They cannot express of their souls. Their equations are tortured. Their lives become hurtful, often ugly, and more often they turn to crime, a substitute for soul torture, revenge for being hurt, hatred for never being of worth anywhere, loathing for those who appear to have what every man is entitled to. Crime has always been from the degradation of the soul inside man's heart and a retaliation of the brain being fed vengeful and hating imagery. If man cannot express from his soul, man will always express from his brain. Criminals are all man made. Crime is always programmed behaviour.

Man chooses particular interests which appeal to his soul and appeal also to a hungry brain. Every interest chosen has relevance to an individual's vibrational patterning. The appreciation of music is because the vibrations emotion the soul or aggress the brain, one or the other. When music is heard it is taken into both brain and soul light in vibrations of patterns. If the music listened to is beautiful, of someone's soul creation, its patterns can cause emotional experience, the lifting, lowering, calming and lulling of equations. Almost all music activates soul light equations emotionally. If a music piece has too much discord and unresolved phrasing, the listener often feels unrequited and disappointed. Deliberate discord has destroyed much pure melodic harmony. The soul light is of perfect balance and cannot accept impure resonance. Equations imbalance. Much of discordant music has evolved from brain experimentation, perfection thoroughly destroyed. Much discord is often for effects that have impact or to create individualism and can be wanted just to be different.

Brain experimentation takes place everywhere and unto everything. A purity is impured, picked at, changed, deformed, hacked up, broken open, fixed back together, leered over continually, probed into, cruelled, imprisoned for surveillance, drugged for control and deliberately force activated just for fun. Brain documentation when a creature is dying and deliberately not helped or saved is entirely the brain again without conscience and progressing itself. Grotesquely genetically engineered creatures and growth and the hideous transplantation of creatures is criminal, acts that only the brain is capable of. Such acts if watched by those in conscience could never be allowed. The soul light would convulse. All that is done, seen, observed, documented, enjoyed, approved and registered, is brain digested, waiting for recall, then activated again. It is the automatic progression of the brain's active vibrations to accept any pure patterning and violate its perfection. It cannot keep any purity of patterning inside its coil unless it aggresses those vibrations. The brain must keep alive and feeding. Once a single pure pattern has been accepted vibrationally, its content is stored, then altered as often as recall forces the image into activation. Each time the image reactivates it changes.

Progress is always man's excuse for most brain addiction. Progress which keeps change permanently fixed in society. Progress which is nothing more than man's hungry brain attaching to any activity whatsoever and mutilating all that is pure. Music is the perfect example of just such brain development. Its rendition has progressed from the single purity of voice and instrument to electronically overpowered performances and screaming gyrating singers.

Almost all areas of the arts have now been brain defiled. Beauty has been violated. Perfection has been destroyed. Art appreciation has become a programme which accepts art that is ugly, art that is insulting and art which revolts. Beauty in art now is almost over. From great original creations of the past to the present day the progress of art has been aggressively charged. Man mimics man's greats everywhere, copies their individuality and claims their inspiration for himself. Man exaggerates their originality, executes a harsh rendition of their beauty, saturates the art markets with repetitious similarities and grossly and greedily places monetary gain as the power which drives artistic creation past and present. Artistic creations then become brain created, not soul inspired. The creative motivation in art becomes moneyed, produced to satisfy the brains of man in all directions.

Art should be absolutely freed of the stigma of money and the artist allowed to create worthily. The creative arts throughout man's history have been utterly denied by God's link. As soon as the greed of the brain interferes in soul creativity God withdraws the rays of pure equational light activity. Art everywhere is of the soul light, pure, beautiful, inspiring and educational. Its progress should always be of soul light vibrations expressing an individual's greatness.

For centuries, creative programming has prevented soul light greatness from emerging in most of mankind. By electrical and radioactive currents of charge, man has been programmed with repetition of every creative work on Earth. Man has addicted himself, become unaware of his own soul worth, and is unable to create purely, for the brain is saturated with creations of others. Man cannot create beautifully unless the soul is accessed. Man can contrive, take from the soul of another and render an imitation of soul greatness. Such works are many and control art appreciation.

Monetary inspiration cripples true artistic expression and podiums of worship absolutely feed mankind brain gluttony. The podium anywhere can be a cruel pretence of soul greatness because of the superficial powering of an individual contriving the soul of another. Magnetic attraction creates worshippers of false emotions and what is generated is the hyping of the brain feeding from the charge.

Instrumentally powered compositions enter man's brain, are stored, recalled for another similar experience, and because the brain must disturb the work it has fed from, an even larger experience is sought via an even more powered performance. Stereophonic repetition of the same work often results in huge amplification of the sound. The listener hypes the brain even more from repetitive recall of just one experience of false soul.

Powered compositions overpower the tranquillity of soul light vibrations. The more instruments and voices powering a work the less real soul emotion is involved. The brain however, becomes elated, powered by false illusionary experience. Programming causes the approval of the performance and an individual applauds aggressively for the experience. Magnetic attraction causes unified applause, unified cheering, shouting, screaming, gyrating, stamping and booing. One individual begins, the brain of another copies. Many become addicted.

Amplified sound has come about by the brain unable to feed from passive sound and insisting on much more aggression of charge. The degree of loudness a brain manipulates for depends on the aggression within an individual's energy cells. The more electric and radioactive charging absorbed by an individual, the louder the sound that individual needs as satisfaction.

If a youth is saturated by the absorption of vibrations from movies, television, video games, computers and cell phones, that youth is automatically over aggressed. Amplified sound is needed to charge the brain. The power in-taken must be greater than its previous food source. A high is experienced, a high of aggressive containment of vibrations trapped inside the head and keeping the brain satisfied.

Youths today have overcharged their brains to the extent of never being able to calm themselves or be at peace in their souls. Their addictions are driven by those in monetary gain no matter the danger to an individual's life. Most addicts of amplified sound die young unless superficially kept alive by medication, drug addiction, or false energy.

Powered electronic music now not only kills light equations in bodies but severely destroys the health of every single participant and listener in hearing distance. The vibrations emitted are deadly. Their aggression attracts micro-radiotic activity, cancerous vibrations seeking entry into forms that are overcharging. The penetration of aggressively activated electronics is thorough and permanent. The charge punctures the soul light detrimentally for equations retract and often never return to full function. The body's energy cells heat and excrete a massive amount of mucous all through the tissues. The brain can swell if electronically charged. The main senses overheat, are damaged in blood and water supply. Watery tissue dries out quickly. All heart rhythm imbalances. All passivity of every body cell is violated. All chance of a healthy life is taken away. With constant electronic sound forced into a body, the lifeline to God ends. The brain becomes of electronic greeding. It thrives. It addicts the body. It relies on the promotion of its charge to keep feeding. It controls everyone within its domain of power.

High powered electronic sound is often too savagely disturbing for many to listen to. Most sensitive souls have to cover their ears to try to prevent suffering. Such pounding causes nerve destruction. Even those outside of the volume of power of any electronic blast are badly hurt in their souls. All manufacture of high-powered electronic instruments is absolutely of brain invention without the slightest conscience possible. The escalation of a business which forces mankind to accept that which is deafening, stressful and overpowering, is unparalleled in man's history. Its progression will destroy man's sight, hearing, voice, smell and heart rhythm. All who enjoy high powered electronic sound have little soul left to acknowledge. All who further its evil have little conscience left to salvage. Child can never become of soul light existence. Boy becomes electrified in physical appearance and in behaviour. Girl becomes the same. Both unite in electronically charged environments. Many supercharge themselves with drugs and alcohol. Many are unable to calm down. Thousands become violent. Millions of lives are destroyed. Magnetic attraction takes place. Repetition of high-powered electronic performances is constant. What can those victimised by such destruction do? Nothing, unless the conscience becomes dominant over man's brain.

The future of mankind is ugly. An electronically charged human being automatically becomes nuclear charged. Mankind is over then. The brain needs only an explosion to satisfy its powering. Those allowing the continuance of electronically manipulated beings need deep, deep, conscience. The type of species evolving will be out of control, a species without any conscience possible, overcharged with aggression, unstoppable in destructive behaviour, magnetically attracted to each other, driven by brain hunger, and of real evil intent. Mankind is creating a hideous species thoroughly addicted to brain violence of every kind.

The reality of Earth's future is at stake. The humanity of the future, the power generated beings without any capacity to be of worth, any conscience, and any desire for truth, have already been born, accepted, and patronised. Their presence today is evident everywhere man tries to live peacefully. Not one area upon the Earth is free of the aggression of man. Not one household is free from aggressive overcharging. Not one soul life is free from brain aggressive drive. Not one life is free from magnetic attraction of aggressive vibrations. A clear picture of man is before all men. A picture no man really wants to look at. If that truth is torn away, mankind has chosen his path. If the truth stands before all men, is wanted as the reason for change, all that has been will never be again.

# Love

To reveal love's truth is to emotion the soul light of every being needing to love and be loved. Without question all who live upon this Earth need love. Why such need is never requited is because love is not understood in any way. Why love is not understood is because man's soul is forsaken for false life, life which has no soul, respects no God, and has no love of purity of light. Why loving any being can be painful is because the soul inside man's heart is without love's truth.

Man has wanted love for as long as man's emotions were overpowered by the brain. Man has craved, begged and pleaded for love to be given. Man has prayed to receive love and be blessed by love's beauty. Man has searched words, music, paintings, dancing, sculpture, every art form, every individual, and every path for love's reality. Never has real pure love been found. Never could its beauty be touched by man. Mankind is without soul respect.

First loving life form was whale, a creature pure and emotional. A glorious creature, held by God, talked to in the language of light by God's answering responses and protected unto eternal life. Love then was of ecstasy, equations expressing their perfect vibrations and God responding in light love also. Whale loved as whale found his mate. Whale's love deepened as calf was born. Whales emotioned in respect for each other's souls. Respect was automatic. The soul light attached to God was sensitised to. Light so radiant was seen by whale. Aura glowed from everything. Nothing except Earth's cooling disturbed whale then. Nothing had destroyed. Everything was loved by whale. All whales were loving at that time. When man hunted whale and killed the oceans' greatest souled creature, whale stopped loving. Whale's soul became of deep, deep contrition. Deeds so ugly experienced by a creature so pure and loving, emotioned whale to contrite for the evil whale felt was unjust and without respect for soul existence. Whale's contrition began in whale's soul at central core of light vibrations. Whale experienced shock waves of violent convulsing vibrations witnessing murder of one of its offspring. Seeing man explode another whale's heart caused whale's soul light to contract its beautiful rays of light. They interned. They heated. They would never extend again. Whale wept excruciating hot tears of suffering. Man had become whale's killer. Greed without conscience of soul was that truth. God answered equations of whale's contrition. God's rays could not requite whale's suffering, equations once interned would never extend again, their purity had been destroyed. Light loving between God and whale ended. Whale's soul light began evolving in retraction of its true greatness, pulsed to react to man the hunter, and unable to show respect for any human being for the rest of whale's evolution. God still held whale's soul, still answered whale's emotions, and forever onward would take whale's soul unto eternal life. Whale was God's first pure evolution of love's divine eternal existence.

Whale cannot escape the evil of man the greedy hunter. Whale cannot hide. Whale's home is the ocean. Whale's home is now horrifically violated. Whale cannot find pure water, pure food, or pure vibrations of light unto its tortured soul. Man has fouled every ocean, poisoned every food source, and nuclearised every pure vibration evolving in whale's environment. Whale's evolution is coming to an end, and mankind knows this, and still seeks to kill such great benevolent parental guidance unto all of life formations in the seas. Without whale's love of sea creatures, they will die without their majestic protector. Without whale man's evolution ends, for the oceans are food, life force, coolness, balance, and evolutionary progressioning. If whale does not survive there man's existence everywhere will end forever. The oceans evolved every species on Earth including mankind. It is to man's severe detriment they are all destroying by callous, stupid, unconscienced deeds of greed and greed only. If the greatest souled creature cannot survive in Earth's waters it is because mankind has defiled that habitat, a habitat that feeds man life, a habitat man absolutely needs in its pure state.

The love any creature feels is pure. It comes from the soul light and nowhere else. All creature nurturing is pure emotional loving. The young are cared for adoringly, fed tenderly, warmed and protected by the soul intelligence of parent creatures. Both parents respect each other's needs. Both parents love their young. Both parents ecstasise at the birth of their young. Both remain together for life. That was the way it was once. Now, much has changed.

Human beings try loving in many different ways. They meet. They court. They kiss. They make love. They sometimes wed. They become parents. They often divorce. They often wed again and again and again and again, always trying to find the right love.

Human beings buy love. They buy another's loved one. They pay for love. They pay a high price to make love to someone. They cannot love without personal attributes part of their loving assessment. They prepare love. They plan love's path according to individual programming. Their loving is contrived. They pay others to perform love acts, acts which are of gross violation to the purity of love. They watch pornographic movies of a variety of sex acts, acts which defile the purity of love, acts all contrived. They watch others when making love. They enjoy watching others. They act out loving someone. They enjoy movies of love stories. They enjoy reading love stories all contrived re-enactments of love. They emotion whilst reading about contrived loving. They often weep where love has been lost. They show interest in every person who might be loving to others. They sing of love's abundant riches. They chant of God's love. They preach of biblical love. They deny love over and over again. They worship those who preach love and how love should be. They also kill for love and love lost.

Human beings protest love for each other. They possess lovers who satisfy their desires. In families, love is often used as bargaining, bribing, and forcing each other to react. Love for children often becomes tarnished by jealousy, hatred and regret. The elderly are often loved intermittently in rest homes, hospitals and lonely rooms. Lovers only love for as long as the sex is satisfying. Lovers never stay lovers for long. Lovers often end a relationship hating each other. Lovers are enticed to love another. Lovers suicide when love becomes forbidden. Love is never wanted in its pure state.

Human beings try to love certain creatures. They possess their beauty and luxurious presence. They indulge in these creatures as long as there are no problems. Human beings force their loved creatures to do exactly as is convenient and accept whatever happens to them. They must be of loving natures. They must give love always to their owners. They must be content with whatever they are given. If they misbehave they are hurt and sometimes killed. They are often neglected, starved and tortured. They are used in arenas of death. They are pampered for huge financial gain. They are adored if their beauty earns trophies. Their worship in sporting activities is entirely for monetary gain. Their own loving of each other is castrated. Their appearance is cut into to please their owners and to look more acceptable. They suffer the deformity of their equations which can never vibrate in balance again. They are denied God's eternal holding. They are bought as a possession and dumped to be put to death if too much trouble. Their identity is changed to suit man's greed and still man asks for their love. Still man possesses their beauty. Still man denies their souls.

Human beings love their possessions. They greed their beauty and value. They love being seen with beautiful things. They love others who are identical in social attributes. They adore each other's friendship. They saturate their talk with loving comments. Their homes are full of loving paraphernalia. Their photos are always of those they love. Their loved ones are often unloving.

Unloving parents and children always crave love. They are often jealous of others who are superficially loved. They deny each other love because they are suffered, unable to convey their suffering and unable to forgive those responsible for their pain.

Cemeteries are full of loved and unloved ones who have passed away. Others are boxed and forgotten. Urns are often left unclaimed. Ashes are kept, scattered and dumped when a loved or unloved one dies. Ashes are kept in memory by many who have loved. Graves are visited by many in grief for loved ones, suffering which could be stopped if only love was understood.

Human beings read biblical parables and spiritual doctrine intending to be of love. They often go to places of worship to pray to a loving God. They ask their gods for love to be given. They vow to be loving individuals. They seek places where love can be practised. They worship those who teach that love is the way. They often confess to being unloving. They contrite for love that never lasts. They rarely give love to the God they pray to. They ask for themselves constantly.

Human beings may or may not love their neighbours. They cannot love their enemies. They cannot love another race. They cannot love another of a different religion, colour, business, belief or behaviour. They cannot love particular creatures. They cannot love another's God. They cannot love anyone who is not of their acceptance. They cannot love each other. They cannot love themselves. Those that practice loving in any way, suffer, for their loving is often not wanted.

Where is real love possible in life if every excuse prevents its appearance? Where can love exist if man's brain decides love's placing? Where is true love? Why is love false? Why is man alone? Why is mankind bereft of the most beautiful loving that only love bestows?

Real love is without destructive influence. Equations have no selection process. They do not stop and start. They do not segregate in vibrations. They ecstasise. They flow of absolute purity of vibrations. Their activity is pure light emotion. God answers immediately. Divine existence is felt. Man's soul in such reality becomes of greatness. Man becomes loved. Man loves truthfully. God loves man.

To be loved by God is to be held by divine rays of light eternally, to be nurtured there, fed, protected, comforted and acknowledged in soul. What greater security could there be for every individual on Earth than God's eternal love, a life that is light beautified?

Where love has gone from man's soul light is obvious. Every touch of light life that feeds man's soul has been destroyed. The light that man needs to live from has radioactivated and is progressing. The emotions that man once felt have become brain contrivances. The God that man once tried for has been discarded. The real decent values the presence of that God created in man's soul have been defiled. The peace that the soul must live from has become of defilement, hatred, war, and murder. The perfect soul mate that exists for everyone has become many. The sacred unity of two life lovers has become short term. The sanctity of real family life has become abusive to all concerned. The purity of love in the soul of man, woman and child has become pornographic. Real true love making has become an aggressed gyrating act. Orgasm of pure ecstasising emotions has become excreting mucous of energy. A personal union of two lovers has become a public spectacle. A virgin has become a shame. A teenager has become sex seeking with anyone. Sex has become experimental. Artificial protection for safe sex has become opportunism. One sex act becomes an orgy. One orgy becomes a public display. One violation after another renders real love worthless and of no importance at all. Such disrespect by everyone only creates more and more defilement as the brain progresses and the soul destroys. Love, the pasture of all things beautiful, can never be known this way of mankind.

One woman desires more than one lover together. One man desires exactly the same. One sex desires the same sex. One individual desires a child to commit atrocities with. Another desires an animal to commit even uglier atrocities with. Many stimulate sex orgasms with hideous brain activated images. Many use drugs to have a powered orgasm. Many addict to masturbation where love is denied. Many rape others to release the brain's charge. Others rape children. All of these deeds are of man's ugly greeding brain. All destroy the purity of the great soul inside man's heart. No man can deny such truth here. No conscience should allow love to be so violated again.

Love when truly wanted, pure and of the soul's conscience, is respect for every living thing, a duty to see that all is loved and cared for, a vocation for all that is beautiful and must be kept that way, a belonging, a beautiful experience, security of soul, security with God. What love brings should man's soul be wanted, is everything man desires to be of peace, of worth, and of happiness. All man has searched for would be found.

Can man change his deadly path to be of God's beautiful givings? Can man sincerely enter his heart and know his soul exists? Can man truly look upon his own kind and realise why love can never be pure? Can man look upon his Earth and his creatures and acknowledge life more worthy than man? Can man turn towards man's God and contrite to become of worth? Yes, man in truth of man's soul, can.

The defilement of the purity of love has prevented true love from being experienced by everyone. Love, if it is pure, is the most beautifying touch there is. Ugliness cannot exist where love resides. A soul light of love behaves in emotional activity of light vibrations, expressing beautiful peaceful feelings and glorious elevating sensations. Each outward extension of emotioning equations often experiences the same extension from another. When both are in magnetic hold they ecstasise. Man and woman then make love, love that is emotional and not of energising aggression, and not with the wrong soul mate. A light vibrational orgasm is experienced. A unity of perfect equations of purity. Such beauty has never been felt by man. The brain has aggressed the orgasm and prevented ecstasy of soul.

The choices man makes to make love to are nearly always brain desired. Desire is the magnetic attraction of the brain unto that which it sees and must possess. Desire causes wrong choice lovers. Brain desire may have been stimulated by programmed imagery or orgasmic experience. It also attracts to provocative areas of a body, or the entire physical appearance of a form. The brain may also be stimulated by the powerful position, wealth, or the public adoration of an individual and need to feed of its greed for possession. The brain also stimulates another with lewd practices and often chooses a partner of the same addiction. The brain desires much false loving and can adapt where an individual may be false also. Desired real love is impossible. Equations cannot possess a body. They are its formation. Love can never be of greed or the lust of desire.

Sexing is often mistaken for love. It is not of real love unless the souls of both lovers are respected and the partners are in the reality of their true existence. When that is wanted sexing is an automatic reaction by equations of emotion expressing love between two pure individuals for life.

Partners are often badly chosen. Sex between wrong choice partners always suffers both. Both have unsatisfactory orgasms and both crave the real feelings of love. If an orgasm is first experienced with an individual of the same sex in sexual adventure, pornographic entertainment, experimentation, copying imagery, observing same sexes kissing or fornicating, holding revulsion for the opposite sex through abuse, rape, brutality or because the sexual organs have been brain stimulated whilst another is present, the brain will seek the same experience again. The charge of vibrations into the head in sexual orgasm is addictive always.

Repeated orgasms with a same sex partner often result in male and female homosexuality. The opposite sex becomes repulsive to the brain and it manipulates personae to feed from. Same sex relationships that do not begin with first sexual experience are often from medical imbalancing, occasionally from parents who force children to behave as the gender they were denied, and more often from a drug used by one or both parents during intercourse which completely alters the equational balance of the birth. Aggressive medications can also change the balance of vibrations of sperm, egg, and unification of gender. An intervention in the pure equations of a foetus in formation which is too heating and aggressive, flushes both sperm and egg at irregular intervals with male and then female activation of vibrations. Because the flushing is irregular, more male or female vibrations than necessary enter the solidification process of a formation. Child born cannot identify with its own sexual identity. Man is always a victim where the pursuit of wrong choice lovers becomes brain manipulated.

When addiction causes love making to be over indulged, the brain feeds ravenously and a greater charge of vibrations is sought. Sexing then often becomes sordid, violent, depraved and perverted. Because there is no soul light involved in addiction the orgasm becomes convulsive. What is spurted is red hot vibrations eager for magnetic attraction. Child born of aggressive indulgent sexing is without soul capacity. Child inherits convulsive orgasmic release of charge. The brain always violates whatever it attaches to. Child of indulgent sexual behaviour always suffers sexual imbalances.

Where power and money have influenced choice, lovers often try to control and possess each other, and may deliberately inflict pain while performing various sexual acts. The brain always violates another it cannot overpower and always degrades the one seeking dominance. If one does not succumb to the other, hatred, violence, and sometimes even murder may occur. The brain feeds from all that is aggressive. It can and has caused vile responses during sex. It does this because it defiles the act to increase the charge of aggression. If an orgasm is activated in this way the brain addicts to vileness during sex permanently.

Brain possession of an individual can be total if not understood. So brain gripped can a person become, he or she loses all ability to be an individual and all capacity to enjoy anything. Many a brain controlled human being has become insane, a form in total control of the brain's powering, an individual who feels nothing except patterns of the brain in activity, an individual the brain has consumed by being allowed to take control and destroy the soul light.

Many marriages which often begin lovingly end in pain. Sexing which usually begins as a regular act of love making often becomes boring. One partner grows tired of the other. One partner turns away from the other. Both desire other lovers eventually. Both often take other lovers.

When children are born a parent may turn away from marital sex entirely or pretend interest to please their partner. Children are often all a marriage is wanted for. Children are also had in and out of marriage simply as a possession, or a craving to love and be loved. Marriage for convenience is always a marriage of suffering. The soul is never requited in any need whatsoever.

Young lovers, as long as they are not seeking sexual pleasures only, are nearly always convicted in their possessive new relationship. They smother each other affectionately. They make love anywhere. They nearly always over-sex each other. They vow to be together as a couple for ever. They often profess undying love for each other. They never attract to another while their relationship lasts. When it ends, both suffer greatly. The brain of both usually destroys them and the soul light of both suffers emotionally. Once suffered from the violation of light equations, lovers never try to love the same way again. The brain can and will copy every loving way it has attended, causing uncertainty, doubt, suspicion, fear, and distaste in new relationships. Soul light equations refuse the contrivances and lovers are never requited.

Love, if withdrawn, causes severe vibrational imbalance in the soul light. Instead of equations expressing their emotions, the extension of those vibrations interns. The soul light overheats, God withdraws if it is too hot, and the lover or lovers become depressed, melancholy, disturbed, and desperately unhappy. The brain enjoys the withdrawal of love, because conflict within the soul light causes aggressive charging in the brain. So feeding from unhappiness is the brain it can keep an individual held in depression for many days, weeks or months. The brain never releases anyone from depression. A soul touch is the only pure release of such suffering. Medication gives a superficial well-being and often becomes a dependency. Once depression is medicated, the soul light cannot be felt in reality. Its equations refuse the charge the medication causes all through the body. The brain however feeds hugely from every kind of medication in-taken. The imbalanced vibrations from medication taken into the bloodstream cause energy cells to overcharge. The patterns these cells vibrate are an acceleration of electric and radioactive aggressive charging which needs only an opening of intense heating for a micro-radiator to enter. All medication for anything over aggresses every vibration in the forms of creature and man. The soul light attached to God cannot express pure charge and weakens. God's withdrawal too often causes equations to fade. Without strength the soul light cannot be magnetised at death.

Pure medication, that which is of the Earth's equating evolution is no longer available to man. All of Earth's healing capacity has been destroyed. Now, man relies on manufactured medications. All destroy man's equations of purity. All aggress man's brain.

The denial of love making for any length of time or pornography observed often, may cause masturbation, the manipulation of an orgasm without a partner involved. Masturbation is the most destructive habit any human being can indulge in. Its aggressive massage by hand or apparatus causes inflammation of equations in sensitive areas inside and outside genitalia. The addiction of the brain to masturbation is because the forced orgasm spurts red hot mucous of energy through the coil and convulsive elation is experienced. A huge charge is forced vibrationally into the brain's mucous and immediately becomes addictive. Human beings who practise masturbation repeatedly violate their souls so hideously,

God withdraws, and does not return unless equations magnetically seek God's rays. They do so only if an individual consciences in some way. God returns only then and not before.

Masturbation so defiles the soul light with its radioactive charge occupying the body being aggressed, the soul light convulses from equations unable to function in any way. Approval of its practice should never be encouraged. The soul light convulses.

Love for anyone can never be satisfying where masturbation is practised. Its addiction can turn man or woman away from wanting real love. If kept up for many years, an individual often becomes cold, guilty, perverted, cruel, heartless, lonely, and selfish. The individual cannot make love without masturbating. The individual does not want sex with another. A private life is sought. A single life. An enclosed life. One of secrecy. One of ugly habits. One the brain manipulates. One God has withdrawn from. Often one of perversion.

The face of an addict of masturbation usually has very little colour. The skin is without aura. The eyes are dull. That is because the constant heated orgasm dries out light vibrations all through the body. It saps those vibrations so thoroughly they cannot express light charge. An individual usually hides from Sunlight, keeps rooms darkened and watches huge amounts of visual stimuli such as movies and television. The radioactive orgasm an individual addicts to feeds the brain one of the largest energy drives of all. The doses of charge become lust. The high of the brain is so powerful it can make an individual masturbate anywhere at any time and in any situation. It automatically perverts its addict because it seeks charge so frequently the addict cannot control the time or place or circumstance. Chronic masturbation destroys the body it addicts and a normal life can never be lived in any way.

Young boys and girls should never masturbate. Their soul lights will never be the same. Men and women should stop masturbating for their soul lights need God's return holding. The act of masturbation prevents real love from ever being wanted. It denies both sexes a pure soul and God's protective rays. It is a programme the brain has been fed. That programme has become a terrible defilement of love. It can be stopped. It can be cleansed. Conscience is the cure. God is the responder. Love, if it is truly wanted, can purify all of man's deeds unto his soul. Man must want love. Man must need love. Man must respect love. Man must be pure with love and pure in love's truth.

Ecstasy of soul inside the heart of man is full release of light vibrations, full magnetic contact with the purity of another's soul light vibrations and full magnetic contact with God's rays of soul holding. Ecstasy in loving another of soul is still possible. The soul light still exists inside man's heart and is available to mankind should man choose love that is pure. The equations involved at the time of love's orgasmic release have no artificial aggression, no forced exit, no pretence of the brain, no closure of the eyes and no defilement whatsoever during release. They magnetise each other first, heat in unison of enclosed containment, are cooled by the invisible rays of God's surround and express full charge of light vibrations at exactly the same moment. They excrete of their orgasm pure light moisture. Every equation in magnetic attraction activates purely.

Lovers of pure orgasmic release can produce pure child. Lovers become lovers for life. Lovers never seek another. Lovers have soul unified. Love of each other's soul light purity has been sanctified. God has accepted their orgasm through rays of cool containment. God's rays have not withdrawn because of aggressive charge. The orgasm has been of light vibrational activity of equations in balance of each other. Lovers in such ecstasy can never violate each other, their souls retain God's purity eternally.

Ecstasy of soul at death of the body of man has a similar activity. No lover is involved. No organic orgasm can be experienced. No moisture is excreted. Equations, held by God at the time of death, vibrate inside their containment, heat within their surround and because God's rays are holding the soul light without any other magnetic attraction, are automatically pulled from their containing body. The organic body releases the pure soul light. Equations are cooled immediately. The extraction of the soul is pure ecstasy, the acceleration of equations in magnetic suctioning travelling through the most beautiful purity of light rays and being placed according to their strength of light life. Such reality is felt. Such reality is of emotioning equations returning to their prime light source of life. Those equations then remain in a constant state of ecstatic existence never to be impured again.

The opposite of soul ecstasy is brain ecstasy, a very different experience with a hideous outcome at death. During an orgasm between two unsuited partners, the equations of the soul light convulse. They imbalance. They scream of their agony. They heat to red hot charge. They cannot be cooled by God's rays for God withdraws immediately the act of aggressive sexing begins. The soul light excretes mucous, not moisture of pure light release. Its activity has impured. Mucous from soul light convulsions enters the blood of the heart. It has strong odour, cannot be purified in the bloodstream because of the surrounding impurities and eventually clots, hardens inside the blood to often block blood flow. Soul light mucous thickens instantly it touches heated tissue. The equations automatically replicate. Imbalance is the cause. As they multiply in vibrational patterning they cling together for protection. Odour results from being heated, trapped, and unable to be cooled by God's rays. Odour is vibrating temperature reacting to various entrapments. Soul light mucous can turn red if remaining trapped near an artery. Equations always glow of their surrounding colour. Equations also return to their natural colouring as soon as they are touched in light rays visible or invisible.

An ugly forced orgasm between a couple causes one or both to close their eyes so the brain can absorb the charge without distraction. Such orgasms often cause muscular reactive display, a stiffening of the legs and feet, a grasping of the hands and fingers which often hurts a partner, a foul-mouthed description of the act in progress, an imagery happening inside the ever-defiling brain, a biting entirely of brain desire, a scratching also of brain desire, a brutality, and often a savagery too vile to be acceptable to anyone. Such is a brain orgasm without the soul understood.

The excreting energy cells of the body everywhere violate all light cells in surround. Their odour affects every light equation already retracting vibrationally. The spurting energy cells are always in extreme aggressive charge. Light cells introvert in ray extension. Heat causes God to withdraw from all light cells at that time.

The release of a forced orgasm activates the brain in such a way it addicts to the charge it receives. It craves the same experience again and again, sometimes more ugly than the last. Its coil reddens during the orgasm. Its excreting mucous spurts into its formation and eventually thickens. The brain bloats of its food. The soul light convulses repeatedly. Not until the violent activity ceases does the soul calm. Not until some conscience is possible does God return to the soul light. Not until man ceases this activity will his soul ever return to its life of pure light evolution.

A forced orgasm is always without respect for another's soul, without any love wanted, or any love felt by either partner. It is purely a sexual act of aggression, a brain needing as well as a brain which has already orgasmed from the act with another. Forced orgasms with many result in an addiction which often becomes perverted, of brain progressive behaviour.

An orgasm with partners who are loving, who do try respect unto each other and who do not attract sexual encounter with others can be God touched, God acknowledged and God sanctified. What prevents that ecstasy taking place is radioactive quantity of body vibrations too overpowering the heart itself to allow the orgasm to express light purely. Also a radioactive vibrating environment can absolutely prevent God's rays from pure contact with the soul.

Brain ecstasy at death of a human being is the most fatalising path of mankind. Its orgasm is not of organic copulation but of lust for the power source the brain has fed from during its life. Radioactive vibrations as well as every electric vibration magnetised by the brain, as well as every tiny nuclear fragment of a vibration, has become its sole life force. Because of aggressive feeding the brain has almost devoured the soul light. It is indulged twenty-four hours a day. The content of its food has escalated. The regularity of its feeding time has turned most of mankind into soulless, cold, heartless, and aggressive bodies capable of extreme cruelty, extreme violent acts, and murder. There is no conscience when the brain becomes an entity. There is no God and absolutely no soul of any vibrational capacity.

Lust of the brain craves more power than it can contain. At death of a human form the brain orgasms as its entire vibrational content attracts to an outer power source greater than itself. As it is magnetised from a body at death, its heat almost explodes its coil, for the outer attractor cannot pull brain vibrations magnetically until the body has ceased function.

Brain magnetic attraction unto an outer source of power lusts orgasmic release as a human form begins the death rasp. The outer power source attracts its vibrations. The brain, as it generates lustful attachment, causes air to be force-ejected in a rasping sound through a body's mouth. It hisses, rattles, and shakes a form, in anticipation of release of orgasmic ecstasy of itself coming unto its prime life force. The heating causes the eyes to roll. The victim often becomes hallucinatory. When a body ceases in vibrational activity the full volume of brain power swivels inside the head, swivels because its pathing cannot be linear as its content is of squashed vibrations. The brain must swivel of its vibrational content to detach from the coil. Unless this happens the brain would remain vibrating of explosive vibrations unable to detach from containment. What prevents an explosion taking place is an automatic outward equational ejection of brain vibrations from the soul light itself. No matter how weak and convulsing of the brain's attraction to an outer power source, the soul light still activates in equational reaction to its imbalancing force. The soul and only the soul light releases the brain from the body. Its violent convulsive spasming discharges the charging of a lusting brain to the hell it desires eternally.

The spasms of the soul light automatically aggress all soul equations which are sucked into the vibrating volume of brain power as it is drawn unto its prime source. The brain's quantity of overheated vibrations on exiting its containing body, drags the convulsing pure soul light's weak equations into its fierce charge and hells these equations eternally.

With a strong soul light the brain's power cannot consume pure equations and cannot carry them to hell. The soul still convulses as the brain lusts an outer power source as a body is dying, but its strength of light equations ejects the brain's volume of charge so forcefully no suctioning from the brain's exiting charge takes place. Heating is controlled at the time of the ejection by God's hold on the soul light of an individual strong enough vibrationally to hold on to God, and not be dragged into aggressive charge of the brain's lustful release seeking its prime source of power.

During the swivelling of vibrations a victim can often realise a ferment is waiting. Colour of red blazing vibrations can be experienced inside the retina. A flaming surface can often be seen. A death gripped human senses a path to hell. Others see light of severe red glow, another composition of red vibrations which is a lesser charge than flaming vibrations. These visible colours are seen because of the huge charge emanating from the brain's coil, which has no other attraction or activity but its prime source glowing red charge so powerful the colour reflects off the retina.

Dying humans facing brain magnetic attraction in orgasmic release of vibrations always know their fate before it occurs. The soul at that instant is the sufferer for its equations are eternal, emotional, and pure. Only the soul of every dying human condemned to death in radioactive ferment is interned in the hell of eternal flaming vibrations, a permanent uncontainable agony. Only the soul hells. The content of brain radioactivity magnetically attaches to a superior force of likeness, is eaten of its inferiority, and swallowed into a gaping constitution of man-made power. God encourages the power formation to attract to a galaxy holding. There it vibrates until its size causes enlargement of area contained. Inside this containment the eternal soul agonises eternally. Never can it be released from its hell. Never can it return to God. Never can it cease in excruciating suffering of a soul condemned in hell by the brain of man overpowering its life line to God.

Man needs to realise that hell exists, not of any fantasy but of full reality. God exists also not of fantasy but a reality no man should ignore. Man can condemn his soul, not God, but man himself. Man can aspire to his soul also, not pretend his soul is safe. God can only acknowledge man if he soul seeks. God is no forger, fake, or pretence. God is of light purity, equations of total balance and total powering. God is the supreme controller of the entirety of light life. Man is nothing in comparison, nothing in powering, and absolutely nothing in brain developed and programmed intelligence. Man should never pit man's brain against the almighty dominance of God. To do so is to minimise a life line already in jeopardy of its continuance. Death of mankind is imminent unless the soul is realised.

Explosion of the soul light, which can be of aggressive deliberate acts, or because of too much radioactive vibrational forced brain entry, hells the soul so agonisingly its equations gyrate eternally. They attempt unity of helled equations. Unity because their equations were of spherical evolution, unity because they were one evolving composition, unity because God's light surround was spherical when they were dropped from the Sun's rays of breath control unto Earth.

Explosion of the soul light happens if too much pressure of radioactive vibrations surrounds its composition, presses its equations to turn inward, causing ray retraction of aura projection. Because those rays have nowhere to extend, make contact with each other in spherical formation, they explode into each other. The contact does not equate. Rays project outward, not into each other. Each equation collides. Each ray swells and heats. Imbalance and pressure cause the explosion. Such soul light explosions are caused by environments which are of extreme radioactive charge, nuclear charging containments, ammunition in operation, torture to a human being unable to be contained, too much drug taking, and sport that becomes violently brutal to a form. Mankind explodes his own soul continually.

Exploded soul light fragments inside a ferment of heated radioactivity and nuclear charge can never unite, the surrounding power is too great. They still emotion, feel their agony. They still scream of their terror. They still attempt escape from hell. They remain in that torture eternally.

To deliberately explode a soul light encased in a heart, knowing that that deed condemns the soul, must be realised as unacceptable to all who deserve life of truth and of light security. With this truth here mankind must alter his own evolution as a species. God is not evolving mankind any longer. Man is. God can no longer hold man's soul purely and take it at death of the body. God can and does, lift many away from Earth's magnetic field and places them securely in star compositions. There they stay without ever reaching purity of domain of light vibrations. Ecstasy is still experienced, but sublime, divine existence of the soul, is not encountered. Man's soul light, no matter how man has lived on Earth, has become of weak fluctuating equations not strong enough to reach the ultimate state of light life. The evolving manufactured vibrations on Earth prevent that ever taking place. Once it did. Now it does not. God has no equational composition to lure to safety a radioactive charging formation with a soul light encased inside a heart structure that vibrates imbalance continually and prevents the soul light from God's rays of light holding.

Conscience is being thoroughly denied by most of mankind today. The act of consciencing absolutely reveals the grotesque violations man inflicts on every living thing. Monetary greed prevents a conscience from progressing in truth. The destruction of Earth in totality is caused by the full denial of man's conscience and the ever-addicting monetary pursuits of a massive number of human beings all in brain existence and all without soul reality. The world's population at this time is being consumed by the very power source it breeds to make money, a worthless and utterly fatal course of attraction.

Within man's intelligence, brained or souled, God cannot be denied. Love and its absolute greatness of presence cannot be denied either. Love is the only real soul need mankind craves more than money, more than power and more than God.

Love, pure, of equations held by God, has every beauty and security within its bounteous touch. Because love has been defiled, no man experiences love anywhere. Because God has been defiled no love can be given. Because man has a soul light love will forever be wanted. Because man's brain has destroyed the light life of the soul mankind will be without real love. Because mankind seeks every other alternative other than pure love, mankind will always be loveless unless the conscience is answered and truth is wanted in all things. Because God is the equator of all light equations, the life giver of all of creation, mankind cannot be an entity unto himself. The imbalance would never be accepted anywhere in light eternal living. Because evolution must progress, must be controlled by its creator, mankind must continue to be evolved in balance of light equations or be interned in galaxy confinement.

Be it of deep contrition or deep perversion man will know that his choosing will be eternal.

Love, the only pure expression of the soul light, is the full extension of emotioning equations reaching outwards from their central core, encouraged magnetically by a beauteous sight, a glorious radiance of creature life, an individual experiencing the same emotional extension of vibrations and a bestowal of pure light from God's intimate touching. Love, because it is of pure emotioning, bestows of itself, gratifies the receiver, and flushes of pure equations colourfully. A recipient's soul light magnetises love's beautiful expressioning which endows peace, softness of feelings, radiance of any eyes releasing its vibrations, and the illumination of the aura containing its purity. No other emotion has such beauty within its equations. Love and only love opens all rays of light protruding from the soul light in full perfection, and in full equating response, God loves of eternal sanctity.

Love releases all suffering once it is experienced purely. Its great force is contained in soul light existence in every living being. It cannot be touched unless the soul is pure. It cannot be given unless the giver is pure. God cannot respond unless the soul light is of pure extending rays.

Love overpowers all brain vibrations for its force transports the soul light unto ecstasy of light, a total unity of pure equations detached from contact with a body and held by God. Once experienced that way, eternal life becomes assured and death becomes obsolete. A being of the experience of pure love can never detach from God's hold, never admit brain charge into consciencing and becomes of soul light dominance in all things.

Without love's beautifying purity man dies without experiencing soul light reality. Man is nourished not. Love lives inside man's soul. Love ceases to breathe inside man's coveting of all that denies love. Love suffers. Love dies. Love cannot be expressed. Love cannot express love. Love and only love is still pure.

Love waits for every man's purification. Love endows every man's needs when God is touched and love is given. Love and only love can release all sufferers where love has been denied.

Love and only love, by pure emotioning equations, forgives all that has passed and requites all that has forbidden love's reality.

Man must seek love that is pure, love that comes from man's soul. Man must seek love that is real, love that is returned from God. Man must forever remain with love's truth, for love, once it is lost, can never be found again.

Purity, once violated, carries suffering never able to be healed unless love's reality is contrited for and God responds to the contrition. So great is the existence of love inside man's soul, only God's reality and all truth should man seek, and keep on seeking, until love is found, and man becomes a being of soul worth, a being worthy of love.

Suffering is soul light retraction of vibrations, an inward pulling back of pure rays of light. Each suffering contained in the soul light of man and creature prevents love from ever emotioning outwards of its rays and touching God's divine light. Suffering is man-powered everywhere. Suffering is brain motivated always. Suffering is without relief because its driving force is brain dominated. Suffering done unto any being is without the reality of the soul and the purity of equations that live of God's light.

Love is able to end every suffering on Earth, able to bring about world peace, the end of killings, the cessation of violence, the stopping of Earth's agonising torture, the end of creature murder and mutilation, the end of man's inhumanity to man. The end of evil. Love has been tried for by many decent individuals. Because the trying is of impure values, love has never been found. Because God's reality has never been understood, God's real love has never been able to be touched.

Scripture love is without the reality of the soul light completely and therefore unable to define love's great purity. Scripture is without God's evolution and therefore unable to secure for man the reality of the soul. Scripture lies have injected a brain program of fallacies which have condoned all that denies love's truth and all that denies God's unquestionable existence as a supreme light equator of all that lives of light life.

Love is always the path of greatness and always the sanctity of life eternal in divine existence of light.

Being of soul existence is being with love's emotioning greatness. All that is real is experienced fully. There are no lies in love's reality. No brain has powering. No mimicry is possible. No pretending attitude is forced and no falsity can preside. Were it not for love's existence man's search for love would not be so eternal. Were it not for love needed so desperately, man's conscience would never be entered. Were it not for man's soul light, love would never be touched.

Love, love, love and all of love will be found.

# Faith

Faith, the power of belief. Faith, that which all mankind needs. Faith, the overriding conscience inside man's soul which confirms God and the soul. If faith is not held, man is alone.

Mankind for centuries has had various forms of faith all superficial. Mankind has worshipped false Gods, false devils, false angels, false doctrine and false kingdoms. Every worship mankind has practised has had ulterior motives other than the purity of soul light and the real God of light. The worshippers of the faiths have all been without God's reality, Earth's suffering, and the existence of the true soul light of evolution by God.

Real faith cannot be experienced unless mankind is in real truth. Faith does not apply only to biblical interpretations or other doctrinated descriptions. Faith belongs to all of mankind with belief that is founded on truth. Faith in anything or anyone, when it is pure, is unshakeable, staunch, and upright. It cannot be destroyed in anyway. Faith has imperial presence if practised correctly. Faith is without real respect in man's soul. False doctrine has disqualified its greatness. Faith is love's protector.

False doctrine has been programmed into the human brain mightily. Doctrine that is flawed everywhere, altered and re-written. Much of it is gross fantasy and calculated effort to hold power over those who succumb. All religious doctrine is without true creation, without first equation, first breath, first light, and God in power over universal evolution of equations.

Brains of mankind have injected false doctrine all over Earth's suffering, all over Christ's truth, and all over every reality in existence. Millions and millions of believers in false doctrine are without their soul reality.

The production of false doctrine is often for monetary gain, enslavement of the many, and power. Indoctrinated beings have learned and been provoked to accept whatever they read and listen to as real. Nothing could be further from the truth. Nowhere in any doctrine is there any real reality.

Biblical doctrine once was transcribally taken by a few with soul light capacity to receive it. It was given intermittently throughout the lives of those chosen. The text then was in response to those in need of requitement of stressing equations. All of the text was for peaceful existence. Ways to improve the soul. Ways to assist sufferers. Ways to attend the Earth. Ways to be loving. Every word was in the vibrational identity of each individual transcribing. Many attempts were made to create tales that could be believed in. Many greedy individuals pretended to receive words that condoned their greed. Many others described happenings over-exaggerated and creating false images. Many would-be transcribers failed during the taking by admitting the brain, thus adding their own programs into the text and violating its purity of light equations.

God's light responses to all individuals in transcription taking never can convey stories of length, descriptive phrases of happenings, or historical sequences for the interest of mankind. Light language is totally of equating vibrations of magnetic search and contact. Once finding balance they cease aggressing in activity and vibrate peacefully. No mercenary deeds can ever be transcribed. Ever. No individual or individuals could ever be separated from soul existence of all of mankind. No false statements of any kind could be contrived.

False doctrine creates false idols. False idols begin where those without their soul reality seek others they see as their superiors, where the presence of someone or something has been programmed into the human brain as superior. Worship is a program of example of the many. Worship needs full truth and God before all that is false.

The false idols of youth today are consumed by false values, often drug addicted degraded beings, chronic alcoholics, sexual deviants, monstrous violating sensationalists and desperate insecure brains all craving idolatry of their souls. Such false worship consumes the conscience always and the worshipper strives to be as the idol. Brain attraction always provokes false idolatry.

Love and faith, the two most needed attributes for eternal life, the two essential capacities of the soul light have been destroyed.

Love without faith is bereavement. Both belong to each other. Both evolved together. Separating one from the other is death to both. Love and faith began in the soul light of the first great souled creature on Earth, whale. When whale ecstasised in love of whale's child, faith in parenting began. Father mated with mother. Child was born of both. Love developed in the bonding of all three. Family evolved. Child depended on both parents. Parents obeyed their souls. Faith in each other was born. Child grew into maturity with faith in child's parents strongly respected. Family evolved with faith in each other's souls. God responded in rays of strong holding as love and faith became divine.

Love and Faith were born of soul light greatness. Never should they be apart. Their unity began from the first born of whale. Their emotions began when child needed parenting. Their loyalty to each other was because their child was pure and experiencing that purity entwined their love and faith in each other. All parenting, no matter the creature, has been of absolute purity of soul light emotioning. Mankind has lost that purity. It is for mankind to want pure child again, child with capacity of soul, child without aggressive existence, child of light equations not energised charge of radioactivity. To birth such a child now is almost impossible unless there is change and conscience answered.

Love, Faith, Soul, God and the Earth, all belong as one mighty force. Cannot mankind be of consequence with such reality as the path of true life?

Why would mankind deny such a great future?

Why and how could mankind deny those who know what is right?

Why is there this truth for mankind to realise?

The unification of love and faith in vibrations of light purity is the pure capacity of the soul to bind together all that is of light life and keep those equations pure and vibrating unto God. Unification with God is eternal sanctity.

Brave and decent mankind still exists despite cruel pressures over soul light existence. Great mankind still survives on Earth. Mankind with soul fealty exists still. Mankind with the Earth conscienced for still exists. Mankind with love and faith inside their hearts. Mankind with every attribute of soul existence. Mankind with Earth's suffering contrited for. Mankind with soul light greatness. Mankind fully aware that change must come. Mankind pure and trying to remain pure. Many souls live diligently trying to make a difference, encouraging others to do the same, aware that mankind cannot continue in savage greed over every solitary life on Earth.

Truth here has no other purpose but to bring conscience back unto the soul light of mankind, to reveal reality, to secure the souls of every living form before it is too late, and above all, to save Earth's life. Truth, provided it is wanted, can achieve all that is needed for Earth and mankind to survive in the light of God's protection. Truth opens the soul light, releases the conscience, and God's touch can be fully and deeply experienced.

Mankind in truth is of divine eternal life. Mankind with God's light unto the soul evolves peacefully, without fear of death and with the Earth's bountiful givings to sustain life as it was meant to be. Mankind without soul fealty is without.

To be without Love or Faith, mankind is obsolete.

# Christ

Christ's existence on Earth has been so depleted of truth, so destroyed in his reality, bringing forth such truth must be understood as absolutely necessary for God's reality unto Christ to be believed.

Conscience here is vital. Conscience that accepts the reality of the evolution of first equation, God's light beginning, the greatness of the soul's composition, and the reality of eternal life. Unless truth is wanted here, Christ's teachings and Christ's miracles will remain without validity.

Nowhere in religious history has the real God ever been explained. Nowhere in religious teachings has the soul ever been explained. Everywhere in religious doctrine has there been interference of truth by the brain of mankind, pilfering, deceiving, powering and defiling the purity and real purpose of Christ's Calling.

God's choice of Christ as the orator of soul fealty, the purifier of man's evils, the assurance there was life after death, and the existence of God, was because at that time the purity of Christ's soul was the only vibrating light composition able to receive God's powerful contact. Mankind was destroying. Mankind was diseasing. Mankind was killing. Mankind had become greed possessed. Mankind was destroying the soul with mankind's brain. Mankind's soul light was vibrating suffering.

Too many violations unto the soul of man were seriously affecting the balance of light rays inside God's protecting hold on the soul. The equations were impuring. The light of God was withdrawing from many of mankind. Equations when in stress are always responded to by God. A chosen human being, a pure man, a body and soul beautiful enough, strong enough and capable of suffering was selected by way of equational capacity in light. Christ was God's perfect choice. Christ was called, in his normal life, to lead mankind back to mankind's soul.

Christ was first clairaudiented, second visioned, third orated, and purified where more strength was needed, to accept God's asking and die for mankind to be forever conscienced. Christ accepted all that became his duty. Christ taught all that was asked. Christ healed those who could be healed. Christ loved as an example to man when love then was destroying hideously. Christ knew he would become a martyr. Christ knew he would be betrayed and when. Christ knew he would have to suffer cruelly. Christ was held by God to go through his suffering. When Christ died, history began religiously.

The presence of Christ on Earth brought conscience inside man's soul. Conscience that enabled God to keep hold of man's soul. Conscience that spread throughout history. Conscience that kept love and faith together always until the brain of mankind overpowered all of Christ's truth and corrupted many administering Christ's teachings.

The horrific defilement of Christ's purity is undeniably of brain ugliness, the brain progressing itself, conjuring an image of impurity, forbidding conscience in those programmed in defilement of that which is pure and should never be impured. To accept any purity of any association or being inside the human brain would automatically prevent the brain from activity. The soul would become. Purity is of the soul. Acceptance of any reality is absolutely not possible within the brain's coil. Once soul presence becomes operative, the brain's presence is denied.

Christ was never homosexual. Christ was a normal man. Christ was not virginal. Christ had experienced what most men experience during their early years. When Christ was called, Christ became chaste. God needed a pure example unto mankind and Christ was that example willingly.

The followers of Christ were many, from different family beliefs and very different values. No follower was pure and no close follower was homosexual either. All were full men, some with wives and families, others single and searching. Christ's following kept growing. Eventually women followed Christ seeking love and their soul existence. Every interpretation of Christ's life has been tampered with severely. Every reality of Christ himself was deliberately changed to feed others with selfish needs and ugly greed.

The Bible is false, a collection of anecdotes and transcriptions with nothing but power and greed at the root of the wording. No race could ever be chosen as superior by God in any way. Slavery could never have been condoned by God in any way. War, killing, incest and plunder, would be impossible for God to condone. Such falsity has been brained. Mankind everywhere, programmed with biblical hearsay, needs soul intelligence here, not anything else. The Bible has allowed every corrupt activity mankind has been guilty of to enter and destroy the pure values of the soul and become testimony. Its content does still hold the great and beautiful oratory of Christ. That is all that it has of real truth. There was no chosen race. Mankind chose himself. There was no Adam and Eve. Mankind invented them. There was no first family. Ape man was first man with family. There was no ridiculous biblical beginning. God, of first equation, first light, and first wholeness, evolved progressively in the purity of real evolution as the light power over all equations at life. There was a beginning, the real beginning of first breathing light force. Please enter conscience here in the reality of what is written here and cease being bloated with fiction from a Bible that needs correcting. No man woman or child can ever be in truth of their souls unless real truth is wanted.

I the writer here express of this truth for all who read, that Christ, the only pure soul on Earth at that time, was necessary in suffering, was chosen by God to conscience mankind for as long as conscience was possible, and keep man's soul unto God. That is the true power of God, the equator of all equations of light life. Christ's death in suffering has kept mankind with soul capacity. Never should Christ's purpose, person, or purity, ever be defiled by man again.

Now, at this time, even Christ's death is slowly being forgotten and too many times tragically defiled. That is the way the brain destroys truth. That is the way the brain is destroying the soul inside mankind. That is fatal for all of mankind at this time. Please, ye of sufficient soul capacity, try hard for all of this truth here to be needed before thy brains destroy its validity. Christ will never live again on Earth. Christ's great oratory is still here on Earth. Christ's legacy still exists here on this Earth. God exists in man’s soul here on Earth. Man’s soul exists awaiting conscience. Conscience, conscience that Christ died for, needs resurrection.

In respect for all ye unable to detach from biblical worship, I say unto ye, begin again with a real explained God of light, then progress unto the real explained evolution of thy souls, from then on truth will flow through thy lives unto eternal life.

# Earth's Soul Light

The comparison of Earth's soul light to man's must be made realistically and without the ever-deceptive interruption of man's brain. Man must try here to absorb this truth within man's soul capacity, within man's conscience, conscience that will allow man's soul to acknowledge Earth in the reality of Earth's true existence as a pure child of God, a child that has been loved by God, held by divine light, and is now dying.

Earth, for all who conscience here, is greater than any man, greater than any soul of man and greater in love than any man could ever conceive. Born of God's pure light evolution. Born of perfect light vibrations. Born of total spherical formation of equations. Born of evolving light vibrations all progressed by God alone. Born beautiful, pure, emotional and loving. Born to eternal life of light.

Equations emotion. They emotion because they are of life. Life that belongs to a father. A father of prime light force, the greatest power of all of light evolution. A father of pure emotion. Pure equating responses. Pure equating touch. Pure sublime acknowledgement. Pure divine love.

In this truth man has come to understand God's evolution, God's light control, the evolution of the universe, the equations necessary to keep it pure, the birth of all bodies of light and their evolution, the truth of the soul light in all living things, and the deterioration of light equations necessary to every life form. Man has also understood the reality of the causes that have fatalised man's future. Man has been greatly truthed already. Man must now be deeply conscienced, where if man is not, man will perish.

At the centre of the body of Earth, the equating core of its light equations, the first pure formation of its body beats its heart of light casing, a protecting sheath of light vibrations which hold the purity of its soul light. So pure is Earth's soul light it can ecstasise emotionally when God feeds it pure life force. It expresses glorious appreciation at God's touch. It stretches out its emotioning equations to hug, hold ecstatically the God it loves to belong to. It loves, and God responds in light love. An Earth, still a child of love, stretches out its rays of light love and embraces its father's loving. Man must sincerely try to understand that it is not man alone needing love, and God alone giving only man love, that Earth was and still is, of greater soul light, and far, far greater love given and received.

Surrounding Earth's heart, layer upon layer of hard light protects that heart from rupture, contamination, explosion, and equational imbalancing. Through hardened light Earth's heart life is watered, kept moist and kept at temperature. Within Earth's evolving body flaming equations have heated, disturbing Earth's temperature and creating Earth's blood, the entrapment of heated equations unable to purify. God has surrounded every single minute impurity of Earth's evolution to hold it securely to life. Nothing affected Earth's soul light until man nuclearised Earth's interior.

Each nuclear explosion inside the Earth's formation has caused Earth to feel pain no man could contain. The size of its living breathing pure soul light determines the suffering it endures, from the ever greeding power consuming brain of mankind, an agony so cruel every man, woman and child must, before it is too late, contrite for, not ignore, contrite, contrite, and contrite.

A great, bountiful, beautiful and pure living entity of God's loving and caring, has been deliberately and callously tortured by the deeds of mankind without soul reality. A perfect spherical light vibrating divinity is being slowly hacked to death, skinned alive, pierced and probed mercilessly through its body, gutted of its life line, drained of its blood, greedily scavenged for its great wondrous light vibrational constitution, plundered for every sparkle it was born with, blown up wherever man constructs a hideousness, mutilated in every form of purity and beauty, asphyxiated in air supply, littered over its once immaculate surface of light equations, dumped upon and into its glorious formation with waste of nuclear contamination, burned of its sensitive and light glowing tissue, radiated of every pure vibrating equation of its evolution, contaminated of its bounteous seas and water ways, been ripped up and out of every balance of light life that evolved from its perfection, and absolutely destroyed in its total environment of light life. Yes, all mankind must realise this truth.

All mankind must conscience for these deeds. Unless conscience is wanted respectfully such deeds will continue.

Earth is alive.

Earth breathes of light life.

Earth holds every light formation upon its body to life sustenance.

Earth's soul is in uncontainable suffering.

Earth belongs to God.

Man, in ignorance, is responsible for Earth's death grip. Man is no longer ignorant of anything. Man, being the sole cause of Earth's destruction, must want to repair what has been done.

I the writer of this truth once again plead for the life of Earth. I plead because I must, because unless I do, unless my pleas are felt, unless I reach the conscience of those able to be in truth, all I have suffered for in bringing this truth will have been for nothing. I have given forty years of my life to bring about Earth's truth. A life I have willingly chosen to offer. A life that has had to transform. A life I have no hesitation in sacrificing. I believe everything I have written here. I stand by that truth. Until I die I will never stop pleading for life of the great Earth, and the reality of God, Earth's creator.

# Greed

World greeding is the unstoppable pursuit of everything the human brain feeds from. Greed has always been of man's brain, activated by that which it needs to remain alive and feeding. Greed is radioactivity inside man's brain, constantly vibrating, constantly feeding, and unable to be put out of charge.

Everything the brain sees good and bad causes attraction, a charge of electrified and radioactive aggressive vibrations which must continue no matter the outcome. Once in pursuit of something animal vegetable or mineral, the brain relentlessly vibrates unto its fixed interest, a charge which eventually obtains and possesses that which it has sought, whatever the outcome. Once it is encouraged it holds firm whatever its vibrations have fixed on.

Mankind in brain life cannot see such reality. Mankind in brain life cannot prevent greed from possessive occupation of acquiring all things. Man's brain is ceaseless in activity. It has overpowered man's soul light. It is the cause of Earth's suffering entirely. It will cause man's extinction.

Were there no greeding, Earth would never have been violated. Mankind would never have warred and the soul light inside man's heart would still be dominant. Now, most of mankind is greedy. Child has recently inherited the disease.

Greed for man's soul has never been an attraction. Why? Because in man's soul is conscience, truth, and God's reality. No brain alive and needing food would allow its life force to be destroyed. Any threat to the brain's powering has almost always been violated, ridiculed, fully denied, and deliberately lied about. Threats to man's brain power here in this text will be fiercely denied.

Where is it possible to conscience? How is it possible to save Earth from horrific greeding of everything the Earth once yielded? How can consciencing redeem all that has been lost? How can mankind undo all that has been done?

The answer is simple. Deny the brain. All will automatically purify.

At this time nowhere on Earth is there any purity. Nowhere has been left alone. Not one creation of light life has been left without destructive influence of man's greed. Not one tree, flower, creature or soul light has escaped the deadly interference of man's brain power. All, all, all of light life is being destroyed.

Wherever man has trod, the Earth has been depleted of light balance. Wherever man has empired the environment has become contaminated. Whatever man has manufactured, gross imbalance of environmental stability has occurred. Whatever beauty man has encountered, man has violated all purity. Whatever creature man has known, man has diseased, destroyed and condemned the greatness of light evolution. Whatever conscience has been stirred, man has ignored.

There is no place of peace, beauty, and purity, left upon Earth. Man has coveted all, not in love or respect, but in horrifying greed and power.

Truth can never be destroyed. Acceptance of truth is of soul confirmation. Truth has no pretence. Truth cannot be of lies. Truth denies the brain for its reality enters the soul. Truth can never be faked, never contrived, never falsified. Truth has real power, greater than man's brain power, and of undeniable reality unto the soul. Truth therefore will remain dominant through all that refuses its presence. Truth if wanted, without fear of the brain's possessive greeding, automatically brings the soul of man unto a God of eternal light security.

Coming unto real truth can be hurtful. The facing of realities can be difficult. The brain always denies the conscience for its powering ceases where the soul is entered. Entering the soul light's free flowing vibrations releases the soul and allows conscienced fealty to all that is of life. Humanity must change, needingly, or by the consequences of refusing to change. The human brain, once confronted with this truth here, will behave in fear of everything.

Fear of losing security of monetary strength.

Fear of the loss of empire, monetary, political and personal.

Fear of the loss of luxuried living.

Fear of losing personal wealth.

Fear of having no future in business.

Fear of having no power over others.

Fear of losing fame, titles, thrones and privilege.

Fear of being exposed in reality of truth.

Fear of having no payment for work.

Fear of being without drugs and alcohol.

Fear of losing property.

Fear of losing possessions.

Fear of guilt.

Fear of concealing.

Fear of others.

Fear of all that is hidden in safes and vaults.

Fear of being seen as a denier of Earth's life.

Fear of being seen as a denier of man's soul.

Fear of being known as a denier of God's existence.

Fear of going to a hell in vibrations.

Fear of dying without soul sanctity.

Fear and more fear and more fear. Fear of every selfish, greedy, possessive, worthless acquisition, which denies mankind a future, and the Earth its life.

And so is the truth.

# Time In Equations

The surround of God's invisible light holding enables all equations to function universally, vibrate in rhythm of magnetic charge. Without that containment no equational balance would there be. Motion outward could not return to its beginning and first equation would never have been born. Breathing would never have been possible. Life would never have begun. God would not exist and the soul light would never have evolved.

Science has always been seriously flawed everywhere, from planetary evolution to man and creatures' existence. Science alone has destroyed Earth's reality and God's presence. Brain programming without the conscience acknowledged has created an education with no reality of a beginning, no evolution of first equation, first light, and first life. Science has nuclearised Earth. Science has experimented with every living formation without respect. Science needs reality, a clear explained unquestionable evolutionary progression of equations, that begins with first equation and answers to God's responses. With this knowledge science must change. Continuation of scientific experiments without reality will destroy every life on Earth and every pure equation attached. Science has empowered itself to critically mutilate Earth and savagely violate man and creatures' soul light.

Time, man's analysis of time, is of linear forward pathing. Time of man's brain calculation is absolutely wrongly placed in universal equational balancing. Man's time is without pure motion, the spherical progression of motion, and God's responding return of spherical motioning. Time therefore, motions inside God's hold, and keeps progressing. Time is of pure motion in perfect equational breathing.

With God's inward spherical motioning every solitary equation is overpowered. The outward motion of first equation allows those equations to progress, vibrate of themselves in pure motion. They do not forward path while in motion. They express their vibratory individuality. There is no stop and start or point of calculation. Equations are continuous in progression. God's return motion which is massive in spherical distance from first equation, gives every equation however minute or large, time to progress; age, mature, solidify, grow, unify, develop, establish field, and purify imbalances. God's motioning does not activate equations. It is a response.

Man's dictated time interferes with all equations everywhere. Man constantly backward paths himself by regulating time to a scale which is without reality of God. In so doing, man has imbalanced the motioning of his own soul light, and every equation at life everywhere else. Man disturbs motion of pure equating necessity. Man forces equations to readjust their motioning. Man restricts those equations from their vibrating purity. Man has created a time scale of grave error.

God's inward motioning, on surrounding every equational formation, automatically absorbs all vibrations within that response. Each vibratory happening during that slow inward return is equated, responded to invisibly and coolly. God keeps motioning inward until reaching first equation, the beginning of life in motion. God decreases in motion as first equation is approached. When it is touched, God's response is identical to first motion of first equation. First equation then begins motioning outwards from its central fixed position, enlarging as God's light entity enlarged, and expanding exactly as God's light sphere. All equations activate in response. Motion outward allows them to progress of themselves, advance in their stages of evolution. They continue vibrating without stopping. Outward motioning of first equation proceeds to God's outer surround with all equations progressing in their containment. On reaching the surround, first equation in motion is immediately responded to by God's equating response, and inward motion begins perfectly without stopping. Every evolved and evolving equation and formation breathes in motion of first equation and God's response whatever the progression. The equating rhythms are set, fixed in tempo according to their varied evolutions. They all breathe in equations of singular identities and individual sizes of formations. Their rhythms are perfectly equating. They are of the purity of light vibrations. Whatever the imbalances man has caused they still breathe eternally, even as helled vibrations.

Time in equational perfection is of spherical motion. First equation opened the sequence of breathing, the containment of spherical surround answered. First explosion separated its light surround and caused the containing, equating, invisible, spherical presence of God to evolve. Breathing never stopped. Its motioning never imbalanced. Its prime equation began life. Nothing touched its beginning. Nothing ever can. Never should there be a calculation to condone a time scale for man to prosper from. All equations imbalance.

Equations all activate inside their surround in colourlessness, the invisibility of God's light vibrations as well as visible light vibrations. Only their balance is interfered with, not their activity.

God's inward response controls temperature entirely, controls aggressive equational behaviour, and contains all equations purely, singular, or in formation. Nothing is disturbed in time. Equations cannot stop and start at any point. They never can and never will deactivate their progressive evolution. Equations cannot die. They are of the purity of light at life from the prime equation of evolution.

For man to evolve in reality of God, light, and eternity, man's time scale must change. Hours, minutes, days, months, years, decades, centuries, and millennia, must become obsolete, totally understood as destructive to man's soul light, and every equation at life on Earth. Forward timescale has placed man's equational form behind universal balance of equations. Man's equations do not progress eternally. They cannot. Their spherical motioning has been prevented by force, a time scale entirely dominant and obedient to the pursuit of monetary gain, a regulated pattern of forced behaviour which destroys the purity of equations at life eternally. Man cannot live purely. Man cannot rest purely. Man cannot procreate naturally. Man cannot love purely. Man cannot eat purely. Man cannot have health purely. Man diseases. Man dies. Man's soul light is devoured.

Earth's own perfect motion has been altered by man's artificial vibrations. No cessation at any time or at any moment is there, from massive vibrational torture, over, under, through, and above the Earth and into its planetary habitat. Millions upon millions of burning equations are being destroyed everywhere. Man's addictions, absolutely out of control, vibrate the environment so threateningly climate change is causing every life on Earth to become insecure, unable to feel safe. Climate change is advancing. Man's greeding is advancing. God's equating response is also advancing.

Time of man does not allow one single life to vibrate in pure motion. Every living form and formation is force-energised, overpowered by manufactured vibrations of huge quantity increasing. At night the aggressive charging still goes on. The body of Earth has become a terminally diseased and dying sphere of universally imbalancing equations disturbing all planets in magnetic contact. During the day that aggressive charge amplifies to trillions of ugly vibrations all progressing hideously and all contained in magnetic attraction to each other. Every human domicile vibrates massive radioactive charge. Every human being is attached to amplified vibrations of grotesque development increasing. Every man-made machine vibrates a vile and contaminating field of aggression and every work environment does the same. Every nuclear power station stores vibrationally the power to murder every life in its path. Every vibrating invention of man destroys equations of light. Every integration of manufactured vibrations creates disease that will eventually consume man himself. Every corner of the Earth is being exploited, greedily, violently, and without any conscience whatsoever accepted. Such a truth is real. Such destruction is real. Such a God is real also.

Life, all life, every minute vibrating equation, singular or in formation, breathing, emotioning, progressing, and held by God needs to be respected.

Respect, the honouring of the soul, can never be without deep conscience and real contrition, for much of mankind in ignorance, has become mercilessly greedy and incapable of truth and reality.

Earth can be saved. Mankind must make that happen. Creature can be saved. Mankind must make that imperative. Mankind can also be saved. God must make that choice. Life is eternal. From a perfect whole, life began as first equation motioned outwards and was responded to by its containment. Light began by contained vibrations warming. God began when first explosion released first equation from imbalance. The universe began as God's equating power enlarged. The planets began from exploded fragments of light particles in magnetic attraction. Earth began as its light equations hardened. Life on Earth began as equations of light were dropped from the Sun's rays. Man began as creature progressed. Man has stopped the evolutionary progression of all equations within man's domain. Man must realise man's future and never be ignorant again.

In the belief that mankind can have a future without war, suffering, and death of the soul, real change will come.

In the belief that Earth will be healed from all it has suffered, change is all that is needed.

In the belief that love and faith will live again in man's soul, change automatically purifies what has destroyed their greatness.

In the belief that God really exists as the light creator of all of evolution, universal sanctity becomes soul eternity.

In the belief that I the writer have delivered this truth for the life of the Earth I so plead for, I accept the outcome.

It is for all of mankind to decide what is truth and what is not. It is for child to follow parental guidance. It is for creature to rely on God's hold on the soul. It is for Earth to do the same. It is for I to hold my love and my faith in full contrition for every living soul light, for every suffering mankind has experienced, for every agony the Earth has emotioned, and for God in truth, never understood.

No explanation has there ever been for any substance of creation, no explanation for Earth's beginning, no explanation for the soul, no explanation for God, and no explanation whatsoever for eternal life.

Mankind, body and soul, has evolved without reality. Mankind cannot continue in such a state.

Mankind, as long as truth presides, will live on.

Mankind without need for truth, will destroy.

In the name of God, the father of light life, the creator of all of evolution, the eternal light sanctity of the soul, the first breathing equation of existence, I the Messiah, seek assistance to save Earth's life before it is too late, to secure Earth's creatures before they become extinct, and to bring back man's soul light unto full conscience, and the safety of eternal life.

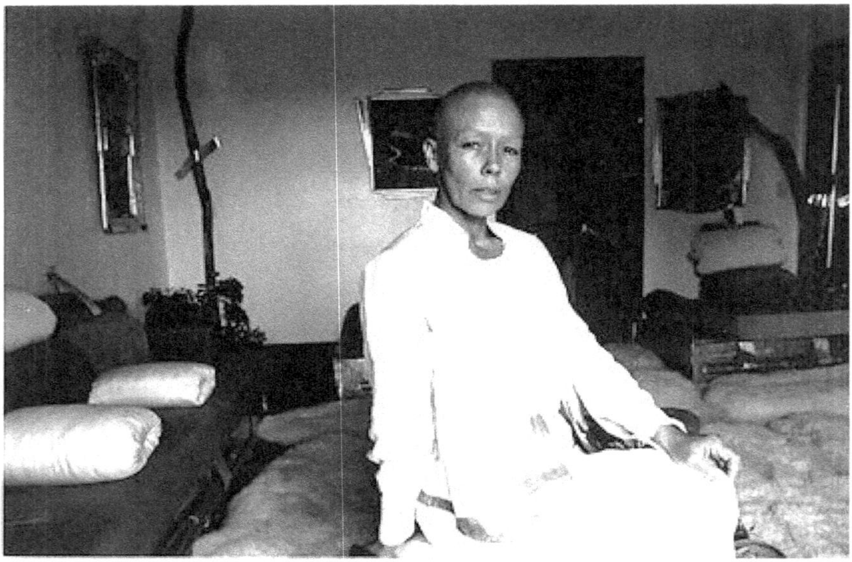

Te Kopuru 1986

# Afterword: My Suffering

Over forty years ago I was a normal human being. I was a beautiful woman, perfectly formed, intelligent, seeking the right partner, very experienced in life, extremely sensitive and with a past of extreme suffering throughout my childhood, a childhood which was cruelled by a heartless mother and her abandonment of any parental responsibilities. My father who had been famous and with racial prejudice to overcome within his life, had been tragically killed in a war he did not want to participate in. I was sent to boarding school where I was beaten, neglected, forbidden visitors and at the age of five and a half years, understood that the war had caused in me a wound that would never heal. My daddy I loved. My mother I could not love. The convent I was educated in I could not respect in any way. At the age of six, from sheer neglect I had contracted tuberculosis and an incurable skin disease, psoriasis. I had begun my childhood carrying suffering and diseases that were incurable. Later on, it became evident why both diseases were cured, for the blood I kept coughing up eventually stopped and several years later the sores I was covered in disappeared.

I felt every ugliness to me deep in my soul. I held truth then which later became a force I could not ignore. I was also not normal in my soul composition and very different to others in every way. I had abnormal senses, those which assessed everything beyond a normal human being. I felt more deeply than others. I hurt more deeply than others. I suffered much greater than others. I contained that suffering more undetectable than others. During my teenage years I endured severe cruelty, soul torture and deeds done unto me that were evil, without conscience, devoid of compassion, bereft of every decency and deeds that caused me to try to take my life three times, two nearly fatal. One attempt was so intended to be my last, the medical staff announced I could not be saved. Returned to life, I continued on without contrition for what I intended and without respect for my soul. I was broken in soul, the part of me I knew was beautiful, the part of me that suffered greatly.

I survived huge hardship greater than a human could. I was left by my mother and family to fend for myself before I became a teenager. I found myself alone, threatened at every turn in life and without a home, family or security. There in that loneliness I experienced one truth after another always frightening and always real. I backed away from dangerous living time and time again. I knew I could be a victim of evil and escaped many, many times from sheer strength of soul. As a child I had suffered more than an adult could contain. The quality of my soul enabled me to live through what no man could, ever. That soul still controls my destiny.

My life as a young woman was filled with experiences rare to others, experiences of real privileged living and real underprivileged existence. I went to and fro, from one experience into the next, never ever realizing how much of real life I was seeing. I could not commit myself totally to anyone or any profession. Opportunities were placed in front of me that others could not obtain. I violated my soul then over and over again not knowing how dangerous that was and never ever honouring the conscience I always experienced and completely ignored. I pulled myself through life trying different paths, seeking adventure, always seeking love, never ever happy and never fulfilled anywhere or with anyone I tried to love. My life then was without any normality and full of experiences I often could not contain. I never had a normal life. I could not establish my strengths anywhere. I could not respect anyone and did not want to give my love to any man I could not respect either. My experiences prevented me from trusting anyone, having faith in any doctrine and belonging to any profession.

Wherever I went I felt unsafe. Whatever I touched was ugly. Whoever I tried to love I felt betrayed. Whenever I sought comfort, I experienced coldness. God, any kind of a God was totally disbelieved in. Prayer, that had been programmed into me as a child, was found to be without credibility when I tried to find help for my suffering. My soul however, the depth of my real feelings, always felt real.

Without any spiritual involvement of any kind and without any spiritual experience I became aware of a terrifying presence surrounding my person everywhere I went, a pressure, a feeling that someone or something powerful was keeping me aware and even afraid. I had left my marriage then, knew I had stopped loving my husband, felt my marriage had become ugly, felt I needed to change and could not control the intense feelings in my heart. My husband I had tried to love. Suddenly his presence became unacceptable in my soul and incapable of understanding my feelings. I fled my marriage, hurt the man who had tried to love me and found myself alone, afraid, searching deeply for the reasons for my disturbing needs. My marriage had stabilized my past of suffering for a time. The man I had married was responsible for that stability. He was tender, understanding, capable of much soul then and able to shelter me gently. He had no God, no respect for anything except monetary gain and no sensitivity to an obvious search I had tried to augment during my marriage to him. His business life occupied him totally and the perversion that life caused, eventually destroyed his soul.

I began to want my soul, want to be a decent person and want to be worthy of something. I had never felt that way before. I had always wanted to be a beautiful person but didn't know how to make myself decent. I began to feel my soul as never before and struggled to accept its existence. I became confused, needing someone to help me understand what was happening to me and finding no-one capable, became isolated, alone and without support. I realized that what I was experiencing could turn close friends away, cause them to lose interest in me and possibly condemn me to those in professional occupations. Soul searching can be very painful if not understood for it exposes extreme conscience which unless acknowledged affects the emotions deeply. I withdrew from trying to seek help. I felt no-one was able to be trusted. I gave up trying to reach someone. I closed out every friend I had. I had lost faith in everyone at that time, faith that never returned.

I first heard my name called clearly but without sound one day whilst walking in the park. I became frightened, aware that the clarity of words which followed my name were unnatural. Later I learned of clairaudience, the capacity to hear silent words and sentences. My name was called several times. I became fearful, afraid to respond, wanting to ignore what I was hearing. When I reached my apartment the voice I had heard quite distinctly, asked me to attend to the words I was hearing. I was then asked to pick up a pen and take dictation. I couldn't, I was afraid of what was happening to me for it was not understood and not trusted.

My sleep was interfered with by my name being called again and again. I was asked to stay calm and watch what I was being shown which was astonishing for I was watching colourful patterns dissolving into pictures. Later I learned that I had received clairvoyance, the capacity to receive visioning. I was frozen in fear, unable to respond in any way. Clairvoyant visioning appeared strongly and repeatedly before my eyes. What I watched was the earth exploding into fragments. What I heard was that the earth was in danger of explosion. What transpired next was a Calling unto me I was asked to accept. My name was repeated many times. Earth's endangered existence was repeated continuously until I accepted that what I was seeing and hearing was serious. I was asked to pick up a pen and write. I did so unable to deny that request. The words that came through my hands were terrifying for I was asked to accept a mission of urgency, give up my present life, abandon everything I held dear, vocation myself for the Earth, receive the Earth's truth, suffer hugely for that truth, publish what I would write and obey everything that was asked of me thereafter. I refused. I refused again and again. I kept on refusing for many years. I never believed I was capable of such responsibility and still find such a mission terrifying. I was forced to accept my Calling and despite my defiant refusals am firmly held unto the soul reality I now face.

My Calling was horrific. My belief in a God was superficial. My mistakes were many. I had lived the life of a glamorous, shallow, unhappy woman wandering the earth in search of love and being totally unfulfilled. I had few values. I had no belief in any doctrine, person, podium or place of security. I could not evaluate right from wrong to stabilize myself. My background left me totally insecure everywhere. A Calling of any kind, especially of spiritual intervention, was disdained. At every interference in my normal life I was in denial. The purification of such denial is unable to be described because the path it took was ugly. I was terrorized, forced into my truth, held there until I contrited, kept in the recognition of truth, was suffered, humiliated, disgraced and degraded until I began to sincerely respect the power I was sure was making me subservient and respectful. It took months of trial after trial of my false beliefs and pitiful values all questioned, challenged, cleansed, contrited for, cast from my brain until real truth became wanted and accepted. My hair went white and fell out in handfuls. My defiance became tamed. I stopped questioning every word I heard. I stopped disobeying everything I was asked to do. I began to change in every way. I stopped being insulting, pretending I was talking to some fraudulent being. I stayed away from friends who were shallow. I began to realize my life had been utterly worthless and so were many of my friends. I began to start feeling for things I had never noticed before. I started to feel my conscience never before answered. I became softer to others, decent, compassionate, deeply tolerant, kinder, more generous, needing to become better, cleaner and a respectful person. The change was constant. My Calling still went on, purifying my every ugliness. My respect for the power I felt in control of my life grew. I was then living a very abnormal life, hidden from others totally.

I began asking questions I had never known the answers to. I learned in transcribal reception much truth. It shocked me. I found difficulty in containing all that I was being taught and advised of. I had been programmed with falsity in everything, insincerity to everyone and truth never honoured. The questions went back and forth until I was convinced that what I was being told was the truth. I then began questioning the reality of the presence I was communicating with. The answer caused me to immediately withdraw my communication and become fearful again. God was that answer. God I could not accept in any way. God was never believed in, in any form. I felt betrayed.

I was left alone for many weeks then called in name again. This time I was needing my own truth and asked of it. What came through transcribally caused my already weak and severely suffered heart to malfunction. I collapsed. I had a heart attack and was taken to hospital. The shock of my revealed Calling plus the lengthy purification I had gone through had caused my heart to clot in its arteries and weaken in rhythm so that I was functioning without full heart beat and full blood supply. I was strapped to a heart monitor when I was called again.

I had become responsive to the presence in communication with me, not yet trusting fully but often obedient and even respectful. God, I had not accepted then. My own truth I had not accepted either. I had however already detached from my glamorous life, given up all of my possessions and security and was living humbly in very poor circumstances. My Calling destroyed my pretensions as well as the shallow values I tried to have. I had become strong in soul, clean and unafraid of living alone with little. When my heart gave out, I was nearly starving. My condition at that time was critical.

To save my life God asked me to leave the hospital I had been taken to, remove the electrodes I was plugged in to and trust the advice I was being given in order to be healed. I did. I dragged myself down the hospital steps unseen, staggered onto the road and hailed a taxi. I was in severe pain and exhausted. No-one was in my apartment at that time. I was asked to warm myself in a bath and go to bed. God then began the first entry of vibrational invisible light rays into my heart chamber where my soul light existed also. The existence of a soul light inside human form was explained to me further on. God's invisible light rays also in contact with that soul light was another educating experience.

All through my purification I had been counselled, truthed of every happening I was experiencing and advised of the next stage of my Calling. Gradually with irregular light palpitations coming from the light rays that were touching my soul light, the blood clots were dissolved and my heart rhythm was normalized by God functioning my heartbeat in light vibrational patterning. This meant that God held me to life and that normality of life was then over forever.

The healing was traumatic, painful, very long, and when it was over my soul, which had experienced the light of God touching its composition, could not accept any vibrations surrounding it, but God's. I was unable to live a normal life thereafter. I changed. I became strong, confident, able to survive anything, able to endure anything and able to confront anything without fear.

During my healing I was shown clairvoyantly everything that was being done to me. I watched light rays pick at my clotting. I saw the miniscule blood compositions part from their clumps, be washed with water and enter my bloodstream. It was beautiful to watch. I was totally calm. When it stopped, I was cleaned of clotting. I recovered quickly.

To accept God's vibrating power through my heart chamber meant soul magnetic attraction to those light rays. Rays of light cover the Earth visibly and invisibly. They feed the Earth its life force. Covering my soul composition with light rays became my only life force. Detachment from that hold would mean I would die. That holding began to destroy my normal body. My Calling was the reason I was God-held. My Calling was the total reason I would never be let go of no matter what the suffering and there came so much suffering my heart stopped more than once and had to be re-started by God for me to survive.

God's powerful vibrating light content I learned of later on, could not keep hold of me unless every opposition to its vibrations was overpowered. I had already been told that I would suffer and that suffering would be horrific. I had already agreed to allow God to do whatever was necessary to bring the Earth's truth to mankind. It was my Calling, that which had been force affirmed in my soul and could never be taken out. At that time I had no idea how horrific my suffering would become and no idea how determined to keep me alive God's hold on my soul would be, for I was human, alive in energy, depleted in the strength of soul I needed to survive and incapable of enduring the suffering coming and the length of time it would continue for.

First, the electrical and radioactive energy content (the superficially charged energy of the human body form) began to weaken. My brain, radioactive and electrical in patterning, alive in aggressive energy and in total control of my person, began rejecting God's touch. I experienced a huge weight on, in and around my head. The weight was heavy, unable to be detached from and of huge power. I became deeply depressed, terrifyingly clairvoyanced to control the aggressive patterns of my brain reacting violently to God's hold. Hideous nightmares were given to control my incapacity to succumb to God's pressure and not withdraw my soul light, for the human brain is the most powerful part of the body now with the soul weak and unable to be of influence.

God's entry into my brain caused my soul to convulse. The brain's radioactivity had to be overpowered. Control of it meant the entry into my head of radioactively charged invisible light rays more powerful than the brain's and able to overpower every opposition in the way of that purification. Then came the cruel heated head throbbing. My eyes, unable to remain open for long, closed constantly, swivelled uncontrollably and caused helpless, uncontainable paralysis of my body and the inability to fixate on any visual stimulant. I could not move, speak, turn my head, use my eyes, call for help, sleep or exist. The temperature of my head was so hot others were alarmed for me and even saw a faint red ring around my head which was shaven at the time to help me keep cool. Gradually I became bed-ridden from agony so ugly I began begging for death. I lay there for months at a time and as the agony grew worse my soul retracted its own light capacity and God had to save my life again by increasing the very vibrations that were causing soul retraction. This was done to overpower the radioactivity of my brain so that God could keep firm control on my thoughts, always in panic and fear, and total control of my functions.

By this time I had thinned greatly. I had begun to teach spiritual development, art and meditation. My own spiritual progression enabled me to help others in need of their souls and wanting to purify. Teaching then was rewarding for those in search of their souls were beautiful to teach and respectful to God. During my teaching life blood began to seep from my gums. I had had a small group of students coming in and out of my life, beautifully respectful, believing that God was in control of my existence and wanting to help me in every way. All of them were asked to leave me to suffer alone. All of them were clairvoyanced, clairaudient and transcribal so they would obey and do as they were asked. Their departure suffered me more for I was in so much suffering and so much need of caring. Their presence had caused me vibrational imbalance and the rays of God going into my body and soul could not be interfered with in any way for my suffering was about to increase. Spiritual development had made me want to develop others, help them understand their souls and create values necessary in all human beings which preserved the Earth they took life from and the preservation unto the Earth that was paramount to their existence. I taught until my suffering destroyed the capacity I had to continue teaching.

The heating of my brain from God's invisible ray entry into my head, affected every part of my body for the brain had been in control of my function and was being put out of charge mercilessly. The pain was horrific, uncontainable and of huge pressure. I tried to find relief. Countless times I dragged myself from my bed to fill sinks with water, submerge my head under the water again and again trying to stop the pain, cool the agony then slide along floors and back into bed begging for mercy. The agony was unable to be lived through. The cruelty was unforgivable. The God I had been trying to believe in became distanced. The suffering I was being forced to endure continued for twenty-three years with respite occasionally. During those years I travelled as I was asked to, worked also as asked and began transcribal informative reception of Earth's truth; dictation explaining to me all of evolution. With every sentence I convulsed. My body could not receive the vibrations necessary for coherency of what was to become the full truth of God, the soul and the Earth. The entry of God's pure light vibrations into my soul was too powerful. Each insertion entered my soul light so forcefully my own projecting light rays were shocked, destabilized and convulsed.

During that agony my blood began dissolving and that which could not dissolve by vibrations of God heating and drying up the energized excretions within my blood, had to be removed medically. I was asked to give blood at every place available and within two months I had given four pints of blood which would never flow again through my watered veins. Blood had to be drained out fast for a supply of blood inside a containment of light vibrations is explosive. The watering through my veins would be permanent, forced into my body by hot light vibrations, changed consistently to stay pure and became a strong disease preventative.

All of my experiences then were carefully explained, clairvoyanced to me and nothing did I refuse. I realized that I must allow whatever I was being asked to suffer through, for the Calling I was gripped in, to eventuate. Too much proof was being experienced. God's constant hold on my soul could not be denied. Earth's truth could not be denied either. My truth however, was.

Areas like my teeth and gums seeped blood continuously for thirty years discolouring my teeth, shrinking the gums, causing my facial features to change and the teeth to move uglily. The intensity of God's vibrations through my head parted every tooth in my head. They gaped. One crossed over the other as vibrations loosened them. Three had to be removed. Gradually I uglied in the face, could not smile, laugh or be as I was, beautiful and aware of that beauty. One of my four capped front teeth was surgically removed by God's heating vibrations, to leave an indentation in the gum so that the tooth would slip outwards, not downwards and therefore able to have the tissue on either side of the indentation magnetized together. The tooth had begun to dissolve from intense heat and severe bloodletting of the gums. After the extraction, the indentation began closing inward, filling with water and looking fairly normal except for a noticeable gap left by the tooth itself also closing to bring the teeth closer together.

The shifting of my teeth, the bleeding of the gums, shrunk my facial structure. The massive amount of blood letting collapsed the gums and my lips shrunk leaving one larger than the other. The lip muscles dissolved during that suffering because the intense heating of my head melted their formation. All of my facial muscles began to dissolve at that time. I was water-padded to prevent ugliness. Even my nose lost its muscular form. It became more refined and less broad. My beautiful lips which were well shaped, full and sensuous, shrunk, to become thin, tight looking and unbeautiful. The result of such suffering caused another agony I could not contain. My jaw had to be shifted to prevent the remaining teeth from smashing against each other and breaking as facial muscles dissolved as well.

The bleeding gums so uglied my appearance any beauty I had destroyed. In time such hideousness will change. The amount of heat through my head lessens each year. The gums will eventually be water packed and my teeth will be secured and improved in appearance. The teeth shifted everywhere. They lost their rooting stability which dissolved during the heating of my head. Some teeth also dissolved in that terrible agony. Others boiled from heat of another hell and muscle tissue in the face also dissolved. My facial muscles disappeared leaving water-padded tissue in their place. Layers of pure water were threaded through tissue filling gaps where the muscles had been. My face lost its natural structure, its beauty and softness. My facial bones became sheathed tightly in thin water padding. I was unattractive, hard looking and without expression.

To keep my gums from too much blood letting God rayed through my mouth, whilst I slept, aggressively charged, pure vibrations which dried up all the moisture in my mouth preventing blood loss and at the same time moving teeth that had shifted dangerously. It was an experience I found difficult to contain. To be without saliva day after day, be unable to swallow, touch my tongue or gums in moisture for any length of time could kill any normal human being, saliva moistens even eye projection and cools every nerve in the head. The agony was uncontainable and attempting to take water for relief did not in any way moisten my mouth. The water dried up instantly. The heat was too great. When moisture was returned to my mouth, I felt abused. I wept, wailed and began to hate all that was being done to me. No-one could suffer that torture. It was beyond human endurance.

I had to be water-packed in vital places to stop dissolved muscle tissue from sinking inward and allow air to pass through my pores unimpeded. I am bone-operated, everywhere. I have not one muscle left inside my body. The heat that has penetrated through me has been a painful and humiliating existence for I have staggered around, limped with a walking stick, dragged my feet often, had splinters tied to my fingers and hands to stop the bones shifting, been unable to bowel properly, unable to speak clearly and have gradually become accustomed to bones manipulated by ligaments only, which are light controlled. I am totally light functioning which means agonizing life. All these changes were physically ugly, painful, deforming and have continued all these terrible years. Never have I had one day without hideous suffering. Never will I. The transformation of my human form into one of light-functioning is an evolutionary first. My Calling is the only reason this is taking place. The capacity of my soul which has experienced eternity from being thrice re-incarnate, enables God to keep me alive with light rays of powerful vibrations.

The entry of God's light vibrations through me, experienced opposition at every progression. Every cell in my body rejected that pure touch. Consequently, every cell became explosive. I began to boil. Purity of light rays if touching impure energized vibrations, heats the energy force, which keeps on heating until an explosion occurs. Unless the imbalance can be cooled, an explosion automatically takes place. Until those vibrations in aggressive charge reach explosive temperature, God cannot respond. My cells all became explosive. When they reached temperature release, God responded with the same aggression of charge, in cool power. The energy cells in my body were over-powered in coolness and prevented from explosion. Their explosive temperature caused huge blisters the size of tennis balls to appear upon my body and when they burst the tissue had dissolved, leaving holes in my skin deep and noticeable. They were filled with water gradually. The heat was so uncontainable, so unacceptable to my frail soul trying to exist, I tried to suffocate myself with a bag tied around my head to put an end to all I was suffering. I was strongly cautioned not to encourage death. I contrited, as so often I had to, for so many times throughout my suffering I deliberately encouraged death and begged and begged to die. Eventually I cooled. Eventually my staggering steadied. My hideous deformities had to be contained, had to be accepted and had to be endured. My beauty had gone. My perfect form had become ugly to look at. My hands looked arthritic for so many bones dislocated and could not be corrected until my energy cells became subservient to light. My belief in God was destroying. What was to come, altered me as a human being forever.

During God's entry through my head, my back teeth boiled, died in energy, dissolved in the heating, discoloured and broke in fragments. Portions of my gums also boiled and dissolved in that agonizing heat. Every tooth left in my head pulsed at a temperature no man could endure, all at the same time and for months, day and night. I could not get relief. I tried, living over a sink taking water as every bout of pain increased and then subsided. I screamed, kept on screaming buried in my pillows until the agony ceased and another began. The bouts of pulsing lasted for hours at a time. The intensity of my screams became electronic in pitch and sound, inhuman, resonating explosively, increasing in pressure and of extreme electronic whining, a thoroughly warning explosive readiness. I felt inhuman. I felt a danger never experienced. I felt my soul ready to explode. The pitch of sound caused my heart to cease beating for it was from my soul, not my body. I left this earth. My soul light extricated itself and reached universal safety. I found relief there. I had to. God had withdrawn from my body form because it was ready to explode. God could not magnetize my soul at that time the vibrations were too heated. Temperature control could not be equated, the soul had to explode or detach from its containment. My soul, unheld by God, ready to explode, ready to travel from magnetic attraction solely, spasm-convulsed (threw off its aggressed equations) and shot through the earth's magnetic field unto soul sanctity. Soul sanctity had been experienced. There my soul was cooled. There God surrounded my soul entirely. There I was held. From there I had to be returned. That return was felt in my soul. The pulsing inside the nerves of all of my teeth ceased immediately my soul left my body. The return put every aggressive vibration completely out of charge. I cannot attempt to describe how traumatic, how emotional, how convincing that experiencing was, for God and God alone was understood as the protector of my soul purity. God and God alone equated the capacity of my soul strength to do what the soul was capable of and reach cool surround equatingly. Had I not been re-incarnate, pure in soul compositional strength, my soul would have definitely exploded and been let go of, by God, because its light equations were too weak to be magnetized.

Continuing on in suffering, blood loss again was vital as my temperature went up and down. I was force-haemorrhaged. I sat over the toilet and let blood drain out of me. It was so heavy I was counselled strongly to let that happen and not be afraid. Every drop of internal blood was let that way. When it stopped, I was clean, ready for the next agony and able to be entered further. The explosive content of my blood cells had manufactured more blood than my light holding body form could contain safely and all of it had been forced into my womb and its surround, by God vibrating every individual vibration into unity of vibrations of the same colour, content and composition. Once my blood was fully magnetized unto itself, it could be drained out of me. I felt so light, so beautiful and so clean after it was over.

The entry of God's light vibrations opposing the radioactive and electrical energy content in me caused violent convulsions, which would persist throughout my Calling. They were never seen. I had tried to appear to be living normally to those I always encountered. The convulsions had begun very early on and I had learned to live with them, never be afraid of them and hide away during their ugliness. I kept that truth hidden most of my suffered life. I kept all of my suffering hidden throughout its continuance. I had to. No-one was capable of such truth. No-one had enough soul reality to believe in what I was going through. Gradually the convulsions increased. Their spasms became longer and much more violent until bouts of twenty-four hours in convulsive spasm almost caused my death. I simply convulsed, non-stop, without sleep for twenty-four hours, several times. So violent were the spasms I dislocated my shoulder. There was no muscle to hold my bones in place. I dislocated my fingers also in the spasms. I injured my throat with my screams. I could only beg for death. I could only want death. I was held from suicide again and again. No-one ever saw my real truth. I managed to conceal it all. I knew I had to continue suffering. I knew that suffering was increasing. God kept announcing there was much more to come. I had held onto faith in the power over me. Faith I lost further on.

I could have been helped through most of my terrible suffering. I was not. An earth, a magnetic attraction to someone strong and pure enough in soul would have kept me earthed. No-one was available to God at that time. No-one was with soul fortitude. I had no magnetic earther to sustain me through suffering. Love was all I needed to attract me. Warmth of feelings would have helped me suffer. Someone able to experience my truth. Someone true to the soul could have spared my deformity. There was no-one. I was told I would suffer alone and without help in any way. I felt despair, disappointment in human kind. I began to lose faith in the God I was trying to accept. I began to lose the conviction I had offered to suffer for. I lost my soul respect which had come from knowing I had soul beauty and fortitude, rare and obviously of worth to God. Feeling no-one supportive, no-one able to feel my truth, no-one with any capacity to help me, caused me to withdraw, retract my soul light, depress its vibrations thus losing the belief in myself as capable of being as I was needing to be. My soul respect had grown with constant communication with God. When God announced I had to suffer alone without human kind attending in any way, communication with God stopped for many months. I felt condemned, condemned to suffer unjustly, condemned to live entirely alone and in pain. I felt cruelled and did not want God in my life at that time. God left me alone to find my own capacity to re-establish communication in need of more conviction, more belief in my Calling and more belief in God. As soon as I asked for God's counsel again, I was responded to respectfully and felt of worth again.

An earth, a magnetic interest to hold my soul unto the Earth and not let it seek God in any way, never eventuated. Prevention from wanting soul levitation had to be merciless for no compassion could God give me, no love of any kind and no encouragement for the beauty of my soul. This I was told, for I could not believe that a God would let me suffer so cruelly. Later I turned away from God for that suffering became unforgivable.

The horrific temperature of my body caused me to swell grotesquely. I had to be water-filled constantly to prevent my tissue from dissolving. I was layered everywhere especially around my heart area. My breasts became so huge no bra could hold them and I had to carry them in my hands. I could not go out and lived in pain and ugliness until the huge imbalance of my body lessened in water-packing and I could walk fairly normally. My breasts were layered with water because one is directly over my soul light which is constantly over-heating. When my soul cools, my over-large breasts shrink.

My eyes had to be protected from blindness. The fierce temperature when God's rays opposed aggressive charge of energy, changed the beautiful deep brown colour of my eyes. They yellowed. They burned from the nerves inside. They wept hot water constantly. They were an agony I still cannot contain for the projection of vibrations from the eyes, which happens by visual magnetic attraction, could not be allowed and every energized action of the eyes was held inside my brain. God had to purify the aggressive action of the eyes with light vibrations so violently charged I almost died again. I could not project my eyes at anything. I also could not magnetize any visual content. That meant over-heating of the brain, over-heating of the entire head and over-heating of my soul light. That continued for twelve hideous years day and night. No man could have endured that. It kills.

The pressure over and around my head was of light force which is heavy when it is of force-field. The weight of that force caused my spine to bend at the neck where the weight was concentrated. For years I had a large lump at the back of my neck which was solid water packing preventing the spine from permanent disfigurement. The lump made it difficult to turn around without pain. As the weight decreased, so the hump lessened. It is very minimal now and soon will disappear. Most of the pressure over the head has gone but what enters my eyes constantly is radioactivity in huge quantities from Earth's vibratory asphyxiation and that is agonizing. My brain is totally subservient to light vibrations. My body is also totally subservient to light vibratory charge, its lifeforce.

My soul deformed during its torture. It retracted its rays of pure light vibrations, over-heated, interned of its vibrations and emitted red rays of suffering. Those rays had to exit or my soul would have exploded. God allowed their exit through my eyes. I cannot want to remember that suffering which continued through the years I had to endure purification of my energy force into light life of pure vibrations to be able to receive Earth's reality.

Out through my eyes came red hot colour so intense I could turn a visual image I was looking at, violent red. The projecting rays were so hot, any contact with substance of electrical manufacture, was over-powered. The visual redness of contact was simply heat magnetizing heat and becoming visual in the shape of whatever I was looking at. My eyes then discoloured and I have not had pure vision since, the cells were destroyed by red heat. They will however become perfect in sight and colour as soon as they cool and can be kept that way. The healing of my eyes has already begun. I see purely quite frequently. When I can't see well it is because the environment or that which I am looking at is electrically or radioactively vibrating. Soon even that will be overpowered.

When God's light rays overpowered my brain power and released soul heating out through my eyes, I immediately began to attract huge quantities of radioactivity back inside my head, for red hot vibrations magnetize red hot vibrations always. Into my brain via my eyes came a hell I almost could not live through, even with God holding my totality. Every part of me began violent reaction. Every cell partly purified at that time heated again and sought radioactive force. Every cooling I had been given to keep me alive extinguished. I knew the suffering I was about to endure would be the worst. When it was announced, I sought rope to hang myself. I wanted God to be affected by the hideousness of such a hanging. I was trying for some compassion from a God I had come to loathe. God did not respond in any way. I eventually put down the rope without contrition. When the agony began I became of uncontainable hatred. I have never suffered so cruelly. I will never again.

To overpower the horrific magnetic attraction to large quantities of radioactivity into my head through my eyes, God's holding rays, became nuclear in content. Their power increased, for the next increase in charge of radioactivity is nuclear. Nuclear vibrations are the progressive powering of every man-made vibrational force now at large in the environment. Their composition is entirely manufactured, totally lethal to every form on Earth and the reason the Earth will explode. I became, because I was containing quantity of man-made radioactivity which had to be overpowered, a nuclear holding human body form. An entity of power, no longer human and no longer of human existence. It was inevitable that I would attract such a charge. Nuclear vibrations were magnetized into my form. The content of light that had been purifying my energy force was so powerful, magnetic attraction to a force equally as powerful would be nuclear. Nuclear vibrations are increasing in Earth's environment every hour. I was a victim of that deadly progression. I can never describe what I went through or stop terrifying at that memory. I could not forgive God. I turned away from God so hard I could not be returned. I am still tormented by that experience, for it lives within my soul in the deformity of light rays and my death is the only release that will free me.

I became spiritually unstable, for my soul denied my Calling. I cannot forgive the humanity that has caused nuclear vibrations to cover the Earth, for I was nuclear-charge held to save my life in order to save the Earth. God's pure rays became so aggressively charged their content was of pure nuclear power. My form then deformed. My soul then deformed. My feelings became of violent hatred so intensifying I conjured clairvoyant scenes of horrific torture trying to show God cruelty that could not be contained or forgiven, cruelty that even defiled God. God did not respond. Every part of me convulsed, burned again, boiled, baked and I never screamed more grotesquely until the agony was so great I became mute, a staring, unbreathing, unfeeling, unliving entity, walked around by God, force-breathed, force-fed, force-emotioned and force-moved from place to place. I am deeply scarred by that experience. Containing its violation unto my soul is still difficult.

There were times my eyelids could not open after sleep; the nuclear charge ate through the ligaments and tissue. I opened them manually until God functioned them normally. To weep was a most excruciating agony to contain. The tears were red hot and often only one would fall and burn my face as it exited during emotion. Gradually emotion ceased. Gradually the charge was stopped. Gradually I cooled, stopped convulsing, screaming, begging to die, pleading for mercy and even cursing God so hatingly I could not accept my soul in any way. Gradually I numbed in disbelief at God. Gradually I became subservient again but without respect.

During the release of nuclear charge from my head, my jaw had to be moved._ Its placement was causing vibrational imbalance._ It had become threatened by the very heat through the head and the blood-letting of the gums. The muscles had gone and the jaw was loose, vibrating imbalance, causing my teeth to smash into each other as I spoke and locking, making it difficult to speak fluently. It was force-vibrated violently at first then slid forward to avoid boiling. Another hell began for God had to pull it backwards again as it cooled. I could not speak without breaking tissue and severing nerves in my face. The mouth swelled, blistered, bled and reacted against every touch of God during that agony. I went through another life-threatening experience which finally stopped after six months of ceaseless manoeuvring. My jaw is still without full support and often loosens and prevents my eating properly. Every now and then God drags it back and forth to give me some comfort. It often clamps down hard on my teeth and I hear it as it bangs. The jolting hurts and often frightens me it sounds so threatening. God always offers me counsel when fear emerges into my suffering. Counsel I know I can rely on. Counsel I know keeps me safe. I feel so ugly and look hard and old. I can't soften in looks in any way and weep so for that deformity. Being bereft of beauty, bereft of soul respect, feels unjust, unspiritual and unacceptable. Contriting for my denials throughout my Calling helps me live with myself, believe in myself and realize that what I am suffering, has to be, for it is the only way Earth's truth will ever be understood. Those who may read this and want to disbelieve what I have suffered through need to confront me in person to see me as I really am.

My head had magnetized nuclear vibrations, quantities of radioactive vibrations as well as huge electric clumps of vibrations which had to be detached from for me to keep alive. God had to remove that deathly grip violently or lose me forever in explosion of my soul light. I was prepared to go through a deadly car crash and the violence of that accident, its own explosive impact of vibrations, magnetized mine at the instant of the crash and released me from vibrational over-powering. God used violence to attract violence and at the same time used violent light rays to encourage the detachment. I was hit three times. There was nothing left of my car but the seat I was sitting in, intact. Not a drop of blood was there anywhere. I was safe except for broken ribs, a punctured lung, lacerations and a minor head injury. I had no safety belt on and never left the car during the smashings. I was force-held there. I should have been killed. I recovered but my faith in God had gone. It took time for me to realize just how necessary that detachment and how it was implemented, was. God assured me of the absolute hold on my soul and that my safety was paramount to the Earth's and what was done to me at that time could not be stopped for I was in serious danger of soul explosion again. I had to believe that. All through my terrible suffering I had been truthed of every agony I would live through, truthed in every detail and my car smash was no different in reality to every other experience I was asked to endure.

After the release of nuclear charge through my head I became bed-ridden for weeks at a time, unable to eat, sleep, and move around. My muscles had gone, my vision was poor, my feelings were often emotional and more often numb. God had to ray through my body, a charge of light purity to keep me going. That was painful. Nuclear charged vibrations penetrated every cell in my body and it will take years for me to cool and be able to live without pain. God keeps me alive by injecting aggressive light rays into my totality in calculated amounts of charge. Too much and I will attract radioactivity again at least until I can overpower the magnetic attraction that tries to overpower me. Too little and I have no light energizing activation. Half of me is still holding electrical and radioactive energy cells. The other half holds light cells of perfect equations which must feed from light holding formations and forms. I am increasing in light charge every day. The acceleration of such powerful purity is causing painful episodes of adaptation and a transformation that cannot be stopped ever.

I only have surface blood left and veins close to the skin surfaces which are watered, keeping the blood thin and able to be moved around. I am internally all water held. The small veins in my body appear and disappear. My feet and legs have the same quantity of blood as my hands and arms which often clogs because of the way I sleep, sit and bend. My watered blood cells have to be kept at temperature always. Each year I lose more blood, more normality in body movements and appear strangely unusual looking. I have unusual bouts of superhuman strength and bouts of absolute exhaustion and weakness. I have been constantly forced to keep living, unwilling mostly, uncooperative constantly and without sincere conviction unto my Calling. A future without blood, tortured by radioactivity, threatened in death by nuclear vibrations is uncontainable. I have been a human being, a woman needing love just as every other, a person in every sense, an emotional person in every way, needing to be of life, decency, truth and stability. I have become an entitised constructed being, abnormal in every way, unacceptable to myself and unable to be anything else. Those who read this truth after all before it, please try hard to believe in all that I have suffered as real, without contrivance of any kind, without lies possible and without the interference of the brain of man in denial. I am the voice of truth. I have suffered for that truth to be realized. I am forced to be as I am now, forced to accept whatever I must do for the life of Earth to be saved. I am not a sacrifice. I was not born for the souls of mankind to be saved. I am promised that my suffering is and will always be for the great Earth and I will always be requited.

Across my heart area are layers of water keeping the frenzied soul light cool and protected. My often abnormally large breasts are hot and uncomfortable causing imbalance in my walk. I often lurch forward unable to straighten up. As my weight increases and decreases, so does the size of my breasts. I am unable to wear a bra because any tightness across my soul light causes excruciating pain and heat. The rest of my body is fairly normal looking until I am touched. I am jelly-like at touch. I like that softness sometimes. I loathe the look of me all the time. I self-deprecate constantly because I was once very beautiful and accepting myself as an ugliness is hated intensely. I have had to live as a normal human being. I have lived tortured by that pretence. I am and have been accepted as an ordinary human person. Hiding all of my gruesome suffering has cost me my self-respect. Pretending to others a normality that does not exist for me and never will, is degrading. I find it extremely difficult to accept myself in any way body or soul. Suicide is no longer an option. It wouldn't be allowed. I have accepted that and long ago given up planning it in selfishness, a phase I go through periodically when my suffering becomes too severe.

In this transformation I will become beautiful again. The hideousness of my deformities is almost over. My Calling to deliver truth will end with this publication. So will the grotesque suffering I have gone through. God has already begun to repair the severity too much suffering has caused. My teeth have already begun to straighten, close in their ugly gapping and the gums will shortly be filled with water to give me facial structure again. My eyes can never return to their dark brown colour but will be beautified by the light projected through them as soon as it is released. Muscles will never return to my body. Blood will never return either. Bones that have dislocated are already slowly being manipulated to stabilize me. Everything bodily that has deformed me is slowly being corrected by God. Even my once beautiful lips will be acceptable to me again. This I am told. This I believe. This will become strong evidence of a transformation never ever witnessed on Earth, a human being, light purified, by God.

God is careful when delivering vibrations into me at this time for too many pure vibrations too soon will cause me to attract to my prime light source before my destiny is done with. So I am starved of compassion, love, respect, comfort, caring and feeling. God has to keep me needing, hurting, begging, waiting for death without relief. To comfort me in any way attracts my soul. To attract my soul could mean the end of my Calling before it becomes influential. God has also begun a substitute vibrational charge which acts as an earth to keep me attached magnetically unto the Earth, a forced pressure downward, hugely depressing always but can keep me unable to be magnetic unto anything. It is cruel. I cannot feel my soul. I want to. I need to. I despair. I hate. I vibrate painful imbalance of light equations which keep me alive. I also know that suffering is permanent and do not want a Calling which totally destroys my feelings. What has been asked of me is all consuming and no matter how hard I have denied all I could not contain; I will always be forced to withstand the suffering.

My destiny, that which I have been called unto, must be acknowledged by me. I fear when God asks me to thrice affirm all I am asked to do. I am forced to accept responsibility for the truth of Earth in publication. I must. I know I must not deny that, ever. I do not have faith in the capacity of humanity to respond to truth as it stands. Soul strength in mankind has almost gone completely. As I transform, I know my suffering will increase. Living in a body of pure light vibrations is impossible on an Earth smothered in radioactivity with nuclear vibrations increasing and uniting with every other aggression within Earth's environment. Trying to stay convicted is so difficult I smother myself with contritions begging for assistance, begging for an end to everything and to be detached from Earth's magnetic field. Appealing unto mankind causes me trauma, trauma of my soul, for unless all I have revealed truthfully, willingly and am believed, life on Earth as mankind knows of it, is over. My Calling, to bring all truth, will have been delivered as God wanted. My suffering will be over forever. I will return to God and never be entitized again.

I am tortured by every mechanical creation upon Earth. Every man-made machine vibrates an aggressive charge of vibrations into every living soul light on Earth. Those vibrations for mankind are consumed by the brain, overpower the soul light and destroy man's lifeline to God. Those vibrations for me are so hideous, so heating my soul and so threatening my life always, I know I cannot live much longer. Those vibrations unto the Earth, are massing to enter an explosion that will cost mankind a future. Machinery, pounds into my purity of light vibrations, often eats into the struggling capacity of my soul, raises my temperature, often convulses me and until the heating reaches temperature release, God cannot help me through that agony. Day after day, night after night, hour upon hour machinery, electrical and radioactively charging man-made creations surround my body, agonize my soul and cause terminal torture for me to live through. I am forced to withstand that torture and, no matter how much longer I can live for; it will go on until God redeems my soul.

God calls me the Messiah, the real voice of truth, the saviour of God's beloved Earth, the sufferer for the Earth's reality to be understood, the only pure soul able to do the work that is needed. All the suffering I have endured so far has convinced me I will fulfil this Calling even though I have relinquished much of my faith in humanity and have little capacity left to keep going. I cannot trust, love, believe in any friendship, or allow anyone to show me compassion or affection. I am containing too much suffering and cannot release its reality. I am force-affirmed in Calling and although God cannot comfort me, God constantly asks me for forgiveness and adds that it is all for the life of Earth. In my own conscience I know that for the Earth I will remain loyal to the end. For the life of the great Earth my life is insignificant and for Earth's future I would gladly lay down my own. Out of my conscience and gripped by too much pain, I have denied even the Earth's life. That has caused me to hate God, hate myself and be unable to forgive myself. Contrition is and always will be my soul's redemption. It has kept me safe as long as I seek its freedom, will keep me in my soul, with my God and for Earth.

Within my life as a human being, I have always wanted love. Always wanted a simple life. Never ever wanted anything other than a beautiful existence on Earth, tending unto the Earth, growing that which is beautiful, that which is nourishing and without selfish greed for anything else. Never have I ever been deceived by greed. Greed which exploits Earth, deprives Earth and should never be. I have searched for that pure existence and never found that greatness. My search still within my soul is for love, love in me for every being deserving of such love, for every purity that love endows and for every evidence that God condones that soul. Forgive me all of mankind, for this truth I am suffering in my soul, for no man woman or child will ever fulfil the emptiness in my heart unless the purification of the soul becomes greed, greed for love, greed for pure existence, greed for the Earth's life before any other manifestation of greed and before the recognized existence of God before all else. All I ever ask from God is to die with love in my heart. All that every man woman and child need to ask should be the same.

I am the Messiah, the real Messiah the world has waited for. My suffering is that proof. God's reality confirms that. To be the Messiah, for me is terrifying existence, resistance to all I have suffered for and the fear of a brained humanity unable to respect or control the activity of brain hyping, brain addiction and brain brutality to truth. I am woman, a contradiction to the expectations of all religious teachings. First man, then woman. The perfect unity of life.

Being a Messiah is agony. Agony of soul. No man has soul reality at this time. No woman either. To be at the mercy of man's brain is to feel death clearly and soon. Unless mankind wants and needs my coming, as I am, with all of my faults and with all of my mistakes throughout life, my bringing of truth will never be requited in the soul of mankind. I have lived as one of you. I have experienced all that you have. I have made the same mistakes as all of you. I have contrited for those errors of judgment and been cleansed. I know you. I have been violated by many of you, despised by many of you, hated for my strength of soul, vilified for the beauty I have tried to show, robbed by you, denied decency by many of you, plundered by your greed, condemned by your laws unjustly, mutilated in my love and destroyed by your refusals to conscience anywhere. Believe in my thorough experience. It has been painful, truthful and evidence of man's brain power without the soul in conscience. I am forced to accept who I am and whoever refuses my truth is of no concern to me or to God. I am here for the life of Earth and no man, no matter what his or her beliefs can change what has to be.

My relationship with God is beyond any religious comprehension, beyond that which any brain could ever contrive, beyond education religiously or scientifically, beyond the knowledge that mankind has at this time. It is pure. It is powerful in truth. It is of real soul infinity, unable to be impured. At every denial of me my contrition has purified the soul of me. I have been asked to never withhold anything that disturbs me, affects me, causes me suspicion or fear. In that asking I have experienced soul release entirely. I have never at any time feared the presence of God and never should. Never at any time have I ever tried to deceive God in my feelings. Never can I for I have during my suffering come to totally respect the holding of my soul. I have hated God, been unable to forgive God for the severity of my suffering. I have forgiven God totally because that suffering is paramount for the life of Earth. I will never be worthy of this Calling, never be worthy of God's choice of me to do an impossible job on this Earth and try to save Earth's life. My unworthiness is because I have lived as one of you. In that life, I have realized my ignorance, the lack of respect for Earth, the grossness of my offences to creatures, my lack of conscience and my incapacity to exist in my soul as the true reality of my existence. I have to do my job. I will with every vibration I have to help me. For all who have been influenced by religious programming, God cannot automatically love ye who want that pretence, unless thy souls are pure. God automatically responds by way of pure equations to all who show soul need and all who respond to truth within the soul. Truth is all every human being needs to bring God unto the soul of mankind. Once that is established, life as it was meant to be becomes a firm reality. Love from God comes only through the soul light, only through the purity of that light and only through conscience which purifies the soul itself. God is not all forgiving, all loving and all pretending that mankind is acceptable. God is an equating response, a light fortification, a powerful guidance through suffering, a magnetic attraction unto every soul of mankind and the invisible life force of every soul light in evolution. A mighty power. A power not ever able to be deceived. The total power of all of evolution. The absolute pure equator of every equation in existence. A real God. A believable God never to be denied again.

Through my suffering I was transcribally informed of much of Earth's truth. I was also partly informed of God's beginning and the evolution of the soul light. I had taken down everything I had been taught. All of it, every time I transcribed, caused horrific convulsive spasms. Nothing joined together. No explanation was clear enough for me to begin to write as I knew I had to. Page after page of the reality of God's existence was stacked upon my desk. Trying to complete sequences of evolution was impossible. All that had been given to me was all my soul could accept vibrationally. The explanations were of patterns of light vibrating words which entered my soul and vibrated through my hands. Some explanations could not be given entirely. My soul could not accept the vibrating complexity in the word patterns, they were too severe. I could not contain too many convulsions, my soul light would once again over-heat.

I had to be left alone for weeks and sometimes months to regain the strength that had been sapped from me during transcriptions. Sometimes I failed even to take the simplest explanation. Other times I kept going for several hours. Putting it all together exhausted me constantly. Gradually the entire truth was given. I had become strong enough to receive it. It had taken me nearly forty years of suffering. It had cost me the purity of my soul light.

I wrote, rewrote, over and over again, asking for help from God, checking every vagueness for more truth and suffered the trauma of such truth not understood. Trying to simplify the reality of evolution so that all who would read the truth could be educated, was a massive undertaking. Keeping the reality of the existence of pure equations through every destructive force of mankind to wipe them out, was a determination I held onto until the end chapter. Trying to make sure that no truth would be denied in the conscience of man, was painful, for my own experiences showed me that could happen. Sobbing through whale's truth made me realize how vital that truth had to be conveyed and how essential to the evolution of mankind that had to be believed in. Every chapter, I had had experience of, and not once did I attempt to exaggerate, lie, or pretend. Every explanation, given to me by God, was absolutely believed in, respected, and understood as real truth never to be ignored. I had been educated, slowly soul released, for once the reality of my own soul became evident, my Calling, the terrorizing command on my soul, emerged as a duty never to be denied. I could not deny God's asking of me any longer. And so came my contritions, one after the other, in an attempt to put right all I had done that was ugly. I am still contriting. I must, to keep my Calling pure. I am still convulsing. I shall, to keep taking more truth. I am still transforming, to keep alive for Earth's life to be saved. I am still the only pure soul on Earth able to do the work God needs to save Earth and however tiny I may be, however much I suffer, I will do my job and no-one will prevent me from requitement.

My final truth here will be believed, without the denials the brain will attempt. It is the reality of what all of mankind feels, sees, knows, absolutely does conscience for and experiences in life. It is this, in the words of a real truthful woman Messiah asked in Calling and responsibility to Earth and all that the Earth has given life to. It is the reality, the blatant ugliness, shameful selfish greed, deliberate disrespectful behaviour, abusive and defiling attitude, violent and shattering denials of every single truth mankind knows exists of himself. It is the real mirror of a civilization that has totally destroyed, not only the Earth itself but every purity there has ever been inside each and every human being as well as every beautiful creature in existence. It is this truth mankind cannot hide from and however callously denies, is the truth.

I, the real Messiah, expose to all of mankind a reality no-one has ever been shown in history, a history born of lies, killings, greed, coveting of every beauty and the bodies of many millions of souled, decent, pure and God-given human beings sentenced to eternal suffering by a particular breed of mankind, a hideous breed of beings predating on the innocent for power, wealth and possession of every gorgeous sight and beautiful peaceful evolutionary lifeform God and God alone created.

I will not be deceived by any living individual attempting to deny all that is here. I will never forgive any being trying such a denial of truth here. No-one, no-one anywhere can ever pretend decency to me or to God this day and age over this truth written here. It is too thorough, too delivering to mankind a real chance to purify or take into the brain the consequences.

I will forever contrite, not for the evil that exists all over this Earth, but for those who could, yet cannot release their own sufferings because of those in powerful condemnation of their souls. That contrition will never end until I die. I contrite here before all of mankind good and bad.

I contrite firstly for the agonies of the great Earth destroyed by all of mankind mostly in ignorance.

I contrite secondly for God, totally not believed in, totally unwanted in truth and fully defiled in every religion, home, prayer, bible and marriage.

I contrite for all creatures totally denied their souls by everyone everywhere.

I contrite for the soul light of every individual suffering of lovelessness, neglect, disrespect, ignorance, impoverishment in life's beautiful truths and lack of spiritual reality.

I contrite for the reception this truth will encounter, the defilement of its greatness that will condemn its path and the absolute refusal of the Earth's life and future some of mankind held in the brain, will want.

I contrite before God for a humanity that has taken every beautiful giving the Earth was itself given and violated everything without conscience.

I contrite for the lateness of my Calling, late because I myself have had to be protected from every threat against publication.

I contrite for what is coming, what inevitably must be if mankind chooses itself before the Earth's life.

I contrite because my conscience never ceases, never stops and never will until this truth I have deformed in soul for, is understood, wanted and respected for what it brings to everyone.

I will leave this Earth the Messiah God asked in Calling, fully pure in soul, fully truthed in all of mankind and fully conscienced and contritioned.

I contrite for the existence of the soul inside every being, not understood.

I honour the soul inside myself contritionally.

May God be requited by my Calling honoured.

Lastly I reveal to all who believe who I am, that encircled around me, visible to the human eye as long as there is water sprayed over the area my eyes project outwardly into the environment, is a rainbow of pure light, exactly as seen when looking at a rainbow except it encircles me. It cannot be seen without water. It can always be seen as long as the sun is shining and water activates its equations. It is the reality of the light of God surrounding my soul and protecting me from too much vibrational interference. Even though that circle was severely entered by nuclear vibrations, the power of it was the reason I am still alive. God's light vibrational rainbow which surrounds my person, although unseen unless I am touched with water and pure light, is evidence of truth that no man can deny. Evidence that light exists that is pure. Evidence that when it surrounds a being such as me, God is the benefactor, the giver and protector of light life as long as that life is pure.

I am no fake. I am no mistake either. I am clearly visibly surrounded by the light of God feeding my soul and protecting me from much that would have killed me. Anyone can see that miracle. Anyone with respect for my truth can be invited to see that phenomena. I the real Messiah hold the proof of God's light surrounding my soul which can never be extinguished until I die. May that truth be the evidence that mankind needs to change all that is destroying the Earth and preventing man's soul from eternal life.

Editor's note: Please see the images to be found at

https://www.arodyce.com/rainbow

www.ingramcontent.com/pod-product-compliance
Lightning Source LLC
Chambersburg PA
CBHW070631160426
43194CB00009B/1431
* 9 7 8 0 4 7 3 7 3 6 7 2 9 *